Representing Jihad

About the Author

JACQUELINE O'ROURKE is an independent research and communications consultant. Since completing her PhD, MA and MEd degrees she has taught at several universities in Canada and in the Middle East, where she has also worked as an adviser. In the conviction that the world of ideas must be connected to practice, she has also been involved in setting up social organizations and youth initiatives. She has published essays and articles of cultural and political analysis and contributed to academic projects, as well as publishing a collection of poetry. She currently lives in Canada.

Representing Jihad

The Appearing and Disappearing Radical

JACQUELINE O'ROURKE

Zed Books

LONDON | NEW YORK

Representing Jihad: The Appearing and Disappearing Radical was first published in 2012 by Zed Books Ltd, 7 Cynthia Street, London N1 9JF, UK and Room 400, 175 Fifth Avenue, New York, NY 10010, USA

www.zedbooks.co.uk

Designed and typeset in Monotype Bembo Book by illuminati, Grosmont
Index by John Barker
Cover design by www.thisistransmission.com
Printed and bound in Great Britain
by CPI Group (UK) Ltd, Croydon CR0 4YY

Distributed in the USA exclusively by Palgrave Macmillan, a division of St Martin's Press, LLC, 175 Fifth Avenue, New York, NY 10010, USA

A catalogue record for this book is available from the British Library
Library of Congress Cataloging in Publication Data available

ISBN 978 1 78032 263 6 hb
ISBN 978 1 78032 262 9 pb

*In gratitude
to Ibrahim, Ishaq and Ya3coub
for the eternal love we share*

Contents

ACKNOWLEDGEMENTS   viii

GLOSSARY   ix

INTRODUCTION *Homo islamicus*: beyond 'good' and 'bad'   1

1 The vanishing jihadist: bin Laden and the Arab revolutions   21

2 Constructing the 'bad' Muslim: *jihad*, Orientalism and
  the militarization of Muslim lands   48

3 Contextualizing 'bad' Muslims: *jihad*, globalization
  and anti-Orientalism   78

4 Ree(a)l jihadists: the media-tion of intentions   107

5 Recovering invisible traces: *jihad* and postcolonialism   141

6 Humanism and Islam: *jihad* and postsecularism   184

CONCLUSION Universalization of universes of resistance   216

NOTES   223

REFERENCES   229

INDEX   245

Acknowledgements

I would like to thank my friends and colleagues for enduring my sporadic moodiness and solitude while I wrote this book. I would especially like to acknowledge my sons Ibrahim and Ishaq for tolerating my irritating habit of intellectualizing the music they listen to and sharing my collection of 'suicide' videos with them. A very special thank you goes to my youngest son, Ya3qoub (Jacob), whose eternal spirit is largely responsible for the will it took to finish this book. I would also like to thank Dr Noreen Golfman and Dr Tariq Ramadan, who made many useful suggestions on my manuscript, as well as my anonymous reviewers. Particular thanks go to the folks at Zed Books for their patience and meticulousness.

Glossary

All explications of Islamic terminology are taken from John L. Esposito, *The Oxford Dictionary of Islam* (Oxford University Press, 2003).

Apostasy 'Renunciation of one's religion. ... The schools vary on the question of whether or not an apostate may be allowed, encouraged, or disallowed to repent, as well as on the apostate's property after death or banishment, but they agree that the marriage of an apostate is void' (22).

Dawah 'Call. God's way of bringing believers to faith and the means by which prophets call individuals and communities back to God. Militant submovements interpret *dawah* as calling Muslims back to the purer form of religion practiced by Muhammad and the early Muslim community' (64).

Din 'Way of life for which humans will be held accountable and recompensed accordingly on the Day of Judgment. The word is the root of the Arabic terms for "habit", "way", "account", "obedience", "judgement" and "reward" and is often translated as "religion"' (68).

Hadith 'Report of the words and deeds of Muhammad and other early Muslims; considered an authorative source of revelation, second only to the Quran' (101).

Halal 'Quranic term used to indicate what is lawful or permitted ...

Often used in conjunction with established dietary restrictions'
(105).

Hijab   'Traditional Muslim women's head, face, or body covering, of
numerous varieties across time and space, often referred to as
the "veil." *Hijab* is a symbol of modesty, privacy, and morality'
(112).

Ijtihad   'Islamic legal term meaning "independent reasoning", as opposed to *taqlid* (imitation). One of four sources of Sunni law.
Utilized where the Quran and Sunnah (the first two sources)
are silent. It requires a thorough knowledge of theology,
revealed texts and legal theory (*usul al-fiqh*); a sophisticated
capacity for legal reasoning; and a thorough knowledge of
Arabic' (134).

Jihad   'From the Arabic root meaning "to strive", "to exert", "to
fight"; exact meaning depends on context. May express struggle against one's evil inclinations, an exertion to convert un-
believers, or a struggle for the moral betterment of the Islamic
community. Today often used without any religious connotation, with a meaning more or less equivalent to the English
word *crusade*' (159–60).

Mujahidin   'Often translated as "warriors of God". Technically, the term
does not have a necessary connection with war. In recent years
those Muslims who engage in armed defense of Muslim lands
call themselves or are called mujahidin' (213).

Shahadah   'Witness. Recitation of the Islamic witness of faith, "There is
no god but God, and Muhammad is the Messenger of God";
the first of the five pillars of Islam' (286).

Shahid   'One who suffers or loses his or her life in carrying out religious
duty' (193)

Ulama   'Men of knowledge. Refers to those who have been trained
in the religious sciences (Quran, hadith, fiqh, etc.)' (325).

Zakah   'Required almsgiving that is one of the five pillars of Islam.
Muslims with financial means are required to give 2.5 per cent
of their net worth annually as zakah' (345).

'But don't be satisfied with stories, how things
have gone with others. Unfold your own myth,
without complicated explanation.'

JALAL AD-DIN RUMI
(*The Essential Rumi*, trans. Coleman Banks)

'patriotism is the last refuge
to which a scoundrel clings.'

BOB DYLAN
('Sweetheart Like You', *Infidels*)

INTRODUCTION

Homo islamicus:
beyond 'good' and 'bad'

The events that occurred on 11 September 2001, commonly referred to as 9/11, magnified, accelerated and popularized the engagement of theory and popular culture with Islam. Following the 1978 publication of Edward Said's seminal *Orientalism*, the issue of the misrepresentation of the Arab world and Islam had tenuously entered the domain of theory. Said had argued that the Occident had created the imaginary Orient through a series of stereotypical images or binary constructions that reaffirmed the Occidental self. These constructions, Said noted, were the cultural accompaniments to colonialism and imperialism. Certainly, the events following 9/11, including the 'war on terror', reinvigorated this discussion as well as extended an analysis on the limits of postcolonial theory, secularism, humanism and democracy, and the metaphysical challenge of a radically militant Islam. It can be argued that until the events of 9/11 there had been a minimal engagement of popular culture and theory with Islamic concepts outside Orientalist and area studies, and that 9/11 popularized a field that, thus far, had remained largely insular, academic and textual. Since then, with the wars in Iraq and Afghanistan in

play, dramatic and spectacular attacks on previously unreach-
able targets in London and Madrid, human rights catastrophes
of Guantánamo Bay and Abu Ghraib, the ongoing siege of
Gaza, and the evolving 'Arab Awakening', media and culture
industries have cashed in on the conflicts, producing a need
for viable cultural translators and commentators. This flurry of
activity has spectacularized the differences between the 'world
of Islam' and the West,[1] and issues such as freedom of expression, women's rights, political reform and radicalism have made
terms such as *apostate*, *hijab*, *ijtihad* and *jihad* part of the popular,
global lexicon. The 'war of ideas'[2] has become the subject of
everyone's conversation and the spoils of that war have been
rapidly consumed. While the theorization of the 'war on terror'
has been continuing for a decade now, both 'suicide bombings'
and attacks on Muslim populations have increased dramatically.
Thus, while theorizing about the *jihad* and popularizing the figure
of the jihadist have become commonplace, hundreds of thousands
of people across the world are still suffering from the effects of
real conflict. It can be argued that this condition demonstrates
a deep dislocation between theory and reality, and that as this
dislocation grows the gap of interlocution grows wider. This
book attempts to highlight this disjuncture and offers suggestions
as to how genuine contrapuntal discourse might begin in radical
criticism. In this book I will argue that the temptation to theorize
jihad, and especially to appropriate the figure of the jihadist,
offers fertile ground for a discussion about the limits of current
theory: including Orientalism, postcolonialism, postsecularism
and cultural studies, particularly regarding the role of Muslim
interlocutors in interpretation, in translating Islam's supposed
challenge to modernity.

Simplified categories have been invented to describe the
multiplicity of perspectives within diverse Muslim cultures and
within the West itself. Islam, particularly, has been compressed
into a monolith when convenient and become synonymous with

fundamentalism. As Edward Said wrote in his introduction to the revised edition of *Covering Islam*:

> It is simply false to try to trace all this [referring to terrorism] back to something called 'Islam,' no matter how vociferously polemical Orientalists – mainly active in the United States, Britain, and Israel – insisted that Islam regulates societies from top to bottom, that *dar al-Islam* is a single, coherent entity, that church and state are really one in Islam, and so forth. (Said 1997: xvi)

This tendency to see Islam as a unitary entity is reversed, however, when the occasion calls for it. After 9/11, for example, President Bush made reference to 'good' and 'bad' Muslims – the 'bad' ones being responsible for the 9/11 attacks and the 'good' ones being anxious to disassociate themselves from the 'bad' ones, clear their names and support America (Mamdani 1995: 15). Throughout periods of high alert, Islam and Muslims are routinely denigrated and stereotyped as enemies of freedom and civilization, victimized as potential holders of threatening ideologies, and even tortured to satiate the public need for perceived security. Other times, philosophers and politicians fragment Islam into convenient differentiations between various 'types' of Muslim: the progressives, moderates, fundamentalists, neo-fundamentalists and jihadists. In fact, those antagonistic to Islam and those sympathetic to it often end up making the same arguments. It has become commonplace to theorize that Islam and the West hold different epistemological frameworks; this assertion comes from the right and the left alike, with neoconservatives such as Samuel Huntington, leftists such as Slavoj Žižek, and Osama bin Laden all singing in the same choir. The politics of representing Islam and Muslims is highly unstable and, as Douglas Kellner notes, 'media spectacles are subject to dialectical reversal as positive images give way to negative ones' (2005: 78).

Jihad has become a central term in this 'war on terror'. Theorists and lay people alike discuss the nature of *jihad*, until recently an obscure concept about which only theologians would converse outside Islamic cultures. In fact, an entire public discourse on *jihad* has developed, and *jihad* itself has been shaped and redefined into various configurations: as a radical revolutionary energy, an agent for peaceful social change, an inner struggle for peace and reconciliation, or a barbarian destructive instinct that opposes civilization. Various commentators on the ongoing Arab revolutions have breathed a sigh of relief that the *jihad* which consumed discourse on the Middle East for the past decade has been replaced by peaceful protests and a secular spirit of revolution.

To be fair, even among theologians *jihad* has held ambiguous meanings, not only in contemporary times but throughout history. Volumes have been written in Islamic scholarship about the doctrine of *jihad*, and only some of these discussions can be explored here.[3] Asma Afsaruddin has noted that throughout the first three centuries of Islam *jihad* developed a multiplicity of meanings largely related to struggling in the path of God, which could mean embarking on the pursuit of knowledge, an inner battle for spiritualism, and a military struggle in defence of Islam. Sohail Hashmi has established that from the eighth to the fourteenth centuries of Islam, considered the classical period, legal jurists ordained *jihad* as a divine struggle in a world divided into *dar al-Islam*, a Muslim state led by a just ruler, and *dar al-harb*, the land of war, where Islam did not prevail. During this period, many scholars aimed at bringing Islamic civilization to *dar al-harb*, under strict conditions, thus developing a code as to how these activities were to take place. This led to the development of a further discourse of *jihad* not only as a defensive struggle against intruders but as a means of spreading Islam to non-Muslim areas. The teachings of Muhammad Ibn Abd al-Wahhab, developed in the middle of the eighteenth century on the Arabian peninsula in direct response to the colonization of Arabia by the Ottomans, have expanded the boundaries of political Islam by positioning *jihad* as a fight against colonialism.[4] Modern concepts of *jihad* largely developed from these historical differentiations, as evidenced in the work of Sayyid Qutb, which grew out of the postcolonial Egypt of Gamal Abdel Nasser.[5] Scholars of Islam had traditionally distinguished between two types of *jihad*: *al-jihad al-akbar* (the greater *jihad*) and *al-jihad al-asghar* (the lesser *jihad*). The greater *jihad* was considered to be the inward struggle of the self against weakness. The lesser *jihad* was directed outward towards self-defence, preservation and justice. However, as Mohammed Fadel notes, Qutb, largely seen as the intellectual forefather of radical Islam, differentiated three types of *jihad al-asghar*: defensive *jihad* to ward off persecution of Muslims, *jihad* to assure freedom to preach Islam without persecution, and armed *jihad* as a means of achieving universal justice. Further development of the differentiations of the lesser *jihad* and the codes for its engagement are relatively modern. African scholar Mahmood Mamdani accentuates this reality: 'After the first centuries of the creation of the Islamic states, there were only four widespread uses of jihad as a mobilizing slogan – until the Afghan jihad of the 1980s' (1995: 51).

It is the lesser *jihad* that is most sharply debated today. John Esposito in 'Jihad: Holy or Unholy War?' summarizes some of the key Islamist positions in this debate. He observes that notable religious leaders, such as Sheikh Yusuf Qaradawi, Sheikh Ahmad Yasin, the founder of Hamas, and Akram Sabri, the Mufti of Jerusalem, have allowed *jihad* only as self-defence in occupied Muslim-predominant countries, including the killing of civilians in these militarized zones. However, Sheikh al-Sheikh, former Grand Mufti of Saudi Arabia, has condemned all suicide bombings as un-Islamic. Sheikh Muhammad Sayad Tantawi, Grand Imam of al-Azhar Mosque and Grand Sheikh of al-Azhar University, has drawn a distinction between acts of self-sacrifice and self-defence and strongly disallowed the killing of non-combatants. Osama bin Laden and Ayman al-Zawahiri, on the other hand, have argued that *jihad* can include attacks upon military and non-military targets inside Muslim countries that are physically occupied by foreign powers, attacks on military installations in Muslim countries that are not formally occupied, as well as attacks within the occupying countries themselves. In the introduction to the highly informative *Princeton Readings in Islamist Thought*, Euben and Zaman argue that bin Laden 'embraces a global jihad that essentially collapses distinctions between national and international, offensive and defensive fighting, enemies at home and those from afar' (2009a: 42), all themes that served as nuanced differentiations in the stances of various Islamists.

To complicate the discourse further, *jihad* is packaged as 'good' and 'bad'. The greater *jihad*, which is inner and spiritual in nature, is presented as benevolent, while the lesser *jihad*, which can take various forms of struggle for social justice, is branded as malevolent. It is this struggle for social justice which is largely the object of public scrutiny. 'Good' Muslims accentuate the inner spiritual journey and work within existing institutions to achieve social justice non-violently. They therefore present *jihad* as compatible with Western neoliberalism or even leftism. The category of 'bad' Muslims can include all those who focus on the social element of *jihad*, whether it involves radically confronting injustice through active social and political organization or through violent struggle. This group of 'bad' Muslims is diverse, and, as Olivier Roy and John Esposito argue, wrongfully groups political Islamists, who aim to institute Islamic political systems, with jihadists, who attempt to disrupt global order through suicide attacks.[6] Euben and Zaman also demonstrate that Islamist politics are remarkably diverse, including strains of Salafism, Sufism, Wahhabism, Shi'ism and modernism, with some Islamists being members of the *ulama* and some not, with diverse viewpoints on issues such as gender, politics, democracy and violence (2009a: 5-46). Though Sayyid (2004: 155) connects the rise of Islamism to a tension between the modernity of Kemalism and the erosion of Eurocentricism, Euben and Zaman (2009a: 6-7) connect it to the continued colonial presence in Muslim lands. In either case, scholars agree that the emergence of Islamism as a political movement is connected to anti-colonial and anti-imperialist sentiments and projects and the internal struggle of Muslims for self-identity. However, this is not a book about Islamism: its focus is the jihadist, whether nationally or globally operational, who shares concerns and visions with various Islamists, but advocates for and employs militant and violent methods, often contrary to traditional Islamist doctrines.

In this book I use the term 'jihadist' or *shahid* (if the jihadist actually manages to die) rather than the term 'terrorist', or 'Muslim terrorist'. In *On Suicide Bombing*, Talal Asad argues 'If one is to talk about religious subjectivities, one must work through the concepts the people concerned actually use' (2007: 44). Contemporary jihadists, such as al-Qaeda and affiliates discussed in this book, consistently refer to themselves as jihadists, *shahid* or *mujahidin*, using an explicit Islamic terminology that rejects the assignation of terrorist. Therefore I use the same terms when I write about them rather than the 'abjected figure of the terrorist' (Redfield 2009: 2) that has emerged to 'haunt' neoliberal Western society, to use a Derridean term originally employed to discuss the spectre of communism, which feeds on an intense fear for one's personal safety. A hunger to know those anonymous others, to theorize their intentions and perhaps even to humanize them is evident in popular culture and theory, particularly over the past decade.

Arguably one of the most useful contributions to naming and describing the figure of the terrorist has been generated by Georgio Agamben, with his discussion of the concept of the *Homo sacer*, which has provoked considerable response in critical circles. Agamben argues that under the spectacle of terrorism a new kind of authoritarianism is created; citizens willingly give up hard-earned civil liberties in order to be protected from the *Homo sacer* – the sovereign-less terrorist, who is seen as less than human, a holder of 'bare life', who can be killed without consequence. In *Beyond the Spectacle of Terrorism: Global Uncertainty and the Challenge of the New Media*, Henry Giroux agrees with Agamben that the fear of the *Homo sacer* has resulted in the privatization of institutions for the public good and that as a result the functions of the state have shifted, leading to a withdrawal into private space in Western society. He also adds to Agamben's formulation, noting that the jihadists 'situate the body both as an object of abuse and torture [beheading videos] and as an agent of resistance [suicide bombers]' (Giroux 2006: 55). While they are the object of indiscriminate killing, they are also the perpetrators. Kellner elaborates that the process of dehumanization, necessary to sustain the threat of the *Homo sacer*, occurs on both sides of the war on terror:

> The terrorist crimes of September 11th appeared to be part of this Jihad, and show the horrific consequences of totally dehumanizing an 'enemy' as so evil that even innocent members of the group in question deserve to be exterminated. (2005: 33)

Even though bin Laden may have been dehumanized for the West, and even though he dehumanized the West in turn, Kellner astutely observes that 'Bin Laden has become a "revolutionary myth", looked upon with awe by millions throughout the world' (2005: 39).

Slavoj Žižek also makes a controversial contribution to this debate about the *Homo sacer* by accusing theorists, such as Giroux, Kellner and Butler, of emptying Agamben of his radicalness in order to appropriate the figure of the *Homo sacer* for the goals of a more inclusionary radical democracy. Like Kellner and Giroux, Žižek notes that though the *Homo sacer* is the man over whom all men are sovereign and who can be killed without consequence, he can also declare a war that is spectral in nature – therefore making him an outlaw. He adds, however, that it is essential to supplement the concept of the stateless *Homo sacer* with the knowledge that he is also the recipient of humanitarian aid, since the dehumanized *Homo sacer* is the object of the West's torture and of its pity. To make this point Žižek draws attention to the fact that both bombs and food baskets were being dropped on Afghanistan at the same time, making the *Homo sacer* at once a 'privileged object of humanitarian biopolitics' and a terrorist. Therefore, Žižek argues,

> there is no place in Agamben for the 'democratic' project of 're-negotiating' the limit which separates full citizens from *Homo sacer* by gradually allowing their voice to be heard; his point is, rather, that in today's 'post-politics' the very democratic public space is a mask concealing the fact that, ultimately, we are all *Homo sacer*. (2002: 100)

As this rather brief review indicates, the figure of the jihadist as *Homo sacer* has been employed by First World theorists as a tool to engage in self-reflection on the state of the democratic project in Western countries. All theorists mentioned steer away from noting the religious nature of the jihadist's intentions and refer to him as 'terrorist' rather than jihadist, robbing him of the particularity of his position and refusing to identify him by the name he assigns to himself. Second, they do not ground the jihadist's stance as a response to the particularities of his own oppression (with the exception of Žižek), and all present him as a reactionary figure without a clear political agenda. There is virtually no discussion of what *jihad* might contribute to the envisioning of future global democratic projects, except as a means to reflect to the West its own inconsistencies and injustices.

It is useful here to recall Maxime Rodinson's much earlier postulation of the term *Homo islamicus*, which specifies the Islamic nature of *Homo sacer* much more transparently than do contemporary theorizations:

> The Oriental may always have been characterized as a savage enemy, but during the Middle Ages, he was at least considered on the same level as his European counterpart. And, to the men of the Enlightenment, the ideologues of the French Revolution, the Oriental was, for all his foreignness in appearance and dress, above all a man like anyone else. In the nineteenth century, however, he became something quite separate, sealed off in his own specificity, yet worthy of a kind of grudging admiration. This is the origin of the *homo islamicus*, a notion widely accepted even today. (Rodinson 1987: 60)

In fact, the theory of *Homo sacer*, as a means of engaging with the jihadist, empties *jihad* of its own rich theoretical position, thereby employing an old Orientalist turn of using the Orient to serve as a mirror of the Occident. If the *Homo sacer* is an object of both fear and pity, the *Homo islamicus* is often the object of both violent oversimplication and a 'grudging admiration' for nostalgic utopian projects. The figure of *Homo islamicus* allows for a more equal dialogue with a full recognition of the jihadist as not merely an image in the Western mirror to allow reflection on the failed democratic project, but as a figure with his own rich tradition of resistance and diverse oppositional discourses. Therefore throughout this book the term *Homo islamicus* is used to refer to the sign of the jihadist and the category of 'bad' Muslim 'sealed off in his own specificity'.

In contrast to the jihadist, the category of 'good' Muslim is used to refer to Muslims of various political persuasions who attempt to translate the sign of *jihad* for a largely uninformed audience. Muslim interlocutors have become central to making visible the spectre of the jihadist, and as such are an important focus of this study. The stubborn curiosity to understand the actions of the jihadists propelled those already engaged in ongoing discussions about Islam and its epistemology prior to 9/11 into the media spotlight. At the same time, 'authentic' Muslims, usually Western Muslims with origins in predominantly Muslim countries, or Western converts to Islam, were solicited as native informants.[7] For the most part, their audiences lie in the West, not in predominantly Muslim countries, and their messages are articulated in European languages, primarily English and French. These intellectuals are tasked with the difficult mission of explaining the jihadist, making him just familiar enough to understand, but exotic enough to fascinate, while keeping a distance from the analysis, ensuring that they in no way express admiration for him. In short, they play the role of 'good' Muslims explaining the motifs of the 'bad' Muslims. Simultaneously, the 'bad' Muslims have developed their own forms and discourses to represent themselves, without the mediation of the native informants. This leads to a vastly heterogeneous discourse which both affirms and rejects dominant ideologies, producing a multidimensional Muslim response.

The 'good' Muslims have gained incredible value by having knowledge of both the cultural capital of Islam, especially the jihadist, and the discourse of First World media and academia. It is useful here to recall Pierre Bourdieu's description of cultural capital in *The Field of Cultural Production*. He argues that capital refers to objects, artistic imagery, texts and music that have meaning and interest for those who possess the code; religious capital, for example, is specific to the religious field and is associated with specialists who guard the corpus of knowledge (Bourdieu 1993: 91). Orthodoxy and heresy, terms openly borrowed from the religious field, are deployed by Bourdieu to describe the struggle for power within any field. In an extension of Bourdieu, Appadurai in *The Social Life of Things* (1986) defines postcoloniality as a system of postcolonial writers working within the neocolonial context of commodity culture, and notes that the writer is only one of the agents of legitimation; others include reviewers, publishers and communities. In this way, cultural industries both produce and appropriate writers to fit into various subject positions in the field. In *The Postcolonial Exotic*, Graham Huggan suggests that the encoding of the exotic has been essential in assigning value to postcoloniality:

> exoticism may be understood conventionally as an aestheticising process through which the cultural other is translated, relayed back through the familiar. Yet in a postcolonial context, exoticism is effectively repoliticised, redeployed both to unsettle metropolitan expectations of cultural otherness and to effect a grounded critique of differential relations of power. (2001: ix–x)

In short, the exotic manufactures Otherness either by rendering the familiar strange or by making the strange familiar in the dialectical process of exoticization (Othering) and appropriation.

It is a 'semiotic circuit that oscillates between the opposite poles of strangeness and familiarity' (Huggan 2001: 13). Functioning as a symbolic system, the exotic assigns the familiar to unfamiliar things and often politics is concealed under this dialectical process. The Other is perceived as foreign and demonized when there is a need to subjugate him, or as friendly and neighbourly when the subjugation will be less violent. Therefore, it is not so much the intentionality of the author that is the focus of interpretation, but the function of the author as a commodity in the process of exoticization. It is the contention of this study that Islam can be viewed as a field within which there is immense competition for both symbolic power and religious capital. Field specialists, theologians and other cultural interpreters define the field and the code of membership. Describing the codes of the field of Islam which have ruptured into popular culture, particularly the code of *jihad*, has been the role of a newly founded group of Muslim writers and intellectuals, who are in competition with their increasingly articulate radical counterparts, the jihadists. This often problematizes the concept of Muslimness itself, with the good Muslims claiming orthodoxy for an Islam which has been 'hijacked' by heretical jihadists. The jihadists, on the other hand, dismiss the good Muslims as heretical pawns who want to reform Islam to make it compatible with the goals of neoliberal globalization.

It can be argued that in First World academic institutions and cultures the value of Muslimness is high if one is considered a good Muslim, but diminishes significantly if the interlocutor takes an unpopular position on the right to *jihad*, in which case she is quickly herded into the group of bad Muslims. The instability of this binary of good and bad Muslims has been demonstrated by Mamdani in his discussion on how the Taliban and al-Qaeda were constructed and how the perception of ally and enemy shifted rapidly in global politics. Muslim interlocutors are acutely aware of this binary and the indiscriminate way they can be allocated to the latter group. Therefore their interventions often remain ambiguous, with an obsessive autobiographical drive to prove both their authenticity as Muslims and their credentials as Western theorists. The moderate interlocutor positions herself as both familiar and exotic, in order to establish a dual credibility in the West and in predominantly Muslim communities. While she maintains credibility in the West, and is perceived as a representative of Muslims, she is often unknown in predominantly Muslim countries. She also has to take particular care in situating her political allegiances since 'good' Muslim has come to mean 'moderate' and neoliberal and 'bad' Muslim has come to mean 'radical' or jihadist. Consider by notable example the persecution of Swiss scholar Tariq Ramadan, whose case became a human rights issue when he was denied a visa by the United States government to take up a post at the University of Notre Dame. Ramadan was accused of supporting fundamentalism because he recognized the legitimacy of *jihad* as the right to fight oppression and social injustice. The international debate regarding Ramadan's case became so heated that Ramadan wrote *What I Believe*, a book outlining his beliefs clearly, in order to avoid charges of doublespeak – that is, presenting one face to the West and another to Islamic audiences. Documenting his work before 9/11, Ramadan notes that because he has overtly positioned himself as a Muslim, he has come under suspicion, even though he is espousing the same ideas and conducting the same work he did previously as a teacher with no obvious religion (Ramadan 2010: 210).

The jihadists, on the other hand, with their spectacular acts of violence, do not worry about ambiguity and clearly speak their messages to specific audiences. However, these messages are continually mediated by others and even stripped of intentionality in the process of being re-presented. In predominantly Muslim countries, their messages resonate and seem direct and obvious, even if they are often rejected, while for Western theorists they remain the rantings of madmen speaking in an idiom that cannot be translated. Firmly located in the group of 'bad' Muslims, the jihadist raises serious queries regarding how he has been represented, playfully engaging in bantering and even comedy to deconstruct his image as a manic medievalist, isolated from Western doctrine.

In fact it can be argued that the debate between moderates and jihadists and the role of moderates in subverting the jihadists' radical messages are a continuation of an internal debate between Islamists and modernists (some Islamists are also modernists) involving the degree to which Muslims should engage with the West and also the core interpretation of Islamic foundational texts, with both claiming recourse to an authentic and genuine interpretation. The objective of this book is not to privilege either 'bad' or 'good' Muslims over the other; neither is it to explore the authentic Islamicity of *jihad* in the global world. The objective is to explore *jihad* as a cultural configuration and the after-effects of its radical message on theory, particularly. In this sense the book focuses on representations of *jihad* – by whom it is represented and for what purposes – and the effects these representations have on theory. *Jihad* is not discussed as a theological concept, but as a cultural configuration that is being circulated in an endless semiotic circuitry in the 'war on terror'. On occasion *jihad* is referred to as a 'sign' relating to the 'master signifier' of Islam as extrapolated by Sayyid in *Fundamental Fear* (2004: 42–8). Further, the sign of *jihad* has a historically unstable meaning while simultaneously it has become anchored to violence in the discourse on the 'war on terror'. In this book *jihad* is viewed as a sign from which one may query how a radical reimagining of the future might look in a postcolonial world. Further, the emphasis in this book is on *al-jihad al-asghar* (the lesser jihad), rather than *al-jihad al-akbar* (the greater jihad), because it is with its contentious claim of the right of violent resistance to oppression that *al-jihad al-asghar* challenges radical theory, particularly postcolonial theory, to examine its anti-imperialist roots. I argue that considering *jihad* as a cultural configuration invites exploration as to how the 'war on terror' has raised issues of urgent importance to intellectuals – particularly as related to issues of representation and interpretation and the role of violence in socio-political transformation.

Some explanation also needs to be given on the use of the term 'contrapuntal' throughout this book. As Mufti argues when discussing the lack of contrapuntality in cultural studies,

> it can be granted that 'they' have literatures and other modes of cultural expression that are worthy of consideration, but only 'we' have theory, the inclination to think in abstract and conceptual terms about language, culture, and the world and about the conditions of possibility of such knowledge itself. (Mufti 2005: 123)

Mufti's comments on contrapuntality are in reference to the deployment of the term by Said, particularly in his widely influential works *Culture and Imperialism* and *Humanism and Democratic Criticism*, where Said makes an impassioned plea for a contrapuntal approach to reading the world and understanding the 'worldliness' of texts. Claiming that 'we cannot deal with the literature of the peripheries without also attending to the literature of the metropolitan centers', Said also argues for reading across disciplines, connecting texts and societies, while not perceiving texts as mere reflections of historical events (1994a: 318). Instead, Said offers a global and comparative approach to understanding texts, placing texts of diverse forms and cultures into a common field, and, in other words, appreciating the genealogy of texts. This approach requires a capacity to read various texts alongside each other, outside their traditional disciplinary fields, in order to contextualize their 'worldliness':

> But this global, contrapuntal analysis should be modelled not (as earlier notions of comparative literature were) on a symphony but rather on an atonal ensemble; we must take into account all sorts of spatial or geographical and rhetorical practices – inflections, limits, constraints, intrusions, inclusions, prohibitions – all of them tending to elucidate a complex and uneven topography. (Said 1994a: 318)

Therefore any study of the figure of the jihadist in theory and literature must necessarily defy the boundaries of traditional disciplinary or national literature studies. First, globalization and terrorism studies, which cross the boundaries of humanities, literature and film, much the way that cultural studies have done, all engage with study of the jihadist and therefore necessitate a cross-disciplinary response. Second, the jihadist is a global figure, not tied to any country or particular geographical sphere, and as such any study of the jihadist defies the approach of traditional area studies, either in literature or in theory. Third, since the figure of the jihadist has deeply permeated popular culture and literature, as well as political, postcolonial and radical theory, an attempt to differentiate between 'high' and 'low' culture or adhere to the limits of genre studies would not allow for a thorough analysis of how cultural hegemony reproduces academic theorization in popular cultural configurations of the jihadist. Finally, this book encourages a dialogic relationship between the works of Muslim and non-Muslim writers in order to explore fully the positionality of Muslim interlocutors in the debate on the figure of the jihadist. In elaborating on Said's concept of contrapuntality, Aamir Mufti calls for a 'comparativism yet to come' (2005: 115), an 'opening up and crossing over' (2005: 114) of texts from different cultures and time periods as a way to elaborate the complexity of concepts – in short, a deconstruction of cultural autonomy. He lucidly argues,

> We come to understand that societies on either side of the imperial divide now live deeply imbricated lives that cannot be understood without reference to each other. It begins to encode a comparativism yet to come, a global comparativism that is a determinate and concrete response to the hierarchical systems that have dominated cultural life since the colonial era. (Mufti 2005: 115)

Following Said's ambitious example, this book situates texts of cultural theory, sociology, philosophy and fiction alongside each other, along with films, videos and political treatises and speeches. As such the book crosses disciplines, genres and 'high' and 'low' culture to offer a contrapuntal reading of the figure of the jihadist. It also places works from the peripheries, from diverse Muslim writers, in dialogue with each other and with those of noted First World theorists.

In popular literature and film, particularly, the jihadist possesses an oscillating strangeness and familiarity. Familiar motives, such as personal despair at the loss of a parent, unemployment, humiliation and alienation, are assigned as possible intentions for his violent act. At the same time, foreign unknowns, such as Quranic incitation to violence, Bedouin codes of family honour, or the politics of faraway countries, also inform these portraits, rendering the jihadist as strange, and alien. Depending on the depiction and even nuances within the same depiction, the portrait of the jihadist resonates as a familiar neighbour, while remaining foreign and unknowable. Further, the line between fiction and non-fiction is consistently blurred in this process of construction, as popular knowledge on actual jihadists finds its way into the fictionalization of jihadist characters. Indeed, the theorists I discuss in this book spend considerable time elaborating upon specific profiles and portraits of individual jihadists, and drawing conclusions as to the intentionality of the *jihad* itself, through the lives of Osama bin Laden, the various 9/11 bombers, and the culprits in the Madrid and London bombings, for example. This analytical approach to the individual lives and motivations of these real-life characters has generated a certain narrative consistency in presenting the jihadists' intentions to a Western audience, an approach derived from critical commentary and fiction and ceaselessly reproduced. Interestingly, fictional accounts of jihadists mirror the non-fictional analysis, in this sense clearly illuminating the historicity of texts. Of course, it can also be argued that these fictional accounts generate, rather than reflect, current popular knowledge about the jihadist. One can argue that the fictional imagery of jihadists presented in contemporary films and novels, for example, which are more readily available and accessible to the masses than is theory, more influential in generating popular knowledge of *jihad* than academic analysis. In either case, the important point is not whether fiction informs cultural criticism or cultural criticism informs fiction, but that both are intricately tied up in constructing a genealogy of terror in a Foucauldian sense.[8] In *Plotting Terror: Novelists and Terrorists in Contemporary Fiction*, Margaret Scanlon (2001) notes that terrorist themes have been prominent in numerous novels from the birth of the genre in the nineteenth century, and many of the works examined in this book fall into this genre of the popular 'terrorist' novel.

This book also argues that a reassessment of theory is required to hear the voices of Muslims speaking in indigenous vocabularies of faith. The debates regarding the disappearance of the jihadist as related to the Arab Spring serve as a pivotal starting and ending point to examine the dislocation between 'good' and 'bad' Muslims. From there the book traces the genealogy of the jihadist in theory and culture since 9/11. Chapter 2 focuses on the re-emergence of Orientalism, which has arisen post-9/11 in the work of Bernard Lewis and Samuel Huntington, and the role of Muslims, such as Irshad Manji, Azar Nafisi, Khaled Hosseini and Yasmina Khadra, either advertently or inadvertently, in supporting Orientalist arguments as the cultural logic for the militarization of Muslim countries. Chapter 3 focuses on the counter-narrative to Orientalism by contextualizing the arguments of anti-Orientalists such as John Esposito, Olivier Roy, Iman Faisal Abu Rauf and exploring the fiction of Slimane Benaïssa and Orhan Pamuk. Chapter 4 examines the intentionality of the jihadist from his own perspective, comparing the direct interventions by infamous jihadists, such as Osama bin Laden, Adam Gadhan, Mohammed Siddique Khan and Shehzad Tanweer, to interpretations of noted intellectuals such as Henry Giroux and Faisal Devji in an attempt to highlight the fault lines that emerge in cultural and political analysis on discussions of the jihadist. Chapter 5 further explores how *jihad* and Islam in general are an invisible trace in postcolonial theory by investigating Said's troubled relationship with Islam and challenges to him by postcolonial Muslim writers such as Anouar Majid and Ziauddin Sardar. Chapter 6 examines the movement beyond postcolonialism towards postsecularism, through the works of Slavoj Žižek, Terry Eagleton, Tariq Ramadan and Talal Asad, arguing that discussions on *jihad* and the Muslimness of Europe have been the catalyst of the exponential growth of postsecular theory. The concluding chapter summarizes how theorizations on *jihad* have contributed to contemporary theory, particularly over the past decade, and reverts to the central assertion in the Introduction that the vanishing of the jihadist in discourse, through various discursive methods, is evidence of an aggressive attempt to secularize postsecular Islamic discourse, particularly exemplified in the discourse on the Arab revolutions.

Finally, the assertion of the existence of *jihad* and Islam itself needs clarification. Sayyid describes the dilemma in which Said found himself – writing about Islam but not wanting to enter Orientalism: 'Said seems to understand that Orientalism totally constitutes Islam, if he starts speak about Islam, he will be re-incorporated into orientalism' (Sayyid 2004: 35). Unlike Said, and like Sayyid, I believe that 'Islam is not a signifier without a signified, but a signifier whose meaning is expressed by its articulation' (Sayyid 2004: 42). Therefore, unlike Said, I assert that there is an Islam distinct from Orientalist representations of it. This Islam, however, is not one with a singular essence, but a master signifier that unifies and draws the limits of its community, the various articulations of Islams, though these limits become areas of contestation. Second, though I am most interested in representations of *jihad* and how *jihad* has infiltrated theory and culture, I do not claim to explain what composes authentic *jihad* according to Islamic exegesis, though I do recognize the existence of *jihad*, as a spiritual and political formulation, separate from its discursive representations.

Further, in this book, Muslim fiction does not refer to religious fiction. Instead, I use the term 'Muslim' to mean practising Muslims, or those born into Islam by birth, or those who have converted to it by choice, and it covers a wide range of allegiance to Islam as a faith, from practising to non-practising Muslims. To this extent, I adopt the criteria which Amin Malak outlines in *Muslim Narratives and the Discourse of English*:

> Accordingly for the flexible purpose of our discussion here, the term *Muslim narratives* suggests the works produced by the person who believes firmly in the faith of Islam; and/or, via an inclusivist extension, by the person who voluntarily and knowingly refers to herself, for whatever motives, as a 'Muslim' when given a selection of identitarian choices; and/or, by yet another generous extension, by the *person* who is rooted formatively and emotionally in the culture and civilization of Islam. (2005: 7)

Because the subject of this book is largely representation and the role of diverse Muslims in representing the varied manifestations of *jihad*, it is only fair that I position my own subjectivity in this debate. Throughout the book I argue that Muslims often identify themselves as such in order to lend credibility to their interlocutions, and the chapters which follow provide various examples of how Muslim interlocutors position themselves as viable commentators. At the same time, non-Muslim writers writing about Islam, especially since Said's *Orientalism*, are self-consciously aware of the risks of being labelled Orientalists. Therefore it is in this context that I situate my own Muslim subjectivity as one most commonly identified as a 'Western convert' to Islam, 'who is rooted emotionally in the culture and civilization of Islam', and who considers herself as part of a community that sees new value in what faith-based belief systems can offer as a radical critique of global capitalism.

CHAPTER I

The vanishing jihadist:
bin Laden and the Arab revolutions

The assassinations of Osama bin Laden and Anwar al-Awlaki, the twists and turns in the Arab revolutions, rebranded as the Arab 'Awakening', and the bipolar positioning of these two struggles, serve as a useful starting point from which to explore the fragility of the binary construction of 'good' and 'bad' Muslims, particularly since 9/11 and the popularization of the rhetoric of the 'war on terror'. Over the last decade, but not limited to this time, Muslims, the majority population in the Middle East and North Africa, now being re-formed through the Arab 'Awakening', have been categorized according to both their position on violence as a tool for revolutionary change and their compliance with the mantra of neoliberal social and economic progress. And, in this sense, bin Laden had always been an easy target that fitted the Orientalist stereotype of the crazed medieval Islamist disconnected from the fine nuances of modernity and progress. Good Muslims are expected to disassociate themselves from bin Laden's violent *jihad* and struggle to implement reforms in their societies according to the narrative that liberalization of the region's economies will finally allow the Muslim world to catch up with Western modernity. The category of bad Muslims, which has become rather heavily populated, includes, but is not limited to, all those who argue that a rupture from Western imperialist interests is necessary for progress and justice, and that this rupture necessitates violence to effect change, whether epistemic or actual. As I have discussed in the Introduction, the sliding measure of 'badness' has been elastic enough to include jihadists, Islamists and, on occasion, nationalists and leftists, as unsympathetic to freedom and universal concepts of liberalization. The Islamophobic trope has been an essential mechanism in culturizing this polarization between 'good' Muslims (who can establish governments whose interests collaborate with those of the United States, the European Union, the World Trade Organization, the International Monetary Fund, the World Bank and, of course, Israel) and 'bad' Muslims (who might reject economic imperialism and its accompanying homogenizing cultural and social programmes). Throughout this book I show evidence of how 'good' Muslims are familiarized as 'people like us'[1] and 'bad' Muslims are exoticized and demonized as enemies of civilization.

Though various anti-Orientalists discussed in this book, such as John Esposito, Faisal Devji and Olivier Roy, have played a vital role in explaining bin Laden's version of *jihad* in socio-political, ethical and secular terms, it can be argued that the environment for hearing bin Laden has always been particularly static-prone. It is likely to remain as such while the CIA pores over bin Laden's diaries and videos, collections of pornography and marijuana plants, leaking information which will further demonize him and his associates.[2] This reinvention of bin Laden coincides with assertions that his methodology of radical violence has been shown to be ineffective by the 'peaceful' protests of Twittering youth 'awakened' to a new pan-Arab struggle, which hopefully will be compliant with American and European interests.

Recent responses to bin Laden's death, from liberals to leftists, have unanimously claimed that he is now obsolete, and had been for some time. Gilles Kepel, for example, confidently declared in a *New York Times* op-ed that bin Laden was 'already dead' before his actual assassination since his message had already been replaced by secular uprisings (Kepel 2011). After Noam Chomsky's controversial article in *Guernica* of 6 May 2011, which highlighted the hypocritical American stance in assassinating bin Laden, Chomsky was compelled to extrapolate in a longer piece on Znet (20 May 2011) in which he noted that bin Laden's death meant less for the Arab world than the West since bin Laden 'had long been a fading presence, and in the past few months was eclipsed by the Arab Spring' (Chomsky 2011b). Likewise, earlier on Znet (6 May 2011) Tom Engelhardt argued that the Arab world had 'largely left bin Laden in the dust even before he took that bullet to the head', again because he had been replaced by 'the massive, ongoing, largely nonviolent protests that have shaken the region and its autocrats to their roots' (Engelhardt 2011). Mainstream Western media have been so keen to discern what Arabs think of bin Laden that the *Guardian*, the *Irish Times*, NPR and CNN all ran extensive pieces documenting Arab reactions to bin Laden's death, issuing a collective sigh of relief that the Arab 'Awakening' will likely serve as a vent for the frustrations of Muslims who might otherwise turn to radicalism.

Faisal Devji's July 2011 policy paper for the Conflicts Forum provides a useful point of entry to elaborate on key points that are discussed in detail throughout this book: first, that the *jihad* has become more relevant to Western societies, which perpetually define themselves in relation to an exotic Other, as evidenced in the wide range of appropriations discussed in this book in fiction, cultural theory and criticism; and second, that the arguments, or content, of bin Laden's *jihad* did not begin or end with bin Laden but are part of an ongoing anti-imperialist narrative and global ethical movement, which, I argue, is evident in the discourse of the Arab uprising. It is the striking continuity of the narrative, rather than its disruption, that is often overlooked by commentators.

To begin with, Devji argues that

> It is only the US public that continues to be mesmerised by Osama
> and his gang, which is appropriate enough given that they had always
> been a factor of America's domestic politics. So the political use to
> which President Obama put Bin Laden's killing was nothing more
> than a fulfilment of his predecessor's strategy, which consisted of
> using fears about security to consolidate his power at the national
> level. (Devji 2011: 2)

I would add that, particularly over the past decade, Western
fascination with the figure of the jihadist has been reflective of a
culture of victimology and fear that has become foundational to
the logic required for imperialist, Euro-American capitalist expansion. In this regard, the exotic figure of bin Laden and his affiliates,
and sometimes an undefined group of Islamists, is the mechanism
which has nurtured this culture of fear. The repetitive replaying of
footage of an aged bin Laden viewing himself on video, combined
with the footage of President Obama and his team watching bin
Laden being illegally assassinated, the morbid celebrations over the
death of bin Laden, and the grotesque Internet postings of fake
corpse photos, reveal a perverse element of the 'war on terror'
which verges on the necrophilic and pornographic. Devji notes
the curious American specificity of this viewing:

> Crucial about this reaction, after all, has been the fact that people
> around the world seemed interested in the event primarily because
> of the extraordinarily pugnacious public response it generated in the
> US, and not for any reason of their own. Thus even in countries like
> Britain and Spain, which not so long ago had themselves been the
> victims of Al-Qaeda's militancy, there was little if any public dem-
> onstration of satisfaction at Bin Laden's death, though it continued to
> be the subject of massive media coverage precisely as an element in
> American politics. (Devji 2011: 1)

In this sense, the American public have taken the position of
voyeur to *jihad* in a 'closed loop of perversion' which enacts 'not
the desire to see and control so much as the drive to make oneself'
(Žižek 1999: 248, 175). In short the 'pervert' is carved out of the

market system for a mass-customized consumer whose perverse desires are an expression of the order's inherent transgression. As Žižek argues, 'the deepest identification which holds a community together is not so much identification with the Law that regulates its normal everyday circuit as identification with the specific form of transgression of the Law, of its suspension' (1992: 225). The celebration of bin Laden's illegal assassination and the killing by proxy of American citizen Anwar al-Awlaki demonstrate this perverse celebration of the suspension of the law. Yet the gruesome lure of bin Laden's demise is more than the utterance of a Wild West rhetoric, 'we got him', by President Obama,[3] but the expression of a diabolical tendency in the American public to see itself, when convenient as a leader of the 'international community' frequently called in to persecute violators of law, and, when convenient, as an outlaw – as outside the law – as evidenced in the bin Laden and al-Awlaki assassinations. The amnesic public celebrates the violence inherent in its transgressions, while simultaneously and hypocritically conceiving of its Empire as a peaceful and benevolent force spreading prosperity and liberalism – economic and hegemonic – across the globe.

It is the latter self-conception that America presents of itself in the narrative of 'the war on terror', particularly evident in its response to the Arab 'Awakening'. One major trend of Western media and Arab protestors is to package the revolutionaries and activists as peaceful in counterpoint to the violence of bin Laden and his radicals. Bin Laden had asserted that violence, including the right to kill oneself in killing the enemy, was an appropriate response to oppression and vowed to use violent means to rid the Muslim world of both its 'near enemy', its autocratic rulers, and its 'far enemy', the imperialist powers.[4] To achieve these ends he approved of spectacular attacks on symbolic targets on Western soil, and attacks on oilfields and various symbols of imperial presence inside predominantly Muslim countries. To the contrary, the Arab revolution has been spun as a peaceful protest, with Tahrir

Square, particularly, as an Arab version of Woodstock. Western support for the 2011 Arab revolutions has been tenuously and grudgingly granted as long as the protesters are 'peaceful'. At the same time the West has virtually ignored the symbolic significance of the violent catalyst of these revolutions, the act of testimony by Mohamed Bouazizi, a Tunisian street vendor who set himself on fire on 17 December 2010, now hailed as a *shahid* throughout the Muslim world. Mohammed Ali Atassi has observed:

> Did not Mohamed Bouazizi commit what – according to traditional Islamic law – is considered the most venal of all sins when he burned himself to inject life back into the veins of the Arab peoples after the tyrants had bled them almost dry? And yet the violation by Bouazizi of such a fundamental principle of traditional Islam was not enough to prevent millions of people from sympathizing with him and turning him into an icon and symbol of the current Arab revolution. (Atassi 2011: 34)

Likewise, did not bin Laden's followers commit similar acts of *shahid*, despite condemnation from numerous Islamic scholars questioning the Islamicity of their actions, and were not they too, much to the distress of pacifist observers, hailed as icons to many across the Muslim world?[5] While both adopted heterodox stances, bin Laden's was considered shameful since he advocated killing others along with the self, while Mohamed Bouazizi killed only himself, making him a hero more acceptable to Western standards of martyrdom. Yet Bouazizi's heterodox act did not prevent him being hailed as a *shahid*, and referred to as such throughout the Muslim world in a language eerily similar to bin Laden's. Even President Obama must have noticed the striking methodological similarity, since he spoke at length to reframe it as difference in an extended commentary on Bouazizi and bin Laden in his 19 May 2011 speech on the Arab uprisings, 'Moment of Opportunity'. On bin Laden, he claims

> Bin Laden was no martyr. He was a mass murderer who offered a message of hate – an insistence that Muslims had to take up arms

against the West, and that violence against men, women and children was the only path to change. He rejected democracy and individual rights for Muslims in favor of violent extremism; his agenda focused on what he could destroy – not what he could build.

Bin Laden and his murderous vision won some adherents. But even before his death, al Qaeda was losing its struggle for relevance, as the overwhelming majority of people saw that the slaughter of innocents did not answer their cries for a better life. By the time we found bin Laden, al Qaeda's agenda had come to be seen by the vast majority of the region as a dead end, and the people of the Middle East and North Africa had taken their future into their own hands. (Obama 2011a)

After emptying bin Laden of intention, and setting him up as the perfect exoticized authoritarian jihadist, Obama eulogizes the saintly Bouazizi:

That story of self-determination began six months ago in Tunisia. On December 17th, a young vendor named Mohammed Bouazizi was devastated when a police officer confiscated his cart. This was not unique. It's the same kind of humiliation that takes place every day in many parts of the world – the relentless tyranny of governments that deny their citizens dignity. Only this time, something different happened. After local officials refused to hear his complaints, this young man, who had never been particularly active in politics, went to the headquarters of the provincial government, doused himself in fuel, and lit himself on fire.

There are times in the course of history when the actions of ordinary citizens spark movements for change because they speak to a longing for freedom that has been building up for years. In America, think of the defiance of those patriots in Boston who refused to pay taxes to a King, or the dignity of Rosa Parks as she sat courageously in her seat. So it was in Tunisia, as that vendor's act of desperation tapped into the frustration felt throughout the country. Hundreds of protesters took to the streets, then thousands. And in the face of batons and sometimes bullets, they refused to go home – day after day, week after week – until a dictator of more than two decades finally left power. (Obama 2011a)

It is quite remarkable how Obama appropriates Bouazizi by comparing him to American revolutionaries and civil rights activists. In this sense, he clearly incorporates the Arab revolt into an

American narrative on the power of the individual in igniting change, and inaugurates the Arab protesters into the American tale of individualism, prosperity and the pursuit of happiness through the politics and economics of neoliberalism. By exoticizing bin Laden and familiarizing the good Muslims of the Arab revolts, Obama uses a practised postcolonial trope. This is explored in detail in the chapters that follow.

Another point worthy of consideration is that Obama's accomplices and new-found allies in the dense political change sweeping the region, who may not measure up to the familiar and 'non-violent' Bouazizi, are conveniently ignored. For example, when he briefly mentions American involvement in Libya, he speaks of 'a legitimate and credible Interim Council', failing to mention that the chairman, Mustapha Abdul Jalil, Gaddafi's ex-justice minister, has been criticized by Amnesty International for human rights violations, and Abd al-Hakim Belhaj, the commander of Tripoli's Military Council, who spearheaded the attack on Muammar al-Gaddafi's compound at Bab al-Aziziya, was a former commander of the Libyan Islamic Fighting Group (LIFG), an organization with historical links to al-Qaeda. As Douglas Kellner has noted, 'media spectacles are subject to dialectical reversal as positive images give way to negative ones' (2005: 78). In this case, Obama's spectacle is operating in reverse as the negative transforms into the positive and his new, familiarized allies are emptied of their radical pasts. In fact, the 'revolutionaries' or 'rebels' in Libya freely speak of their armed and violent struggle as *jihad*, and Abdul Jalil has stated that he wants a civil state in Lybia with *sharia* as its major source of legislation.[6]

In fact, the narrative of non-violence that has accompanied the familiarization and reversal of the jihadists' sacrificial tactics has been a major theme in how the revolutions have been packaged. The following comment by an Egyptian participant/blogger in the uprising is self-explanatory and worth quoting at length:

The revolution (like any other revolution) witnessed violence by the security forces that led to the killing of at least 846 protesters.

But the people did not sit silent and take this violence with smiles and flowers. We fought back. We fought back the police and Mubarak's thugs with rocks, Molotov cocktails, sticks, swords and knives. The police stations which were stormed almost in every single neighborhood on the Friday of Anger – that was not the work of 'criminals' as the regime and some middle class activists are trying to propagate. Protesters, ordinary citizens, did that.

Other symbols of power and corruption were attacked by the protesters and torched down during the uprising. Revolutionary violence is never random. Those buildings torched down or looted largely belonged to Mubarak's National Democratic Party.

In a number of provinces like in N Sinai and Suez, arms were seized by protesters who used them back against the police to defend themselves. State Security Police office in Rafah and Arish, for example, were blown up using RPGs, hand grenades and automatic rifles, while gas pipelines heading to Jordan and Israel were attacked.

Am I condemning this violence? Totally not. Every single revolution in history witnessed its share of violence. The violence always starts on the hands of the state, not the people. The people are forced to pick up arms or whatever they can put their hands on to protect themselves.

May all our martyrs rest in peace. Their blood will not go in vain. Revolution continues... (3arabawy 2011)

3arabawy makes a critical point: revolution is always violent; people protect themselves from state violence through violence and they are willing to die in the struggle. Yet, strangely, the Arab revolutions have been packaged as non-violent protests, intent on effecting change peacefully, antithetical to bin Laden's radical message, and converging with Obama's narrative of social progress.

In fact Obama's speech demonstrates a crude rewriting of history as he articulates the reasons for the revolution as a lack of self-determination and blocks to economic and social progress, while failing to mention that these deterrents to freedom and justice were perpetrated by the very regimes his administration, and those before him, supported throughout the region. There is no mention of the debilitating effects of American foreign policy in the region, except a vague promise that they have learned their lesson, established democracy in Iraq and Afghanistan and so will now leave. What Obama does not mention is that the revolutions in Tunisia and Egypt demonstrate media savvy on the part of a new generation of Muslims, who clearly have learned lessons from the past decade when it comes to positioning any protest originating in Muslim-majority communities. All attempts by both Arab dictators and American and European media, in the early stages, to label the revolutions 'Islamic' failed, thanks to the youth who initiated the movement. This generation grew up with the rhetoric of the 'war on terror' and is familiar with the tenuous categorization of 'good' and 'bad' Muslims. It has lived in a world where simply being Muslim has become a highly contentious and visibly political stance and does not suffer from collective amnesia. One critical reality is that this revolution is not only a revolution against Arab dictators, but a revolution against the humiliation Muslims have faced in the post-9/11 global landscape. The Arab/Muslim people are not just enraged on account of political, social and economic oppression; they are also angry with their rulers' complicity with imperialism, particularly American and Israeli. For example, Martin Scheinin, the UN special rapporteur on the protection of human rights, has detailed how Tunisia's counterterrorism laws and policies played a central part in the former government's crushing of political opposition and argues that the autocrats of the region were cooperative with the CIA's controversial 'extraordinary rendition program'. It is evident that the shameful and awkward baggage of the 'war on terror', particularly in North Africa, is coming to haunt the West.

In short, revolution has erupted from Muslim societies as a result of internal oppression *and* as a response to political, economic and cultural imperialism with which the post-9/11 youth are intricately familiar. And there is evidence that Muslims throughout the region are wary of America's friendly overtures of assistance. The May 2011 issue of *Perspectives*, 'People's Power: The

Arab World in Revolt', offers a diverse collection of analysis from Arab participants in and commentators on the ongoing uprisings, and as such provides an intriguing counter-narrative to Obama's mantra. For example, one such essay by Ramy Zurayk, 'Feeding the Uprisings', elaborates on the caution with which the Arabs are receiving the belatedly extended hand of assistance from the Americans:

> One must learn here from the experience of Latin America where the US accepted and even supported the overthrowing of dictators. Instead, it fostered pseudo-democracies where political power is spread among a class of neo-liberal political elites closely associated with the global business sector.
>
> In the Arab World, a strategy of this type would ensure that the ruling class continues to provide access to oil and minerals; and to markets wide open for manufactured goods among which food will continue to occupy the lion's share. It will promote a neo-liberal economic environment that will cultivate capitalist market fundamentalism and a political and economic and cultural normalization with Israel. (Zurayk 2011: 124–5)

In this regard, the international community, including President Obama, seems to have missed the message – that this revolution is as much against its hypocritical and condescending manner of dealing with Muslim societies as it is against Mubarak, Ben Ali or Gaddafi. Instead, Obama's speech delineates an intention to continue much of the same politics as before the revolutions began. He outlines a pragmatic plan for the continued spread of economic liberalism throughout the region, ensured by more loans from the World Bank and the International Monetary Fund, the promise of relieving 'a democratic Egypt' of up to $1 billion in debt, and an Enterprise Fund to invest in Tunisia and Egypt. In other words, Obama initiates a critical intervention to save neoliberal discourses and US foreign policy with a series of corporate bribes. He seems not to have heard, at all, the criticisms of these policies which emanate from the uprisings themselves. Mouin Rabbani, for example, explains in 'The Arab Revolts: Ten

Tentative Observations' how these very policies are the objects of the uprisings:

> Many if not most Arab regimes are facing similar crises, which can be summarized as increasing popular alienation and resentment fuelled by neo-liberal reforms. These reforms have translated into growing socio-economic hardship and disparities as the economy and indeed the state itself is appropriated by corrupt crony capitalist cliques; brutalization by arbitrary states whose security forces have become fundamentally lawless in pursuit of their primary function of regime maintenance; leaders that gratuitously trample institutions underfoot to sustain power and bequeath it to successors of their choice – more often than not blood relatives; and craven subservience to Washington despite its regional wars and occupations, as well as increasingly visible collusion with Israel proportional to the Jewish state's growing extremism. (Rabbani 2011: 10)

Intervening in an attempt to salvage American imperialism in the region, Obama utters a thinly veiled warning as to what Tunisia and Egypt, and other regimes, must do in order to ensure compliance with America's directive: continued support for and protection of Israel and normalization of relations, and a pledge against the acquisition of nuclear weapons in reference to the growing power of Iran across the Arab world.

Perhaps most incredible is how Obama erases his own nation's complicity in the conditions which fermented the revolutions in the first place, and his arrogance in continuing to reassert these very same conditions by focusing on the spontaneous nature of uprisings forged from an act of individual defiance. Though there is no doubt that youth such as Google executive Wael Ghonim, to whom Obama refers,[7] played a crucial role in organizing popular demonstrations, the uprisings are the product of a cumulative evolution in response to policies and dictators cradled by the Obama administration and those before. The ignition struck from Bouazizi's match, of which Obama speaks, was kindled from long-standing sentiment and organizing, growing from many years of smaller demonstrations and confrontations with security forces, from innumerable mass actions and interventions by trade unions, youth groups, women's organizations and environmentalists, not to mention Islamist movements, including the jihadists' radical militancy. In fact, it can be argued that the reasons cited by activists for the uprisings, though diverse in various regions, had been articulated by bin Laden himself throughout the preceding decades.

Though it cannot be argued that bin Laden's messages were innovative or unique, one of his distinctive contributions was the collapsing of the near and far enemy and the globalization of the concept of *jihad*. As Euben and Zaman note, his various messages reveal 'not a shift in focus from the domestic politics of Saudi Arabia to the dynamics of foreign power but rather the increasingly blurred boundary between the two' (2009b: 431). Bin Laden's assessment of Saudi society is intricately connected to his critique of Saudi cooperation with neo-imperialism. In 'Declaration of War Against the Americans', for example, he argues for both military operations in Saudi Arabia and economic boycotts against America as a dual strategy for liberation and notes how Saudi 'is the world's largest buyer of arms from the United States and the area's biggest commercial partner with the Americans who assist their Zionist brothers in occupying Palestine' (bin Laden 2009a: 449). Likewise, the Arab revolutions have focused on a reassessment of relations with Israel, particularly in Egypt and Tunisia, and the complicity with imperialism on the part of their leaders, whose fortunes rested safely in Western banks. Commenting on the uprisings, Fawaz Traboulsi summarizes the arguments of youth activists on the 'contractual agreement' between regimes and the American governments that was 'concretized' after September 2001, which 'stipulated an adherence to the Western agenda in the region and protected Western interests in return for supporting the continuity of these regimes' (Traboulsi 2011: 17). He argues that the transparency of this contract has been a major catalyst for the uprising, as the contract was based on

> preserving the neo-colonialist order under the pretext of prioritizing and maintaining 'security and stability' – meaning, the security of American military bases, facilities, airports and ports; securing oil and gas pipelines; ensuring the continuous turnover of high returns on deposits; securing employment in Western economies and bonds in Western treasuries; and ensuring markets for Western exports. (2011: 18)

The similarities between these arguments and bin Laden's convergence of Saudi domestic politics and the interests of the 'far enemy' are self-evident.

Bin Laden also focused on the economic impoverishment of the region, claiming, again in 'Declaration of War Against the Americans': 'People are deeply concerned about their everyday living; everyone talks of the deterioration of the economy, inflation, ever-increasing debts, and jails full of prisoners' (bin Laden 2009a: 439). These are the very same complaints that have dominated the discourse of the Arab revolutions. As Asef Bayat argues,

> [T]he current neo-liberal turn has failed to offer most of them [college graduates] an economic status that could match their heightened claims and global dreams. They constitute the paradoxical class of 'middle class poor' with high education, self-constructed status, wider worldviews, and global dreams who nonetheless are compelled – by unemployment and poverty – to subsist on the margins of neo-liberal economy as casual, low paid, low status, and low skilled workers (as street vendors, sales persons, boss boys or taxi drivers), and to reside in the overcrowded slums and squatter settlements of the Arab cities. (Bayat 2011: 53)

This 'middle class poor' are the new proletariat of the Middle East, and at the heart of the revolutions in Tunisia and Egypt.

It is also interesting to note that the methodology used by the 'middle class poor' to organize was also used by bin Laden and al-Awlaki themselves: Internet and social networking. The growth of jihadist discourse has become a major concern for governments worldwide, with numerous websites being shut down daily. In 2009 al-Awlaki released '44 ways to support *jihad*'.

Number 29 in his list, 'wwwjihad', describes how to become 'internet mujahideen':

> The internet has become a great medium for spreading the call of Jihad and following the news of the mujahideen. Some ways in which the brothers and sisters could be 'internet mujahideen' is by contributing in one or more of the following ways:
> - Establishing discussion forums that offer a free, uncensored medium for posting information relating to Jihad.
> - Establishing email lists to share information with interested brothers and sisters.
> - Posting or emailing Jihad literature and news.
> - Setting up websites to cover specific areas of Jihad, such as: mujahideen news, Muslim POWs, and Jihad literature. (al-Awlaki 2009: 12)

Al-Awlaki's bullet points serve as a blueprint for actions actually taken by young Tunisians and Egyptians in spearheading the revolutions. Through a series of interviews with bloggers and Internet activists, Doreen Khoury discusses the role social media played in organizing the community. Her interview with Ahmed Gharbeia describes how youth used social media:

> The great conversation on the Internet that started on forums and mailing lists, and later became all encompassing on the blogosphere was crucial. Even our open-source events: they helped revolutionize the youth against an archaic, unjust, and inefficient system, or way of doing things. (Khoury 2011: 83)

However, Gharbeia and other bloggers are quick to point out that the Internet is a tool, not a source of revolution.

> Many activists were introduced to activism and incorporated in the groups of activists by first making contact on the web. The Internet was a medium of theorising, campaigning, and organising. All in all it was a method of 'activating' the community. (Khoury 2011: 83)

Though the ideology differs, methodologically are not these youth, highly cognizant of the uses of social media as a tool for change, the inheritors of al-Awlaki's call to become 'internet mujahideen'? It is ironic that Obama lauds the use of the Internet

by the youth of the uprisings, praising their adeptness and creativity, considering that al-Awlaki advised on the same strategy.

Even the language of the Arab 'Awakening' was contained in
bin Laden's messages. 'Awakening' evokes a nineteenth-century
imaginary of Arab unity and reclaiming of identity as envisioned
in 1938 by the Palestinian-British intellectual George Antonius in
his famous book *The Arab Awakening*, which describes the *Nahda*
– 'Awakening' – as a secular, literary and cultural renaissance,
which pre-dated the populist Arab unity movement of the 1950s
and 1960s. The original *Nahda* focused on constructing a collective
identity and community, though bin Laden used the metaphor
of awakening for his own purposes. In fact, bin Laden often
emphasized his intention to jolt the masses from their slumber. In
one of his most widely analysed speeches, 'The Solution', which
addressed the American people on the occasion of the sixth anniversary of 9/11, bin Laden speaks at length about the debilitating
effects of capitalism. He argues that capitalism and democracy had
detrimentally affected people of Iraq and Afghanistan through
war, the people of Africa through displacement, and mankind,
in general, through global warming, and that despite the talk
of democracy by Bush, Blair, Sarkozy and Brown, these figures
displayed a 'flagrant disregard for the intellects of human beings'.
The 'solution', bin Laden argues, is for the American people,
and the people of the world, to wake up from the not so sweet
slumber of capitalism:

> This is why I tell you: as you liberated yourselves before from
> the slavery of monks, kings, and feudalism, you should liberate
> yourselves from the deception, shackles and attrition of the capitalist
> system. ...
>   The capitalist system seeks to turn the entire world into a fiefdom
> of the major corporations under the label of 'globalization' in order to
> protect democracy. (bin Laden 2007)

Here, bin Laden posits Western populations as victims of their political leaders and capitalism, living in a state of false consciousness,

or slumber, under a false sovereignty. His call is international, and interestingly he assures his Western audience that as they managed to free themselves from the false consciousness of their religion through secularism, they could now transcend secular capitalism to engage in a greater morality by sharing in the utopian vision of Islam. Bin Laden even points to sources that would assist the audience in waking from its slumber – the works by Noam Chomsky on the 'manufacturing of public opinion' and Michael Scheuer's explanation for the reasons for 'the losing of your war against us' (bin Laden 2007). In a 2009 statement he repeats this call for awakening, and refers to Mearsheimer and Walt's book *The Israel Lobby and U.S. Foreign Policy*, arguing 'it is time to free yourselves from fear and intellectual terrorism being practiced against you by the neoconservatives and the Israeli lobby' (bin Laden 2009b).

The threat of Israel is a major, recurring theme in bin Laden's messages, and the reality of this threat has become increasingly discussed in the discourse on the Arab uprisings. Thus far, the West feels insulated from the repercussions of the Arab 'Awakening', but it is unclear if this will remain stable if the 'Awakening' threatens the slumbers that sustain the nightmare of American imperialism in the region. A taste of what could happen was felt on 17 May 2011 when tens of thousands joined in protests called to commemorate the 63rd anniversary of the Palestinian *Nakba*. Israeli troops opened fire with live ammunition on protestors who demonstrated on Israel's borders with Syria, Lebanon, the West Bank and Gaza. In all, sixteen people were killed and over 400 wounded. Meanwhile in Egypt the military-dominated regime sent troops and police, who fired tear gas, rubber bullets and live ammunition into the thousands who had assembled outside the Israeli embassy in Cairo in solidarity with the Palestinians. This type of 'Awakening', of course, was not welcomed warmly by President Obama, who two days later made this position clear in 'Moment of Opportunity':

> As for Israel, our friendship is rooted deeply in a shared history and shared values. Our commitment to Israel's security is unshakeable. And we will stand against attempts to single it out for criticism in international forums. But precisely because of our friendship, it's important that we tell the truth: the status quo is unsustainable, and Israel too must act boldly to advance a lasting peace. (Obama 2011a)

The 'shared history and shared values' barely hide the Judeo-Christian alliance against Muslims of which bin Laden often spoke, and Obama's threat to block Palestine's bid for nationhood in the United Nations with his veto and cutting off $200 million in aid if the Palestinians insist on pushing forward is evidence that the position new Arab governments take on Israel will be a deciding factor in their relations with America. The one-line rebuke to Israel, 'The status quo is unsustainable, and Israel too must act boldly to advance a lasting peace', is presented as the advice of a friend in contrast to the firm hand of authority over Palestinians and the Arab nations struggling to be reborn. In a further speech delivered to AIPAC on 22 May Obama stated his unequivocal support for the security of Israel, justifying 'why, despite tough fiscal times, we've increased foreign military financing to record levels', and boasting of the Iron Dome anti-rocket system which protects Israel from attack. He praises Israel as an ally against Iran, Hezbollah, and Hamas, condemning any alliance between the PLO and Hamas, and pledges that a vote for an independent Palestinian state will not pass through the United Nations; he affirms, again and again, Israel's right to defend itself, including, no doubt, against the unarmed protesters that gathered at its borders on 17 May. The speech refers to 'a new generation of Arabs' who are 'reshaping the region', slightly wistful for the days when 'a just and lasting peace' could be 'forged with one or two Arab leaders' (Obama 2011b). President Obama's message is clear: as long as the protestors do not threaten imperial interests in the region, including Israel, they can be managed. Yet it seems the protestors are not as obedient as Obama would wish. An even more dramatic event occurred on 9 September 2011 with the attack on the Israeli embassy in Cairo. While many in Egypt have condemned the attack, Arab commentators are quick to point out that it was in response to the 18 August 2011 incident on the Egypt–Israel border, in which several Egyptian soldiers were killed. Obama's response was decisive, with US Secretary of State Hillary Clinton ensuring that Egyptian Foreign Minister Mohamed Kamel Amr cooperated with the protection of the Israelis.

Though it has become common in academic discourse and in presidential addresses to argue that bin Laden is irrelevant to the Arab revolutions, it is evidently not so. His methods and messaging are present in the revolutions, but require a deconstruction of the methodology used to divide Muslims into 'good' and 'bad' post-9/11. The final bin Laden message, released shortly after his assassination, offered support for the Arab uprisings, noting that the region was at a 'serious crossroads' that offered a 'great and rare historic opportunity to rise with the Ummah and to free yourselves from servitude to the desires of the rulers, manmade law, and Western dominance' (bin Laden 2011). Obama's 'Moment of Opportunity' attempted to spin a counter-narrative to bin Laden's lingering, posthumous warnings.

In fact it has been argued that bin Laden's assassination was directly connected to the Arab uprisings, particularly the instability facing Yemen. In the Spengler forum on *Asia Times Online*, Goldman argues that bin Laden 'was crushed between the tectonic plates now shifting in the Muslim world' (Goldman 2011). He claims that until the uprising the Saudi royal family preferred to allow some of its more radically inclined members to provide support to bin Laden on a covert basis in return for al-Qaeda's de facto agreement to leave the Arabian peninsula in peace. While al-Qaeda had drawn funding from both Saudi and Iranian sources, with the advent of the Arab uprisings its activity tended to serve Iranian rather than Saudi interests, considering the instability in both Yemen and Bahrain, where Saudi Arabia has implicated

Iranian involvement. With the destabilization of Yemen, such Saudi politics became obsolete as 'In the slow-burning civil war in Yemen – a proxy war between Riyadh and Tehran – al-Qaeda acted as an Iranian ally'. Goldman argues that precisely because Saudi Arabia was a critical financial support base for al-Qaeda, Saudi intelligence, knowing the whereabouts of the recipients of their money, 'called in that favour in Pakistan' (Goldman 2011). The result was the assassination of bin Laden by American forces inside Pakistan.

Whether or not one considers bin Laden a casualty of the tectonic shift in the Middle East, it is evident that the tremors of this shift are just beginning to be experienced. Hamid Dabashi expresses optimism that we are at a crossroads of postcoloniality:

> After Gaddafi's speech on February 22, the discourse of post-coloniality as we have known it over the last two hundred years has come to an end – not with a bang but with a whimper. After that speech we need a new language – the language of postcoloniality, having had a false dawn when the European colonial powers packed and left, has just started. After forty-two years of unsurpassed banality and cruelty, [Gaddafi] is among the last vestiges of a European colonial destruction of not just world material resources but far more crucial of a liberated moral imagination. There are a number of these relics still around. Two of them have been deposed. But still the criminal cruelty and the identical gibberish of many more – from Morocco to Iran, from Syria to Yemen – are to be taught the dignity of a graceful exit, an ennobling silence. (Dabashi 2011)

Dabashi goes on to argue that what we are witnessing in the recent revolutions across the Arab world is a 'deferred postcolonial defiance', and that the liberation of the Arab states, particularly North Africa, from the oppressive remnants of postcolonialism will open 'a new imaginative geography of liberation, mapped far from the false and falsifying binary of 'Islam and the West', or 'the West and the Rest'. He rightly argues that this liberating geography goes far beyond the Arab and even the Muslim world:

From Senegal to Djibouti similar uprisings are brewing. The commencement of the Green Movement in Iran almost two years before the uprising in the Arab world has had far-reaching implications deep into Afghanistan and Central Asia, and today as far as China there are official fears of a 'Jasmine Revolution'. (Dabashi 2011)

No doubt Dabashi's observations are right on target, even predicted in the work of Edward Said and Frantz Fanon, who drew their extensive theories of postcolonialism largely from case studies on Palestine and Algeria. But one critical point needs to be added to Dabashi's observations: political Islamism will, no doubt, play a defining role in the 'new imaginative geography of liberation' and has the historic opportunity of transforming the binary which has dominated Orientalist politics between 'Islam' and the 'West'. The realities of the past decade have shown that a true contrapuntal discourse between the 'West' and Muslim societies cannot take place through the interpretations of Western Muslim interlocutors and academics alone, who are confronted with the dilemma of articulating the demands of Muslim societies to a rather secular and unsympathetic audience. As long as the category of bad Muslim remains so broad-based, and includes all Islamists from al-Qaeda to the Muslim Brotherhood in the same ferocious tribe, genuine engagement between Muslim and non-Muslim societies, and even between Muslim thinkers themselves, will not be fruitful, and the moment for Dabashi's 'new imaginative geography of liberation' will once again be deferred.

On this point, Olivier Roy's (2008) categorization of four major ideological players in the Middle East is particularly useful. These categories contain Islamists who 'campaign for a political entity' (51); 'fundamentalists ... who want to establish sharia law' (51); jihadists who 'undermine the pillars of the West' (50) through symbolic targeted attacks; and cultural Muslims who advocate for 'multiculturalism or community identity' (50–51). Roy points out that the four movements often contradict each other, reflecting 'a tension between deterrorialization and deculturation on the one hand, [terrorists and multiculturalists] and reterrorialization and acculturation ... on the other [Islamists and fundamentalists]' (2008: 51–2). Globalization carries with it both the desire to deculturate and become part of a more expansive and universal community, and the opposing desire to position identity and culture as paramount in the face of the homogenizing cultural effects of globalization. Thus, the real division is not between secularism and Islam, Roy argues, but between the forces pulling between deculturation, which takes the form of a universalism often associated with secularism and global capitalism, and acculturalization, which argues for a delinking from the universal of globalized liberalism and a revival of indigenous knowledge. It is this natural dialectical process that best explains the current tensions within Muslim and numerous other societies. Roy argues that the differences between the Islamist groups and nationalist ones, such as Fatah and Hamas, for example, are not ideological; nor can the alliances between Hezbollah and Aoun's Christians in Lebanon be explained by maintaining the conservative binary of a secular and religious divide. In fact, the tolerance of Islamist movements has been demonstrated by nationalist intellectuals in Egypt and Pakistan, as they both define and defend social and cultural norms and mobilize popular support. Roy succinctly concludes: 'In short, there are countless examples, but nowhere in the Middle East is there a war with Islamists on one side and the secular democrats on the other, whereas media debates in Europe give the impression that this is the main difference' (2008: 60).

It is interesting to note, for example, that the first three of Roy's groups are all cast in the discourse on the 'war on terror' as 'bad' Muslims, with no differentiation between them. This construction of a rather large group of 'bad' Muslims is a fabrication that endlessly defers a genuine engagement with arguments originating in Muslim-majority countries – claims that Islamic ethics can indeed offer an alternative or an 'oppositional politics'.

In this regard, Alastair Crooke's *Resistance: The Essence of the Islamist Revolution* (2009) is a unique and valuable contribution as it concentrates on systematically analysing the philosophical, ethical, cultural, religious, economic, psychological, national and political values of Islamism. Crooke focuses on philosophical and ethical differences between Islamism and Western traditions which have been translated into operational politics by a number of powerful personalities, including Sayyed Qutb, Mohammed Baqer al-Sadr, Musa al-Sadr, Ali Shariati, Sayyed Mohammad Hussein Fadallah, Ayatollah Ruhollah Khomeini, Sayyed Hassan Nasrallah and Khaled Mesha'al. Crooke argues that Islamists seek to recuperate an alternative consciousness – one drawn from its own intellectual traditions that would stand in opposition to the Western paradigm. For Crooke the Islamist revolution is much more than politics; it is an attempt to shape a new consciousness – arguably, a postcolonial consciousness.

It is interesting to note that parallels have recently been drawn between the Arab revolutions and the Eastern European, Central and South American revolutions in the 1980s. We should recall, however, that moves towards democracy throughout Central and South America were deeply engaged with Catholic liberation theology. In Brazil, for example, religious institutions played a key part in its transition, and the Workers' Party (PT), which currently holds power, was formed in 1978 as a union between labour agitators, religious activists from the Catholic Church and human rights groups. Likewise, the revolutions of 1989 in Eastern Europe can be traced to Poland where, throughout the mid-1980s, Lech Walesa's Solidarity Movement was solidly supported by the Catholic Church. So, why are Western commentators so anxious about the role of Islamist coalitions in the Arab revolutions? There is evidence in Egypt and Tunisia that the people, having come this far, will not accept the replacement of one dictator with another, compliant with American interests, and are eager to explore diverse alliances which include political Islamists. In

Egypt the Muslim Brotherhood has become a vocal part of this negotiating process. In Tunisia Rashid Ghanooshi's Al-Nadha Party has been legalized and has won a large number of seats in the elections. The situation in Libya is much more complex because of the absence of a strong civil society due to the extreme suppression of Islamism of all sorts by Gaddafi. For this reason Libya runs a greater risk of falling prey to the agendas of more radical Islamist and jihadist factions. Certainly we can predict that any acts of violence or bigotry by splinter groups of radical Islamists in the region are bound to be highlighted as evidence that Muslims are simply too medieval and infantile to determine the destinies of their own societies.

The debate between Orientalists and anti-Orientalists, which is explored in more depth in Chapters 2 and 3, is also evident in the discourse on the Arab revolutions. For example, Thomas Friedman's 1 March 2011 column in the *New York Times* is an Orientalist text *par excellence*. Friedman outlines five ridiculous reasons for the Arab revolutions, which include: the inspiration of President Obama, particularly as exemplified in his Cairo speech; the ability of Arabs to see their world through Google Earth and realize that some of their homes are smaller than others and therefore become aware of the inequalities; the democratic example of Israel, whose former prime minister, Ehud Olmert, had to resign because he was accused of 'illicitly taking envelopes stuffed with money from a Jewish-American backer'; the fact that China got the Olympics and the Arab world didn't, generating a case of envy for development; and the new form of responsible government introduced to the Middle East in the past three years by Palestinian prime minister Salam Fayyad (Friedman 2011a). Friedman's reasons are so far-fetched that at first the reader may mistake his Orientalism for irony due to the absence of the obvious reasons for the revolutions, related to corruption, exploitation and imperialism, as discussed in the works of Arab activists throughout this chapter. But, unfortunately, Friedman's Orientalism is shocking simply because it is transparent and becomes even more so in the columns that follow the developments of the revolutions. For example, he articulates explicitly the pragmatism with which America has approached the revolutions: 'We don't want the Arab democracy rebellions to stop, but no one can predict how they will end. The smart thing for us and Israel to do is avoid what we can't manage, and manage what we can't avoid' (Friedman 2011c). And of course he warns of Islamist extremism in the absence of Arab autocrats to keep them at bay:

> These Arab regimes have been determined to prevent any civil society or progressive parties from emerging under their rule. So when these regimes break at the top, the elevator goes from the palace straight to the mosque. (Friedman 2011b)

These warnings are repeated with the prediction that if the Muslim Brotherhood wins a plurality in Egypt's elections they 'could inject restrictions on women, alcohol, dress, and the relations between mosque and state' (Friedman 2011d). And as Friedman prepares for the inevitable onslaught of Islamism, crediting the deposed Arab autocrats of 'holding together multiethnic/multi-religious societies', albeit with an 'iron fist', he advises that since such alliances have now broken down, 'hope for the best, prepare for anything' (Friedman 2011e).

To the contrary, the anti-Orientalists, aware of the overt Islamophobia generated over the past decade through Friedman and his allies, attempt to assuage these fears by erasing the presence of Islamism from the Arab revolutions. Olivier Roy, for example, attempts to curtail the concerns over the revolutions turning Islamist, but makes a similar claim as President Obama regarding Bouazizi's act of sacrifice:

> The young Tunisian street peddler who triggered the revolt by publicly burning himself reminds us of the Vietnamese Buddhist monks in 1963 or of Jan Palach in Czechoslovakia in 1969 – an act of precisely the opposite nature from the suicide bombings that are the trademark of present Islamic terrorism.

> Even in this sacrificial act, there has been nothing religious: no green or black turban, no loose white gown, no 'Allah Akbar,' no call to jihad. It was instead an individual, desperate, and absolute protest, without a word on paradise and salvation. (Roy 2011a: 52)

Further to this he argues that although the Islamists have not disappeared, they have become 'democrats' or retired from political life into private religiosity, and that the mass populations of the Middle East are 'post-Islamist' (2011a: 53). In 'The Paradoxes of the Re-Islamicization of Muslim Societies' Roy clarifies that post-Islamism is related to the individualization of religiosity, largely the result of the failure of Islamist politics, questioning of the *ulama* and the reconstruction of Islam by youth on the Internet:

> Religion (theological corpus) did not change, but *religiosity* (the way the believer experiences his or her faith) did, and this new religiosity, liberal or not, is compatible with democratization because it unlinks personal faith from collective identity, traditions, and external authority. The usual religious authorities (ulema, or Islamist leaders) have largely lost their legitimacy in favor of self-appointed, and often self-taught, religious entrepreneurs. Young born-agains have found their own way by surfing on the Internet or joining local groups of peers: very critical of the cultural Islam of their parents, they have tried to construct their own brand of Islam. ... Religion has become more and more a matter of personal choice. (Roy 2011b)

However, in his intention of quelling the fear of Islamism, Roy fails to note that the three factors he mentions are all directly relevant to the impact of bin Laden over the past decade. As I have noted in this chapter, bin Laden often opposed the dictates of the *ulama* and was rejected by the majority of Islamists and the *ulama* alike as he voiced concerns about their relevance. Further, his and al-Awlaki's insistence that young people discover the 'truth' about Islam by using the Internet reverberated not only in his messages, but in the ensuing Orientalist discourse that placed severe restrictions on radical discourse on the Internet. My point is not to argue that bin Laden is in any way responsible for the

Arab revolutions, but to highlight that in the highly politically charged field of Islam, in the battle between Orientalists and anti-Orientalists, the Islamists and jihadists, grouped together as 'bad' Muslims, are either put in the forefront of the debate on the future of Middle Eastern societies (Orientalists) or allocated to the back of the room (anti-Orientalists). In the end, anti-Orientalists, sometimes inadvertently, end up in agreement with President Obama's diagnosis, declaring that the revolutions are evidence of the failures of 'bad' Muslims to offer alternatives, and close the door on the continuity of a reasoned radical critique.

I have argued that although bin Laden can be viewed as a 'casualty' of the Arab uprisings, he was hardly irrelevant, as his strategies of sacrifice and Internet warfare have been critical methodologies for the uprisings. Further, his messages, though not unique to bin Laden, are echoed in the discourse of activists of the Arab uprisings. The al-Qaeda (2011) statement on bin Laden's death promises that 'Sheikh Osama did not build an organization that will die with his death and leave with his departure.' Though many theorists have claimed that al-Qaeda is merely clamouring to catch up with the revolutions it was largely left out of, I have argued that bin Laden's methods and messages have been present in the revolutions, but that the categorization of discourse into 'good' and 'bad', secular and religious, and the processes of familiarization versus exoticization, present a formidable challenge for analysts and scholars in understanding the complexities, continuities and discontinuities of the narratives of liberation coming out of the Middle East and North Africa. It is the unfortunate division of existing interpretive communities, that either essentialize Islam and place it centre-stage or make it vanish in their discourse on narratives by or about Muslims, that is largely responsible for this deep scar on the body of Muslim discourse. It is to this genealogy that this book now turns in the hope of tracing backwards the development of this disjuncture by exploring the cultural configurations of the jihadist.

CHAPTER 2

Constructing the 'bad' Muslim: *jihad*, Orientalism and the militarization of Muslim lands

Through the events of 9/11 it became increasingly clear that globalization was not proceeding as smoothly as predicted by neoconservatives such as Francis Fukuyama in *The End of History* (1992), and since then Islam occupied centre stage in globalization discourse. A wide and diverse range of social theorists have argued that today's world is organized by accelerating globalization and increased militarization.[1] Douglas Kellner has persuasively theorized globalization as a highly complex, contradictory and thus ambiguous set of institutions and social relations, as well as involving flows of goods, services, ideas, technologies, cultural forms and people (Kellner 2007). There is no doubt that within the global landscape, Islam has occupied a pivotal place for at least the last decade. 9/11 and its aftermath have revealed that globalization both divides the world and unifies it; it produces dominant cultural hegemony and counter-discourses that contradict it. As Kellner notes,

> The experience of September 11 points to the objective ambiguity of globalization, that positive and negative sides are interconnected, that the institutions of the open society unlock the possibilities of destruction and violence, as well as democracy, free trade, and cultural and

social exchange. ... Some saw terrorism as an expression of 'the dark side of globalization', while I would conceive it as part of the objective ambiguity of globalization that simultaneously creates friends and enemies, wealth and poverty, and growing divisions between the 'haves' and 'have-nots'. (Kellner 2003)

In short, the events of 9/11 and their aftermath highlight some of the contradictions of globalization and its dialectical functions, both as a homogenizing force of sameness and uniformity, and as a source of heterogeneity, difference and hybridity. They also reveal globalization as a contradictory mixture of democratizing and anti-democratizing tendencies, which allow more and more voices to be heard while simultaneously escalating attempts to curb civil liberties. Grasping that globalization embodies these contradictory tendencies – that it can be a force of both homogenization and heterogeneity – is crucial to understanding the current manifestations of Orientalism as the cultural logic in militarizing the Middle East.

There has been an obstinate effort to insert Islam into cultural analysis by reactivating old Orientalist absolutes to justify militarization of predominantly Muslim countries. In *Orientalism* (1979) and *Culture and Imperialism* (1994), Edward Said had noted that cultural imperialism went hand in hand with colonization and that, in the case of the Middle East, Orientalism was the cultural companion to imperialist designs on the region, assured by a growing militarization. Likewise, in various notable essays after 9/11, Said continued the argument in light of the wars in Afghanistan and Iraq and the flourish of rhetoric that was produced on the 'war on terror' (Said 2001, 2003a, 2003b). In many of his post-9/11 articles, Said attempted to place reasoned arguments into the debate about the violent nature of Islam, arguing that historical situations and politics of the day have to be considered in interpreting the tragic events.[2] He also spoke out more fervently as an American about the dangerous rebirth of evangelism and nationalism (Said 2002b).

In this regard, perhaps the most interesting of Said's late articles is 'Dreams and Delusions', published in *Al-Ahram*, the last before his death (Said 2003c). In this charged piece, Said laments the bigotry and Orientalism that is sweeping American society, summarizing the derogatory view of Arabs spouted by Francis Fukuyama, Thomas Friedman and Fouad Ajami as too ridiculous to be taken seriously. He then examines the terminology that was hypocritically being employed to justify the Iraq War, such as democracy, liberalism and secularism, and speaks directly to Arab and Western intellectuals, whom he believed had a common aim:

> As Arabs, I would submit, and as Americans we have too long allowed a few much-trumpeted slogans about 'us' and 'our' way to do the work of discussion, argument and exchange. One of the major failures of most Arab and Western intellectuals today is that they have accepted without debate or rigorous scrutiny terms like secularism and democracy, as if everyone knew what these words mean. (Said 2003c)

In the same article he makes an emotive appeal for the intellectual and citizen alike:

> I urge everyone to join in and not leave the field of values, definitions, and cultures uncontested. They are certainly not the property of a few Washington officials, any more than they are the responsibility of a few Middle Eastern rulers. There is a common field of human undertaking being created and recreated, and no amount of imperial bluster can ever conceal or negate that fact. (Said 2003c)

Said continued to emphasize the importance of culture as a site for the current militarization of the world, particularly the war in Iraq, and placed hope in intellectuals and citizens to see through the rhetoric.

Despite Said's reasoned arguments, the neoconservatives have positioned Islam as the antithesis to globalization, with the assumption that the 'Islamic' world-view, usually presented monolithically, is violently challenging the current path of secular

humanism. The old Orientalist arguments, which Said deconstructed so well, have been upgraded to take into account technology and the transfer of Muslim populations to the West. The
line runs roughly like this. Muslims are envious of the freedom
and technological advantages of the West. Their society has
been in decline since the scientific advances of medieval Europe.
Instead, they try to use the West's technology against itself.
Whether it be airplanes, viruses or chemicals, Muslims have
appropriated science for the purpose of terrorism. Consider, for
example, Thomas Friedman's assertion that

> terrorists can hijack Boeing planes, but in the spiritless monolithic
> societies they want to build, they could never produce them. The
> terrorists can exploit the U.S.-made Internet but in their suffocated
> world of one God, one truth, one way, one leader, they could never
> invent it. (2003: 46)

According to this narrative, not only have Muslims appropriated
the technology of the West for this battle, they have also appropriated its citizenship and territory, with European Muslims
particularly presenting a grave challenge to democratic processes.
Of course, this is a rather simplified version of the narrative, but it
does highlight two central points around which the globalization
debate circulates. First, the history of Muslims is presented as
on a direct course of confrontation with the West, requiring an
erasure of the influence of Muslim influences on the development
of modern thought in Europe.[3] This requires that the role of
Muslims in European history be actively erased, and repositions
the contemporary Muslim in a parasitic position – feeding off
Western ingenuity while plotting to destroy it. This argument
weaves through the work of diverse sources: Samuel Huntington,
Bernard Lewis, and Muslim 'reformers' such as Irshad Manji.
Second, the debate about Muslims and their roles as citizens in
Western societies has placed Muslim theorists under the micro-
scope, challenging them to prove their Americanness or Euro-
peanness over their Muslimness. This debate is, of course, part

of a much larger discussion around identity, statehood, citizenry and globalization.

The major perpetrators of the argument that Muslim history has been on a collision course with the West and that Islam is basically incompatible with Western progression have been Samuel Huntington and Bernard Lewis. It should not be overlooked that while Huntington popularized the Islam-versus-the-West debate (2003), Bernard Lewis in his 1990 'Roots of Muslim Rage' warns of a resurgence of Muslim rage rooted in fourteen centuries of conflict with the Christian tradition and the humiliation of modernization, which bypassed the Arabs. He concludes that the rise of anti-American ideas is a mixture of Marxism and Muslim rage – the inability of Muslims to accept domination. Soon after 9/11, Lewis endorsed the US overthrow of the Saddam regime and set out his later version of Islamic history in *What Went Wrong? The Clash between Islam and Modernity in the Middle East* (2002). As Lockman notes, though the book was written before 9/11, it offers a distressed American audience and policymakers explanations and a rationale for their response (Lockman 2005: 250). Here, Lewis virtually ignores the impact of colonialism and the complexities of Muslim responses to it, and claims that Muslims have failed to respond to modernity, remaining religiously inclined to authoritarianism. The Afterword he attaches to the book after 9/11 describes the attacks as 'the latest phase in the struggle that has been going on for more than 14 centuries' (2002: 164), and argues for policies in the 'cause of freedom' that will 'triumph' as they did 'over the Nazis and the Communists' (2002: 165). In another book, written after 9/11, *The Crisis of Islam: Holy War and Unholy Terror* (2004), Lewis rehashes his arguments about the failure of Islam to modernize and insists on the necessity and rightness of American foreign policy, articulating that it is American's role to lead the Arabs to democracy.

Samuel Huntington lays out his vision for the post-Communist world order in his widely quoted *The Clash of Civilizations and the*

Remaking of World Order (2003). Huntington maintains primarily that future conflicts will not be ideological or economic but cultural, and he identifies the major civilizations that will conflict with each other – Western, Slavic Orthodox (Russia and Eastern Europe), Islamic, Confucian, Japanese, Hindu, Latin American and African civilizations – arguing that it is precisely where the civilizations meet that conflict will occur. He also predicts the emergence of alliances between Confucian and Islamic civilizations set against the West, and so advises the West to strengthen its military superiority.

The work of Lewis and Huntington has been at the forefront of the American foreign policy agenda in the Middle East for the past decade. Their perspective is supported by mainstream media. For example, the *New York Times* columnist Thomas Friedman's *Longitudes and Attitudes* (2003) extends these arguments and further divides the Islamic world into medievalists and modernists. Friedman follows up on Huntington's recommendation to exploit the interior differences and conflict among Confucian and Islamic states. To do so, he advises strengthening moderate and secular Muslims in the war against the radicals, raising direct questions about the role of Muslim interlocutors in the 'war on terror'. One such Muslim interlocutor who fits neatly into the Huntington/Lewis/Friedman triangle is Irshad Manji, a Canadian writer who is currently director of the Moral Courage Project at the Robert F. Wagner Graduate School of Public Service at New York University. Manji's book *The Trouble with Islam Today* (2005) has been published in more than thirty languages, and she has narrated a PBS documentary, *Faith without Fear*, which was nominated for a 2008 Emmy award. Manji takes great pains to position herself inside her faith and speaks from the subject position of a concerned and dedicated Muslim, leading a brave reform for her faith. Her website, for example,[4] opens with a flash of Irshad in reflection (though not in Islamic dress), praying, with the caption 'I am a faithful Muslim'. Then

various images of 'bad' Muslims inundate the viewer: men being
hanged, women being stoned and buried alive, and raging masses
of Muslim demonstrators, followed by the caption 'I speak out
against violence and human rights abuses in the name of God.'
Following the various scenes of violence and remarks about
courage, a photo of Manji as a child, in Islamic dress, appears
with the caption 'I am Irshad'. In this way, as in all her work,
Manji credits herself as an insider, bravely positioning herself
against the bad Muslims to redeem and reclaim her religion. She
is also frank about who her audience is. First, to all Muslims
in the West, who obviously still have the hope of being good
Muslims, she poses the question, 'Will we remain spiritually
infantile, caving in to the cultural pressures to clam up and
conform?' Second, to non-Muslims she asks, 'Will you succumb
to the intimidation of being called fascists?' In this way, Manji
positions herself in relation to a Western audience, raising the
firm hope that reform can come from Western Muslims who
refuse to be as infantile as the violent jihadists, all of Oriental
personage, images of whom flash across the screen.

Manji also positions herself as an anti-intellectual outside the
academic mainstream and attempts to appeal, in style and content,
to a mass popular audience. Resonating with Bernard Lewis's
What Went Wrong? and *The Crisis of Islam*, her work *The Trouble
with Islam Today* offers 'expert' opinion in all areas of Islamic
exegesis: Muslim diasporas in the West, Islamic law, the treat-
ment of women, fundamentalism and terrorism, the relationship
between Islam and democracy, the Arab–Israeli conflict, and much
more. Manji explains for a confused audience that the problems
with Islam are related to its patriarchal, homophobic and violent
outlook on life, based on her own experience as a lesbian Muslim
under the control of a domineering Muslim father. The cover
of the book, with its title taped across Manji's mouth, her eyes
looking sadly upwards, accentuates her stance as one who refuses
to be quiet, despite the risk.

Tarek El-Ariss (2007) offers a valuable insight when he notes that in *The Trouble with Islam Today*, Manji takes an anti-intellectual position in order to popularize her argument and make herself familiar to her audience. He refers to the prologue to her book, written by Dr Khaleel Mohammed, an American professor, who praises Manji for not writing for an academic or intellectual audience but for speaking to the people in their own voice. Certainly, throughout the book Manji uses a conversational tone, cracking jokes, often irreverent ones, for her audience.

It has been argued[5] that Manji's interpretations are rather superficial and her choice of references rather selective. For example, her feminist interpretations omit the achievements of major Muslim women figures, as well as the Islamic context of property and marriage laws. Her historical analysis largely ignores the depth of the Muslim history of Spain, including the post-crusade diaspora when Muslims and Jews cooperated in fleeing Christian oppression. In fact, Manji tries to erase Muslims from European history, paving a clean path to contemporary thought from the Ancient Greeks to postmodernism. Further, the only attention she pays to the contemporary politics of the Middle East is in one chapter, where she emphasizes how Israelis treated her better on her trip to Israel than the Palestinians did. Elsewhere she focuses on contemporary Muslim immigrants, especially European Muslims, whom she accuses of being ungrateful for the freedom granted to them by their host countries. Here she places herself as a member of the First World, not of an immigrant community, and claims that 'in order to defend our diversity, we'll need to be less tolerant' (Manji 2003: 199), advocating for the necessity of the Patriot Act.

Perhaps Manji's major achievement lies in the movement from *jihad* to *ijtihad*, two very closely related terms in Islamic theology. As noted in the Introduction to this book, in the contemporary repertoire *jihad* refers to violent revolutionary action *and* an inner spiritual search. *Ijtihad*, on the other hand, which has become a

favourite code of Muslim reformers, describes the process of critical thinking and questioning that is inherent in Islamic theology.
Manji's *ijtihad*, however, is not merely Muslim self-reflection upon
the failure of Islam in developing Muslim societies; rather, she
positions herself as the leader of 'Operation Ijtihad'. Her plan
for Operation Ijtihad and the reform of Islam explicitly posits
post-war Iraq as the starting point in the Middle Eastern region,
directly connecting her agenda to the political one (Manji 2005:
185). As El-Ariss notes, it is no wonder that Manji's work has
received recognition from Friedman, who connects her work on
Operation Ijtihad to Operation Iraqi Freedom, as a process of
reform and democratization (El-Ariss 2007: 93).

Manji's move from *jihad* to *ijtihad* is significantly more than a
linguistic manoeuvre, for in order to advocate for *ijtihad* Manji
first attempts to deconstruct *jihad* for a Western audience. For
her, *jihad* remains dehistoricized and associated with the authoritarian nature of Islam. She rejects the argument made by
other Muslims post-9/11 that Islam was 'hijacked', and claims
that attention must be paid to the 'nasty side of the Koran and
how it informs terrorism' (Manji 2005: 42). To do this, she takes
two approaches: first, she quotes inconsistencies in the Quran
(without annotation, and so it is difficult for the reader to check
against a noted translation), and she points to the use of violence
in the Quran. She dismisses the qualifications that scholars have
attached to these verses, claiming 'I've read the scholarship that
explains these verses "in their context" and I think there's a
fancy dance of evasion going on' (2005: 43). However, she does
not give the reader the privilege of this 'scholarship', since she
does not document it. By highlighting apparently contradictory
positions in the Quran on *jihad*, she concludes that 'compassion
and contempt exist side by side' (2005: 45). She asks, 'What if
the Koran is not perfect? What if it's not a completely God-
authored book? What if it's riddled with human biases?' (2005:
45). Therefore the deconstruction of *jihad* for Manji necessitates

a call for *ijtihad*, at the core of which is a questioning of the Quran itself, a revised copy of which she provides on her website, entitled *Reformist Quran*.

The second strategy Manji uses to deconstruct *jihad* is to home in on the figure of the jihadist, particularly Mohammed Atta, the 9/11 bomber, attributing his motives to 'unfettered access to dozens of virgins in heaven' (Manji 2003: 45) and the 'perpetual license to ejaculate in exchange for a willingness to detonate' (2003: 46). She asks, 'What if Mohammed Atta had been raised on soul-stretching questions instead of simple certitudes' (2003: 47) about the perfectibility of the Quran? However, she contradicts herself, since Atta *was* indeed raised in a secular environment. Manji can only despair that, despite his secular upbringing, his engineering degree, and his German postgraduate education, Atta was 'incapable of (or uninterested in) questioning Islam's autocratic interpreters' (2005: 161). Thus, by using the example of Atta, Manji attempts to show the tragic results of trusting a faulty text. Manji never attempts to contextualize Islamic political activism, including *jihad*, with reference to its socioeconomic and historical root causes.

This practice is evident in Manji's documentary *Faith without Fear* (2007), as she travels through various Muslim communities to rediscover Islam. One of the most telling conversations is with Nasser Ahmad al-Bahr, supposedly a former bodyguard to Osama bin Laden. The voiceover tells us that jihadists claim Muhammad as their role model, stating that 'Ahmad sees the present as a dark age racked by the same struggles as 7th century Arabia', again placing *jihad* in the context of a dark Muslim past, rather than in a historically informed present. This past looms over the entire documentary, and, in fact, is a more valid explanation for the violent present than any other elucidation; Manji notes that 'what happened in the past is key to understanding why there is so much violence and silence in the present.' For Manji, *jihad* remains dehistoricized, much in the way it is for Huntington and

Lewis, a blind enacting of the Quran's inconsistent provocation to violence and the promise of sensual pleasure. Her discussion of *jihad* remains locked in an Orientalist framework of unchangeable and fanatical violence sanctioned by a faulty text in need of reform. As a supporter of the Iraq War, Manji serves to put a Muslim stamp of approval on the militarization of the land of *Homo islamicus*.

This conservative rhetoric in the 'war on terror' is further reproduced in popular fiction, as can be demonstrated in the work of two of America's most beloved fiction writers, John Updike and Don DeLillo. Updike's 2006 *Terrorist*, a *New York Times* bestseller, manipulates numerous Orientalisms to present the character of Ahmad, son of an absent Egyptian father and an Irish-American nurse's aide, who prepares to blow up the Lincoln Bridge, but fails. Ahmad is drawn to Islamic radicalism after being brainwashed by a neighbourhood sheikh. He interprets his world through a distorted Quranic text, which Updike intersperses throughout his novel (and which he confesses in a 2006 interview for the *New York Times* was translated for him by a graduate student). In the same interview, Updike states his intention in creating a humanized jihadist:

> I think I felt I could understand the animosity and hatred which an Islamic believer would have for our system. Nobody's trying to see it from that point of view. I guess I have stuck my neck out here in a number of ways, but that's what writers are for, maybe....
> I sometimes think 'Why did I do this?' I'm delving into what can be a very sore subject for some people. But when those shadows would cross my mind, I'd say, 'They can't ask for a more sympathetic and, in a way, more loving portrait of a terrorist.' (McGrath 2006)

Unfortunately, Updike does not succeed in drawing this 'loving portrait': Ahmad remains undeveloped and unconvincing as a character. The hatred he feels for the society around him is never fully crystallized except through the clumsy Quranic translations, which seem to be echoing permanently in his head. Ahmad also has no transformation of any sort. At the beginning of the novel he notes 'These devils seek to take away my God' (Updike 2006: 3); at the end he utters 'these devils ... have taken away my God' (2006: 310). Further, Ahmad's plan is subverted by his mother's lover and his high school Jewish counsellor, Mr Levy, perhaps the most memorable character in the novel, who, in an unconvincing heroic moment, foils Ahmad's plan. In fact, Ahmad even remains unmoved by Mr Levy's arguments to circumvent his act of terror, just as he is unmoved by the children looking at him, soon to be his victims, in the next van. Ahmad aborts his act only when faced with his arch-enemy's attempt to foil his plan. Ahmad is left unredeemed, foiled by a Jewish antihero.

The critics are merciful with the book when they note that, when faced with a plot relying heavily on coincidental connections and undeveloped heroes, 'it seems meant as a fable, and any good fable requires some derring-do' (Stone 2006). In general the book was praised for giving the reader the terrorist's point of view (Leonard 2006), with the failure of credibility in the character of Ahmad being due to the fact that he is too Updikean, too aesthetic, to be a real suicide bomber, rather than pointing to a failure in Updike's craft (Adams 2006). If the novel is indeed intended as a fable, the old Orientalist argument here is very thinly veiled: there is no hope of redemption for the jihadist; the solution lies in intervention, perhaps by a Jewish neighbour.

Though it is arguably a much more successful novel than Updike's, Don DeLillo's multilayered *Falling Man* (2007), which refers directly to 9/11, also stops short in humanizing the character of the jihadist. Critics eagerly awaited DeLillo's intervention as a long-time chronicler of the relationship between the terrorist and the writer, with many praising his insightful reflection on the victims of 9/11, while noting the decline in his writing when he writes about the jihadist himself (Litt 2007). As Frank Rich notes in his 2007 *New York Times* review: 'When "Falling Man" sporadically leaves Keith and Lianne behind to retrace 9/11 from the point of view of the hijackers, that spell is broken. These brief interruptions seem potted, adding little beyond mellifluous writing to the journalistic record' (Rich 2007).

The narration of *Falling Man* is split in terms of perspective between Keith and Lianne, survivors of 9/11, and the jihadist identified only as Hammad, a follower of Mohammed Atta, whom the novel puts on the first plane to crash into the World Trade Center. As a fictional character, Hammad, like Updike's Ahmad, is not particularly persuasive. DeLillo's account of his actions in the period leading up to 9/11 follow the same formula as Updike's, with the same process of radicalization being articulated: the long political conversations, the dull monotony of rituals, and the dehumanization of the victims. Below is typical of these Hammad reflections:

> There was the feeling of lost history. They were too long in isolation. This is what they talked about, being crowded out by other cultures, other futures, the all-enfolding will of capital markets and foreign policies. (DeLillo 2007: 80)

When Hammad has a temporary attack of conscience about his victims, he quickly resolves his conflict: 'The others exist only to the degree that they fill the role we have destined for them. This is their function as others (2007: 176).

Perhaps one of the most interesting achievements in the novel is DeLillo's presentation of a near nihilistic view of the relationship between the jihadist and the victim, each caught in the mad meaninglessness of the present, each dependent on the other for its necessary implosion. This becomes evident in the last chapter when the attack itself is recounted through the eyes of both Hammad, the jihadist, and Keith, the victim, so it is difficult for the reader to discern where Hammad's narrative stops and Keith's begins:

> He fastened his seatbelt.
> A bottle fell off the counter in the galley, on the other side of the aisle, and he watched it roll this way and that, a water bottle, empty,

making an arc one way and rolling back the other, and he watched it spin more quickly and then scatter across the floor an instant before the aircraft struck the tower, heat, then fuel, then fire, and a blast wave passed through the structure that sent Keith Neudecker out of his chair and into a wall. He found himself walking into a wall. He didn't drop the telephone until he hit the wall. The floor began to slide beneath him and he lost his balance and eased along the wall to the floor. (DeLillo 2007: 239)

This is DeLillo's most explicit connection between the two men, but the similarity in their behaviour is already present throughout *Falling Man*. Both discover blood on their clothes without knowing where it came from; both seek solace in ritualistic acts – for Hammad the physical preparations he makes for the attacks, for Keith the rules that govern his poker playing and the physical therapy exercises he compulsively repeats. Both distil their lives down to the essentials: Hammad 'prays and sleeps, prays and eats' (Updike 2006: 176); Keith reduces his sleep to five hours to have more time at the poker table. DeLillo, like Updike, seems to be suggesting that the jihadist and the victim are caught up in one process of self-annihilation. However, the reader gets an Orientalized jihadist from both DeLillo and Updike: the jihadist is made more familiar, simply because he lurks in a familiar landscape, but he remains largely foreign, exotic, and not quite human enough.

On the other hand, Muslim writers have played an important role in humanizing Muslims, as evidenced in the growth of Muslim autobiographical or semi-autobiographical fiction. The value of these interlocutors is largely connected to their perceived ability to interpret the code of *jihad*, seen as the driving force behind Islam's confrontation with modernity and globalization. In *The Anarchy of Empire in the Making of U.S. Culture*, Amy Kaplan (2002) demonstrates the link between domestic and foreign affairs in imperial projects and discusses the role of metropolitan postcolonial intellectuals in discrediting their native culture of resistance and winning the hearts and minds of domestic American voters. Muslims strategically position themselves in the discourse on 'bad' and 'good' Muslims that presents *jihad*, in particular, as the antithesis to modernity. Muslim 'reformers' often refer to reclaiming an Islam that has been hijacked by the jihadists, asserting their recourse to an authentic and orthodox Islam, while demonizing the hijackers. This is especially evident in recent fiction set in Iraq, Iran and Afghanistan, the focal points of the 'war on terror': Afghanistan because it housed al-Qaeda; Iran because, as a member of the 'Axis of Evil' and alleged would-be possessor of nuclear weaponry, it can at any time unleash its legion of jihadists on the West; and Iraq for a similar reason, to depose the despot Saddam Hussein and bring 'democracy', or perhaps Manji's *ijtihad*, to the region.

It has become common knowledge, however, that the desire to control the vast oil reserves of Iraq and gain access to the reserves of the Caspian Sea is a major economic incentive to 'democratizing' the region. And, surely, the 'war on terror' has been good for the American economy. In 2009 the USA signed arms deals worth $22.6 billion, and on 14 September 2010 the Obama administration announced a weapons sale to Saudi Arabia worth $60 billion, reportedly the biggest in US history, with an indirect effect on 77,000 jobs in forty-four states (Brauchli 2010). But not only has the American government gained; there are numerous new opportunities for private contractors (Gregory 2008).[6] Enormous amounts of money have been paid out to private contractors for security, estimated by the Congressional Research Service to make up 54 per cent of the Department of Defense's workforce in Iraq and Afghanistan (Schwartz and Swain 2011). An estimated $100 billion has been paid out to contractors in Iraq (Risen 2008), who are allegedly major culprits in torture and murder, now a matter of public record with the October 2010 Al Jazeera exposure of over 390,000 classified US documents, leaked to whistleblower website WikiLeaks.[7] Similarly, contractors in Afghanistan, whose number is significantly higher than that of military personnel (Cole 2009), have come under attack for similar cases of indiscriminate killing of civilians. Though the exact amount paid to these contractors has not been released, up to $15 billion was paid to just two firms, to build and support US military bases throughout Afghanistan (Gregory 2008). These examples could be multiplied many times over, and the connections within the military–industrial and media–entertainment complexes have become more intricate, as has the relationship between the military and private contractors and the alarming numbers of civilian casualties and human rights abuses. It has become increasingly obvious that this is no 'Operation Ijtihad', or Huntingtonian process of bringing democratization to *Homo islamicus*. Instead, it is a process of commodification and dehumanization, consistent with the brand of Orientalism that has underwritten the 'war on terror' since its inception.

A cursory look at some of the popular novels by Muslim writers from or about Afghanistan, Iran and Iraq clearly demonstrates how the authority of an authentic Muslim voice has been complicit, willingly or not, in the process of empire-building by constructing 'good' Muslims and demonizing 'bad' ones. Of particular interest are Azar Nafisi's *Reading Lolita in Tehran* (2004), Khalid Hosseini's *The Kite Runner* (2003) and Yasmina Khadra's *The Attack* (2006) and *The Sirens of Baghdad* (2007). These Muslims can be considered examples of the kinds of native informants of which Said and Dirlik have written, who profit from the essentialization of marginal people to whom they marginally belong, and of Appiah's 'comprador intelligentsia', 'a relatively small, "Western"-style, "Western"-trained group of writers and thinkers, who mediate the trade in cultural commodities of world capitalism at the periphery' (1996: 62).

Azar Nafisi is a visiting professor and the director of the SAIS Dialogue Project at the Foreign Policy Institute of Johns Hopkins University's School of Advanced International Studies in Washington DC. She is best known as the author of the bestseller *Reading*

Lolita in Tehran: A Memoir in Books, which has been translated into thirty-two languages, was on the *New York Times* Best seller list for 117 weeks and won the 2004 Nonfiction Book of the Year Award from Booksense, the Frederic W. Ness Book Award, the 2004 Latifeh Yarsheter Book Award, an achievement award from the American Immigration Law Foundation, and the 2006 Persian Golden Lioness Award for literature (Yale Office of Public Affairs and Communications 2008).

Reading Lolita in Tehran is an autobiographical account of Nafisi's experience as a teacher of literature in Iran, where she constructs a secret reading group so that she and her students can discuss the classics of literature. The memoir unfolds around her students, the texts they read, and the discussions she holds with them about classics by Jane Austen, F. Scott Fitzgerald, Henry James and, especially, Nabokov, about their own lives, and about the political atmosphere in Tehran. Endorsed on the cover by Margaret Atwood as a 'literary raft on Iran's fundamentalist sea', Nafisi's work has achieved international acclaim. The book has come under harsh scrutiny by postcolonial anti-Orientalists such as Hamid Dabashi, a friend of the late Edward Said, who argues that the book received immediate validation because 'it seeks to provoke the darkest corners of the Euro-Oriental fantasies and thus neutralize competing sites of cultural resistance to the US imperial designs both at home and abroad' (Dabashi 2006). Commenting on the close relationship of Nafisi to neoconservatives such as Paul Wolfowitz and Bernard Lewis, and their validation of her work, he accuses her of being a 'comprador intellectual'. In what is perhaps a more tempered argument, Fatemeh Keshavarz makes similar criticisms in her work *Jasmines and Stars: Reading More than Lolita in Tehran* (2007), in which she questions why numerous memoirs written over the last decade alone by Iranian women political activists, who have suffered and survived heroically under both the Pahlavis and the Islamic Republic, are virtually unheard of, but Nafisi's memoir became a bestseller.[8] She also notes that the historical background of the revolution is obliterated in *Reading Lolita*, and that Iran is presented as a patriarchal, oppressive state crying out for liberation. Though the novel's literary merits are questionable, its characters undeveloped and its plot predictable, it is interesting to note that it is Nafisi's role as a native informant that has mostly come under attack. Of particular relevance is the fact that Nafisi serves as a trustee for Freedom House, a highly controversial US nongovernmental organization that advocates for American-style democracy abroad while receiving a large portion of its funding from the United States government. Its chair is ex-director of the CIA James Woolsey, and both Samuel Huntington and Paul Wolfowitz have served as board members. In *Manufacturing Consent*, Edward Herman and Noam Chomsky pinpoint Freedom House as a propaganda machine for American foreign policy:

> Freedom House fulfils its function as a flak machine, attempting to bully the media into a still more thoroughgoing conformity with the propaganda requirements of state policy by methods that are a travesty of honest journalism (let alone scholarship) – all, of course, in the interest of 'freedom.' (1988: 227–8)

It is this allegiance that is relevant to our discussion here. As a Muslim interlocutor, Nafisi provides a narrative that mainstream American society is ready to hear: how democracy must be brought to Iran to liberate the citizens from the grip of medieval theocracy. With America's ongoing Cold War with Iran over its nuclear programmes, and the lingering threat of military action, *Reading Lolita* puts a stamp of approval on such intervention, just as Manji's *The Trouble with Islam Today* does for the Iraq invasion. It is not as if the American government requires this approval from Muslim interlocutors, of course, but it does aid the neoconservative agenda of militarization of the Middle East if Muslim writers, authentic voices, familiar enough as Americans and Canadians, assist in their propaganda to support the argument that Muslims need to be liberated.

Furthering this argument, it is interesting to compare briefly Nafisi's *Reading Lolita* with *The Bathhouse*, published in the same year, by an American Iranian contemporary, Franoosh Moshiri, who teaches literature and creative writing at the University of Houston. *The Bathhouse* is a chilling account of a teenage girl's imprisonment and torture at a detention facility located in what had been a public bath. The setting is presumably post-revolutionary Iran, though specific historical and contextual details are scarce, and even the city is not named. In contrast to *Reading Lolita*, *The Bathhouse* does not elucidate much about the particular history of the Iranian Revolution, but is an in-depth personal and literary probe into abuse and torture. Moshiri, however, has been articulate in her interviews and essays about what she sees as religious 'fundamentalism'; at the same time, she condemns the Bush administration for its colonizing of the Middle East.[9] She also notes the difficulty she has faced in publishing her work, commenting that the market is interested in memoirs, not fiction.

However, it can be argued that fiction sells well if it is 'on message'. For example, *The Kite Runner* (2003), the first novel published in English by American Afghani Khalid Hosseini, has sold over 8 million copies, been translated into more than forty languages and been made into a major motion picture. Hosseini's novel is certainly more nuanced than Nafisi's; it tells the story of enduring friendship in war-torn Afghanistan, as it highlights the ethnic tensions between the Hazara and Pashtun. The main character, Amir, an American Afghani like Hosseini, leaves Afghanistan after the Soviet invasion and returns during the Taliban regime to rescue his childhood friend Hassan's son, Sohrab. The novel's great hero, Amir's father Baba, is secular and loves America, while his nemesis is the paedophiliac Taliban executioner Assef. Amir is a developed character, familiarized to his audience as an American but also an Afghani; so too are Baba and Hassan, since much of the novel's plot is tied up in the daily activities of the two friends and the inhabiting of these partly fictional characters.

The Western response to Hosseini's book has been fairly positive, with critics hailing it as a postcolonial masterpiece written for a broad Western audience, a humanization of Afghanis, about whom Americans knew little (Singh 2007). In a 2007 interview with *Salon*, Hosseini concedes that while the events of 9/11 and its aftermath helped to get the book published, his novel humanizes the plight of the Afghani people, promoting sympathy for them among the American public. However, it can be argued that it humanizes *some* of the Afghani people, while demonizing others, particularly the Islamist Afghanis, who are all presented as violent and lawless examples of *Homo islamicus*. The reception of the novel in Afghanistan was certainly not as warm as in America. When the book was turned into a film, using Afghani child actors, the scene in which the young Hassan, a Hazara, is raped by Pashtuns stirred up great anger, so much so that the film director, refusing to cut the rape scene in response to Afghani demands, arranged for the removal of the three young actors and their guardians from Afghanistan to the United Arab Emirates before releasing the film (Milvy 2007). It can hardly be considered accidental that the controversial rapist is Pashtun, the major ethnic contingent in the Taliban, against whom the American government and NATO are fighting a war.

Likewise, Hosseini's follow-up novel, *A Thousand Splendid Suns* (2007), also slated to be made into a film, paints a dark picture of polygamist fundamentalists, while also telling an endearing tale of friendship and courage between women. As with *The Kite Runner*, *Splendid Suns* weaves together dramas of personal struggle and regional politics, and perhaps that is exactly where it achieves success. Again, Hosseini has been applauded for humanizing Afghanistan for Western audiences and for bringing the abuses women have suffered in Afghanistan graphically to the fore.[10] It appears that Hosseini has found a successful recipe, familiarizing 'good' Afghanis, particularly women and children, who await redemption from their paedophiliac and fundamentalist men, invariably Taliban-like figures, representatives of *Homo islamicus*. In *The Kite Runner*, Amir, who can be read allegorically as America, flees Afghanistan with the Soviet invasion (just as the Americans deserted the *mujahidin* after using them for years of battle with the Soviets); he then returns to save Sorab from the Taliban (just as the Americans have returned to save Afghanistan).

In short, endearing tales that humanize the Afghanis and Iranians in Hosseini's and Nafisi's works succeed because they also demonize perceived potential enemies to globalization and 'democratization'. This is not to say that Hosseini and Nafisi are pawns in the neoconservative military machine, though a stronger case could be made for Nafisi as a native informant than for Hosseini, who does not fit so easily in the neoconservative think-tank clique. Instead, Hosseini has positioned himself as a humanitarian working as a Goodwill Envoy for the United Nations High Commission for Refugees (UNHCR) and establishing his own humanitarian foundation for Afghanis.[11] It is interesting here to recall Žižek's criticism of humanitarianism, as discussed in the Introduction to this book. For Žižek, humanitarian aid is the cover that disguises the oppression of *Homo sacer*. In *Welcome to the Desert of the Real* (2002) he insists that humanitarian organizations play a similar role to that of military institutions in robbing *Homo sacer* of his sovereignty and humanity. The fact is, regardless of the politics or the intentions of Hosseini and Nafisi, both novels provide a convincing supportive argument for the American need to save both Iran and Afghanistan from their oppressors. The books have achieved mass popularity because of their perceived insight into a brutal and oppressive world, a world with which *we* are at war. The writers themselves, through memoirs and fiction, are perceived as offering authentic insight into the troubled worlds of Afghani and Iranian jihadists. Both Hosseini and Nafisi are familiar Americans, and yet they remain exotic, belonging to places that they are asking *us* to save. Simply put, as empires are being built, intellectuals and writers are taken into the fold, intentionally or unintentionally, and their work is selected and packaged to suit the dominant ideology. From the images on their covers (the shy Muslim girls reading an unseen book on *Reading Lolita in Tehran*, the boy hiding from an impending shadow on *The Kite Runner*, the wind-blown women in burkas of *A Thousand Splendid Suns*) to the endorsements from the literary and politically establishments, the books are given value as an insider and victim's look at Islamic radicalism. In short, the production and reception of the books, as well as the content, contribute to the justification of the ongoing 'war on terror'.

Perhaps one of the most prolific fictional chroniclers of this war on terror who deals directly with *jihad* by painting portraits of fictional jihadists is Mohammed Moulessehoul, an ex-officer in the Algerian army, who adopted a female pseudonym (his wife's name), Yasmina Khadra, to avoid military censorship. His most recent books all focus on violence in currently politically volatile places: *Wolf Dreams* (2003) in Algeria, *The Swallows of Kabul* (2004) in Afghanistan, *The Attack* (2006) in Israel, and the *The Sirens of Baghdad* (2006) in Iraq. Notwithstanding the publication of many successful novels, Moulessehoul only revealed his true identity after leaving the army and going into exile and seclusion in France. The unveiling was a shock to France's literary establishment:

> The woman who had written several well-received novels in French and who had as a result been clasped to the Gallic literary bosom as a writer, who would, finally, give an insight into what Arab women were really thinking, turned out to be a man called Mohammed Moulessehoul. And not just a man, but an Algerian army officer with three decades of military experience behind him. And not just an army officer, but one who had led a struggle against armed Islamist radicals and who, as a result, faced opprobrium in the French media for being tainted with the blood of civilians killed in brutal oppression by the north African state. (Jeffries 2005)

The revelation of Moulessehoul's real identity deconstructed his literary persona as an 'authentic' voice of the oppressed Muslim woman, such as Azar Nafisi, commenting on the patriarchal oppression and religious totalitarianism in her homeland. The unveiling also questioned the very notion of 'authenticity' itself. Moulessehoul is not a suave, familiar interlocutor, a UN special envoy, humanitarian and Afghani American medical doctor like Hosseini, but a writer–soldier who had fought a brutal war against the Islamists in Algeria. Moulessehoul was attacked in the French press, his credibility seriously threatened. In *Le Monde* and on French television he defended Algeria's army against charges that it too massacred civilians; in 2002 he asserted in the *Guardian* 'I can only say what I have seen. In eight years I never witnessed anything close to a massacre by the army' (Tremlett 2002). As a result of his defence of his military actions, Moulessehoul claims, his funding was withdrawn by the International Parliament of Writers (IPW), which had offered his family support for two years while he established himself outside Algeria. The IPW, set up in 1993 in the wake of the Rushdie *fatwa*, has provided physical safety and financial support for writers such as Salman Rushdie, Wole Soyinka and Vaclav Havel (Drabble 2001).

Is Moulessehoul a 'good' or a 'bad' Muslim? When he was merely Yasmina Khadra and not Mohammed Moulessehoul, he was a 'good' Muslim. However, now that his military background is transparent, the falsely constructed objectivity of the cosmopolitan Muslim interlocutor has been called into public scrutiny. Perhaps it is the transparency of Moulessehoul's anti-Islamism that so troubles France's literary establishment – the quality that is also fuelling the popularity of the English translations of his books. In 2004, *Newsweek* acclaimed *The Swallows of Kabul* as a 'masterpiece of misery' (Piore 2004), and on the back cover of the Vintage translation the Nobel laureate J.M. Coetzee observes that 'Yasmina Khadra's Kabul is hell on earth, a place of hunger, tedium and stifling fear' (Jeffries 2005). *The Swallows of Kabul* was shortlisted for the International IMPAC Dublin Literary Award in 2006. Who better than an Algerian army officer to explain the brutality of jihadists to an already convinced and prepared English-speaking audience? Unprotected by neoconservative authorities such as Lewis and Friedman, unlike Manji and Nafisi, Moulessehoul has to struggle harder to prove his impossible position of objective distancing. This is exactly what makes his fiction so duplicitous when it comes to describing the intentionality of the jihadist.

Citing the influence on his work of Camus, Nietzsche and Dostoyevsky, thereby placing himself in a Western intellectual tradition, Khadra (Moulessehoul still uses the pen name) simultaneously positions himself as a viable Muslim interlocutor for various sites of conflict. In a 2005 interview for the *Guardian*, for example, he speaks of his right to interpret Afghanistan, a place he has never visited:

> I have never been to Afghanistan but I met a lot of journalists who worked there who told me that they read the book, and said, 'I see these incidents all the time, but I never noted them. ... All my literature takes place in that space – it deals with that which has not been attended to. I wanted to bring a new look from a Muslim on the tragedy of Afghanistan. And to bring to it a western perspective at the same time, I have written a western tragedy, but also a book that is filled with eastern storytelling. When there are two perspectives there's a better chance of understanding. (Jeffries 2005)

He then points to the photo of a woman in a burka on the front of his novel *The Swallows of Kabul* and comments, 'This could be the Saharan village where I was born.' Khadra implies that whether Algeria, Afghanistan, Iraq or Palestine, all are being ravaged by the same monster – the jihadist and radical Islam. It is to his novels on Iraq and Palestine, also places Khadra has never visited, that we will now turn our attention.

In *The Sirens of Baghdad* (2007), Khadra stresses the location of *jihad* as an effect of political and personal humiliation by chronicling the transformation of a young apolitical Iraqi through some rather awkward narrative strategies: the first-person thoughts of the jihadist himself, and political conversations between various representative, one-dimensional mouthpieces. The novel moves from Beirut, to Kafr Karim (an imaginary Iraqi village), to Baghdad and back to Beirut again. Khadra utilizes the nameless narrator's impressions of these places to describe the psyche of his jihadist. The narrator's disappointment in Beirut, his judgement of its falseness and schizophrenia, opens the novel:

> I'd imagined a different Beirut, Arab and proud of it. I was wrong. It's just an indeterminate city, closer to its fantasies than to its history, a fickle sham as disappointing as a joke. Maybe its obstinate efforts to resemble the cities of its enemies have caused its patron saints to disown it, and that's why it's exposed to the traumas of war and the dangers of every tomorrow. (Khadra 2007: 1)

In fact, for the narrator, Beirut, representative of the contemporary Arab world, is guilty of its own schizophrenia, the cause of its own disasters, its inability to be either Arab or Western: its 'gutless illogical pride, for the way it falls between two stools, sometimes Arab, sometimes Western, depending on the payoffs involved' (2007: 2). Thus, from the opening pages, Khadra's narrative manipulates some of the very Orientalisms we have discussed in the work of Friedman and Manji – his jihadist is consumed with a blind and egocentric Arabism, and a belief in the incompatibility of cultures.

In contrast, life in Kafr Karim, a traditional Iraqi village, is presented quite differently. Until the Americans violently descend on the village, it is a quiet place, untouched by the ravages of war. The characters are loyal sisters and young men who gather to engage in political discussion, playing dominoes and watching television. This is a typical small-town story, in which the mores of Arab tradition are respected: codes such as respect for the elderly, generosity, and social order are kept firmly intact. Discussions focus on timely issues, such as the mixed Iraqi feelings regarding Saddam Hussein, and the rise of Islamist politics in the country. The conversations between the young men in the village highlight the debate on the relationship between religion and politics and focus on the complicity of the Arab region in its own political turmoil. This complicity is considered to be a fatal turning away from tradition towards modernity: 'If the Americans are here, it's our fault. By losing our faith, we've also lost our bearings and our sense of honor' (Khadra 2007: 37).

It is the code of honour, the mysterious code of the noble *Homo islamicus*, that becomes the main impetus for the narrator's violent choices. When the narrator witnesses the heavy-handed symbolic humiliation of his father, at the hands of American troops who enter his house, this anger spirals out of control. The sight of his beaten father, pushed to the ground so that his genitals are revealed to his family, drives the young narrator over the edge:

> The blow was struck, and the die was cast. My father fell over backward; his miserable undershirt flapped up over his face, revealing his belly, which was the concave, wrinkled and gray ash belly of a dead fish... And I saw, while my family's honor lay stricken on the floor, I saw what it was forbidden to see, what a worthy respectable son, an authentic Bedouin, must never see: that flaccid, hideous, degrading thing, that forbidden, unspoken-of, sacrilegious object, my father's penis, rolling to one side as his testicles flopped up over his ass. That sight was the edge of the abyss, and beyond it, there was nothing but the infinite void, an indeterminate fall, nothingness. Suddenly, all of our tribal myths, all the world's legends, all the stars in the sky lost their gleam... A Westerner can't understand, can't suspect the dimensions of the disaster. For me to see my father's sex was to reduce my entire existence, my values and my scruples, my pride and my singularity, to a coarse, pornographic flash. (Khadra 2007: 101–2)

This excerpt is particularly rife with Orientalist stereotypes that accentuate the irrational masculinity of *Homo islamicus*. The father is symbolic of Iraq, which has been emasculated through the American presence. The Bedouin code of ethics serves as the driving force for the narrator, not the injustice of the American occupation. This code of ethics is not understandable to a Westerner, as the narrator states; it is a mysterious, apparently irrational, intention. It is seeing his father's penis, not the American invasion itself, that drives the irrational Bedouin into a murderous quest for revenge: 'I was condemned to wash away

this insult in blood.' And, of course, the easiest way to do this is
to find a mechanism, Islam, which by its nature accommodates
violence, through which he can reclaim his identity and honour:
'I wanted something greater than my misery, vaster than my
shame' (Khadra 2007: 102, 108).

This symbolic desecration of the body of the father and the
forced desertion of home and identity, leads the narrator to partake
in ideologies of which he is never quite convinced. Baghdad is
the Kafkaesque landscape of the *jihad*, where people are unjustly
kidnapped, robbed and killed, and no one is as he appears; this
is very similar to the lawless Algeria of *Wolf Dreams* and the
Afghanistan of *The Swallows of Kabul*. In this picaresque tale full
of destruction and villainy, all the young jihadists share a sense
of having been dishonoured: 'Various motivations activated these
men, but they all shared a single, blindingly obvious objective'
(Khadra 2007: 158), namely to reclaim their honour. As the narrator shares stories of dishonour with these men, he begins to
feel as a member of a victimized but powerful group who are
bonded together through waiting and ritual. The period before
the bombing is one of preparation for death, in which the narrator is disassociated from his own body: he isolates himself in his
hotel, which he compares to a tomb, and allows himself to be
injected with a virus, which he will spread to others on a flight to
London, his body becoming his tomb. Like Manji's (2005) account
of Atta, the narrator loses his sense of self in a codified world of
rituals and violence, until he is an empty shadow, ready to use
his already deserted body as a weapon.

The decision of the narrator not to commit the act of terror
at the end of the story is mysterious and unconvincing, even
sentimental, being solely connected to people he sees at the
airport, particularly a couple kissing each other: 'They deserved
to live for a thousand years. I have no right to challenge their
kisses, scuttle their dreams, dash their hopes' (Khadra 2007: 306).
Thus, the narrator rejects violence when he remembers himself as

an individual, directly asserting old Orientalist narratives of the collective nature of Islam and the loss of identity and self required to be Muslim. His humanity is returned through the simple act of seeing a Western couple kissing in the airport, which allows the deranged and dehumanized Bedouin to learn humanity, at the last moment, from the sensitive and humane West. Perhaps most significant is his assertion that no one is to blame for the devastation of Beirut and Baghdad, absolving the West (as exemplified by the old lady, the kissing couple and a mother in the airport) of its responsibility for its part in the destruction of these Arab capitals. In fact, the would-be victims on the flight to London, all described curiously as Western, are the human forces which jolt the dehumanized *Homo islamicus* back to his senses and rescue his sense of humanity. Though reminiscent of Hosseini's very similar message in *The Kite Runner*, there is no chance of redemption in *The Sirens of Baghdad*, since the body of the jihadist has already been contaminated and therefore must be destroyed by his own friend. Perhaps we could also read this allegorically, as we read Amir's rescue of Sorab. The jihadist (representative of Saddam Hussein, or perhaps even Osama bin Laden) cannot be redeemed, and his only redemption is to be killed by his friend (America, considering America was once Saddam's and bin Laden's greatest ally). Thus redemption occurs only for Amir, the moderate Western Muslim, not for the already dehumanized jihadist.

Khadra had already told a similar tale of the jihadist in *The Attack*, published in 2005 in French, immediately following the London bombings, and translated into English by 2006. This time the landscape is Israel and the war-torn occupied Palestinian territories. Khadra tries to illuminate the nature of the relationship between the jihadist and the victim, and to explain some of the causes of the Palestinian resistance. The main character in *The Attack* is Dr Amin Jaafari, a Palestinian living in Israel, working in a hospital. Amin is a non-practising Muslim, thirsty for success and material prosperity, who wants to live a life free

of conflict and who sees himself as apolitical – as a healer, a
surgeon. When his wife Sihem is identified as a suicide bomber,
his constructed identity unravels and he begins a journey back
through the wasteland of the Palestinian territories, trying to
grasp the intentionality of his jihadist wife. The fact that Khadra
makes his jihadist a woman is significant, given there has been a
great deal of discussion on the rising number of female jihadists,
particularly in Palestine.

Interestingly, *The Attack* begins and ends with a fragmented
account of an attack. The reader is subsequently led to assume
that this refers to the attack perpetrated by Sihem, perhaps as
recounted through her own eyes, the only instance of her perspective throughout the novel. However, by the end of the novel,
when the same description of the attack closes the narrative, the
reader is made aware that the narrator of the scene is actually
Amin, who has become a victim of another attack, which he
himself has failed to prevent, perpetrated this time by his niece. In
this way, Khadra seems to suggest that not only does the jihadist
lurk within, among those closest to us, as chillingly learned from
the London bombings, but that there is no discrimination among
the victims of the jihadist: even those who attempt to understand
and prevent her can fall prey to her violence. Though his landscape
is Palestine, and he does on occasion use mouthpieces to articulate
the Palestinian resistance, his real landscape is the spectral space
where the jihadist could be your next-door neighbour, or even
your wife. By making his two jihadists female, Khadra's novel
references the growing trend of female jihadists, particularly in
Iraq and Palestine. The close relationship between the victim
and jihadist, the uncertainty of perspective in the opening and
closing scenes, the posing of the question as to whose perception
of reality is correct – all can be read as an assertion that jihadist
and victim are inseparable in the cycle of violence.

It is evident from the works examined in this chapter that
the Orientalism of both Muslim and non-Muslim writers in

cultural criticism, journalism and fiction in relation to *jihad* and globalization is complex and multilayered. There is no doubt, however, the militarization of Iraq, Afghanistan, and Palestine is continually justified by Muslim authors themselves. Muslim writers present themselves and their characters as both exotic and familiar, exotic enough to have access to the intentionality of the jihadist and familiar enough to recognize the immorality of these intentions and appeal to Western audiences. In all cases, redemption lies in reform and militarization at the hands of the West. One message is consistent: the jihadists must be conquered at all costs since they offer no hope for dialogue or redemption, and their mentality is based on primitive codes of honour, a sense of victimhood and deprivation, and even an irrational rage, which can never be addressed. The articulation of the necessity of military intervention may be direct or subtle, or even ambiguous, ranging from Manji's support for the Iraq War to Nafisi's plea for a reimagined Iran, to Hosseini's positing of a Taliban-oppressed Afghanistan in need of Western redemption, to Khadra's despair at lawless war-torn Iraq and Palestine. In all cases, there is little hope that indigenous characters will manage their own changes and progression. They are trapped in cycles of endless, irrational violence. These Muslim reformers forewarn us that we are all possible victims of the jihadist, and therefore insecure even in our own metropolitan centres of power, where we desperately need to be protected.

CHAPTER 3

Contextualizing 'bad' Muslims:
jihad, globalization and anti-Orientalism

In the previous chapter, I argued that cultural criticism and fiction by Muslim writers, particularly as related to the figure of the jihadist, should be read in the context of the value of such work in reinforcing imperialist designs in predominantly Muslim countries, such as Afghanistan, Iraq and Iran. However, an active counter-discourse to the one described has also developed, which attempts to locate the reasons for the *jihad* not in a medieval Islam but in the socio-political realities of globalization. Basically, two major trends have arisen across the humanities to explain the intentionality of the jihadist, outside the traditional Orientalist argument of the inherent violence of Islam. The first argument firmly connects the intentionality of the jihadist to the foreign occupation of Muslim lands and to Western alliances with corrupt regimes in these lands. It notes that even when the jihadists are Western in education and culture, they identify themselves with the plight of their Muslim community and see their struggle as a political one with a specific purpose. The second argument tends to disassociate the European jihadist from his Middle Eastern progenitors and posits him as a deculturated individual, alienated from Western society, and symbolic of the global discontent of numerous minority communities. In this perspective the jihadist assumes an ethical, rather than political, posture. As with those engaged in the neoconservative debate, Muslim interlocutors who attempt to explain the intentionality of the jihadist circulate around these two basic arguments.

The first argument is advocated by John Esposito, Professor of Religion and International Affairs and Islamic Studies at Georgetown University, founding director of the Prince Al-waleed Bin-Talal Center for Muslim–Christian Understanding in the Walsh School of Foreign Service, who has served as a consultant to the US Department of State, various governments, corporations, universities and the media worldwide. Esposito, whose books have been translated into thirty languages,[1] has emerged as a leading figure on political Islam and the rise of the *jihad* post-9/11. If Esposito has been at the forefront of the American academy and media in explaining *jihad*, Olivier Roy, representative of the second line of argument described above, has held a similar position in the European academy and press. Roy is a political scientist and scholar of the Persian language and civilization, professor at the École des Hautes Études en Sciences Sociales in Paris and a senior researcher in political science at the CNRS (French National Centre for Scientific Research). He was a consultant to the United Nations Office of the Coordinator for Afghanistan (UNOCA) and to the French Ministry of Foreign Affairs. He has written numerous books, including on Iran, Islam and Asian politics.[2]

Both Esposito and Roy are academics; at the same time both have been called forward in the post-9/11 world to advise foreign policymakers on the role of Islam in the changing world, and how best to fight extremism. Both are highly valuable commodities in understanding the intentions of the jihadist, and both have also had their arguments misrepresented on Campus Watch's 'howler of the month page', which the organization claims 'demonstrate[s] the moral obtuseness, politicized outlook, and rank absurdity in the field of Middle East studies, and thus the need for Campus Watch'.[3]

Esposito is perhaps the most prominent non-Muslim scholar to attempt to highlight the socioeconomic and political root causes of *jihad*. His work focuses on the rise of political Islamism in predominantly Muslim countries, which he sees as the root of the formation of *jihad* in both Muslim countries and in the West. As early as 1996 in *Islam and Democracy*, co-authored with John Voll, Esposito uses the case studies of six Muslim countries to argue that Islamism is a diverse and multifaceted phenomenon, which he places in its political and socioeconomic context, and that terror is firmly rooted in political realities rather than in an ideological or religious agenda. He connects the causes of Islamic radicalization to the continuing failure of governments in Islamic societies to respond effectively to social and economic problems, since the incompetence and corruption associated with a number of authoritarian regimes has led many across all segments of society to seek in Islam a hope for reinvigoration of their society. He also specifies American and European foreign policies in the region as being a major cause of radicalization. Esposito further contends that the tendency to dismiss political Islam is erroneous since its more articulate adherents constitute a new elite that is engaged in a sophisticated debate about how best to rectify the cultural contradictions that beset the Muslim world.

Esposito's opening question in *Unholy War: Terror in the Name of Islam* (2002) sets the framework for his argument regarding the nature of the *jihad*. With reference to Osama bin Laden and al-Qaeda, he asks, 'Have they hijacked Islam for their own unholy purposes, or do they, as they claim, represent a return to the authentic teachings of the faith?' (2002: xii). His answer to this question involves humanizing the figure of bin Laden himself to help explicate the choices that he made and the historical and geopolitical circumstances that shaped his destiny. Esposito looks at bin Laden in the context of the environment in which he grew up in the 1970s in Wahhabi Saudi Arabia and the growing Islamic resurgence of the period, noting influences on him such as Dr Abdulla Azzam, his professor at King Abdulaziz University and a Jordanian member of the Palestinian Muslim Brotherhood; Dr Mohammad Qutb, another of his teachers, the brother of Sayyid Qutb; and his deep intellectual friendship with Ayman al-Zawahiri, considered the ideologue of al-Qaeda. Furthermore, Esposito considers bin Laden in the context of the 1967 Arab–Israeli Six Day War and the 1973 oil embargo. Of course, later events include bin Laden's time in Afghanistan as a *mujahid* and his disillusionment with Saudi politics upon his return, and his subsequent exile in Afghanistan and Sudan. After painting the landscape in which bin Laden navigated, contextualizing the political history which formed him and became part of his personal history, Esposito notes that 'Bin Laden played to the Muslim sense of historic oppressions, occupation and injustice at the hands of the West', and that bin Laden's *jihad* against America started with his 'outrage at the injustice in his homeland' (2002: 22). He explains that bin Laden held the American people, who elect their president and Congress, directly responsible for actions against Muslims, particularly Palestine, and that he rejected charges of terrorism (2002: 24).

Esposito reviews bin Laden's statements to demonstrate how he integrated key issues such as politics, honour and retribution into his philosophy of *jihad*. At the same time, Esposito argues that while *jihad* began as a local response to authoritarianism, a very particularized and unusual element of political Islamism, it migrated into a more universal movement, while still rooted in the political realities of the Middle East. *Jihad* has become 'a new form of terrorism, born of trans-nationalism and globalization. It is transnational in its identity and recruitment and global in its ideology, strategy, targets, network of organizations, and economic transactions (2002: 151). Thus, in describing the intentionality of *jihad*, Esposito uses the real political and historical figure of bin Laden to contextualize the struggle, taking it out of a purely Islamic setting and locating it in the political landscape of both the Middle East and the new global transnational reality. In doing so, he challenges the loud claims of neoconservatives who argue that Islam itself is inherently incompatible with Western values and warns that unless Muslim grievances are addressed wisely and the economic and political conditions that engender terrorism amelio-rated, terrorism will continue to plague the West and authoritarian Muslim regimes. This argument is further elaborated in Esposito's later (co-authored) work, *Who Speaks for Islam?*, which reveals the results of a Gallup poll across Muslim countries and concludes that 'The religion of Islam and the mainstream Muslim majority have been conflated with the beliefs and actions of an extremist minority' (Esposito and Mogahed 2007: x). The debate is located outside the Western metropolis to show that 'moderate' Muslims are in fact the majority in the Muslim world and that the only way to avoid a continued conflict with Muslim communities is 'by winning the loyalty of the people in the region' (2007: 165).

Imam Feisal Abdul Rauf, who since 1983 has been imam of Masjid al-Farah mosque in New York City, argues, like Esposito, that violence is not inherent in Islamic doctrine, but that *jihad* has been taken up by a minority of radicals. Like Esposito, Rauf focuses on the socio-political reasons for *jihad*, as well as on the psychological and cultural contexts. In contrast to Irshad Manji, discussed in the previous chapter, Rauf assumes an oppositional response to Bernard Lewis in his book *What's Right with Islam is What's Right with America* (2004), directly addressing Lewis's criticisms of Islam. While Rauf condemns the 9/11 attacks as unIslamic, his call on the US government to reduce the threat of terrorism by altering its Middle Eastern foreign policy has often been met with controversy. For example, in an interview with Ed Bradley on CBS's *60 Minutes* in 2001, Rauf stated that the United States was an 'accessory' to the crime of 9/11 and that bin Laden was 'made in the USA', referring to the CIA support for him in Afghanistan in the war against the Soviets (CBS 2001). In 2010, his plans to build Park 51, an Islamic community centre two blocks from Ground Zero in Lower Manhattan, met with a mixed response. Rauf has been accused of doublespeak, particularly by Ibn Warraq, self-proclaimed Muslim apostate and author of *Why I am Not a Muslim* (1995) and *Defending the West* (2007). Ibn Warraq claims that Rauf belongs to a group that 'still has not learned that 9/11 had nothing to do with US foreign policy' and argues that 'Rauf says one thing to Western audiences and another to Muslim audiences' (Ibn Warraq 2010).

The difficulties faced by Rauf and Esposito lie in the layers of their messages which do not fit the prevailing Orientalist narrative as neatly as those of Manji or Ibn Warraq. An example is that the postcolonial *jihad* as employed today is not orthodox Islamic belief but in fact heretical; another is that *jihad* needs to be understood in the context of American foreign policy. In order to explain this message, in *What's Right with Islam is What's Right with America*, Rauf sets out to describe the compatibilities between the Islamic and the American traditions. To do this, he positions himself, like Manji, as a native informant of a different kind: as an insider of both cultures, hoping to inform Americans about Muslims and Muslims about Americans. He notes that Islam comprises 'my essential identity as a human being' while America is 'a land whose values I cherish' (Rauf 2004: xviii). Consequently, he strategically positions himself as a hybrid with an authentic essential Muslim identity that allows him to interpret the current clash of civilizations for America, and as an American who cares about the preservation of American values.

If Manji takes pains to position herself as an authentic anti-intellectual, Imam Rauf firmly positions himself inside the Western intellectual tradition. On numerous occasions he attempts to draw parallels between the Western intellectual and Muslim traditions, including the Kharijites and General Patton.[4] He specifically draws on theories of Western psychology and sociology, to explain the phenomenon of 'suicide' bombers in particular, to uproot it from the Quran and put it in a language Americans can understand. For example, he borrows Richard Dawkins's controversial theory of the selfish gene to explain how an individual exhibits suicidal aggression to save the community. He notes that what might appear to be selfishness may be explained by game theory, in which the pay-off for a variety of behavioural traits is computed. The pay-off benefits less the well-being of the individual than the well-being of the gene, and it bypasses our conscious behaviour (Rauf 2004: 125). Rauf also refers to social theorist Émile Durkheim, rather than to the Quran, to offer further explanations for 'suicide' bombing. Noting Durkheim's observation that those most inclined to resort to suicide are not necessarily those who suffer the most, and that high-income groups have high suicide rates, he applies these factors to the World Trade Center bombers, all middle-class professionals. Referring to Durkheim's theory of 'altruistic suicide', he categorizes suicide bombing as an example of an altruistic desire to ameliorate the oppressive conditions Muslims live under in occupied countries, for suicide bombing is often used as means to fight occupation or dramatically bring attention to social ills. Rauf argues that suicide bombing is 'extreme altruism', a 'profound anomie' caused by a 'deep tear in the traditional society and culture' (2004: 146). He concludes that 'Suicide bombing in the name of Islam is therefore a sociopolitical phenomenon, not a theological one' (2004: 147).

Rauf, unlike Manji, is intent on rescuing the Quran from heretical interpretation. He therefore asserts his religious authority as imam and quotes specific verses from the Quran which place clear restrictions on aggression and assert that 'When people kill in the name of God they are usually really doing so in the name of their own ego, their struggle for power, or their desire to obtain some other asset' (Rauf 2004: 134). Urging a *jihad* for peace, Rauf wishes to rejuvenate the 'true' tradition of *jihad*, the inner spiritual striving of which *ijtihad* is a component, by discrediting the roots of contemporary political violence as *jihad* masquerading in an Islamic tradition. He also places his argument in a political context and proposes long-term solutions, which for him are only partly anchored in the critical thinking of 'Operation Ijtihad' and the transformation of Muslim interpretive conservatism. He calls for a reform of American foreign policy to encourage the growth of modern societies in Muslim countries: economic freedom for Muslims, application of the rule of law, democratization and a separation of powers. The goal of *jihad* for peace would be to support 'a free society stated in Islamically orthodox vocabulary' (2004: 260). His appeal is remarkably similar to Esposito's call for just foreign policy.

In contrast to Esposito and Rauf, the second major counter-narrative to neo-Orientalism and neoconservatism focuses not on socio-political reasons for the *jihad* rooted in geographical realities, but on the process of acculturation and deculturation to articulate a vague and unstable intentionality for *jihad*. In *Globalised Islam: The Search for a New Ummah* (2004), Olivier Roy presents the *jihad* as a secular, ethical movement, rather than a religious movement, noting the striking parallels between today's jihadists and Europe's radical left of the 1960s, with both movements drawing from similar social pools of alienated, dislocated youth and having similar targets: imperialism, globalization and Americanization (2004: 46). Roy argues that today only two Western currents of radical protest claim to be internationalist, 'the anti-globalisation movement and radical Islamists' (2004: 324). Thus, for Roy the *jihad* is at the intersection of a tradition of radical Third World Marxism and Islamic radicalization (2004: 47). Understanding the jihadist, therefore, cannot be accomplished by looking in Quranic text for the justification of violence but must be sought in a larger international political context.

Perhaps one of the most interesting observations Roy makes in his work is on the nature of the new *umma* in relation to what he characterizes as the deterritorialized nature of modern Islamism. This can be discerned, for instance, in the personal histories of bin Laden and his followers: no national group dominates al-Qaeda; many of its activists appear to be drifters, often hailing from regions where Muslims live as minorities; and what unites them is a sense of shared alienation and the desire for an 'imaginary community'.[5] Roy notes explicitly in *The Politics of Chaos in the Middle East* that the issues of the jihadist are becoming increasingly disassociated from Arab and Middle Eastern issues, elaborating with the following examples: there are few Palestinian members of al-Qaeda; no European jihadists have returned to their country of origin to fight; and that up to 25 per cent of radical jihadists are converts (Roy 2008: 143, 144, 146), including al-Qaeda's spokesman in Pakistan, a Jamaican American who was involved in the 7 July 2005 London bombings, and the converts accused in August 2006 of plotting to destroy transatlantic commercial airlines (2008: 146–7). He reaches the dramatic conclusion that 'there are more converts in Al Qaeda operating in the West than there are individuals of Middle Eastern origin in the strict sense (i.e. excluding North Africa)' (2008: 148). Yet Roy also qualifies this remark by noting that there remain two basic kinds of *jihad*: that which is connected to a nationalist agenda, such as in Palestine and Chechnya, and that which is deterritorialized and symbolic and targets the West or the system (2008: 53–4).

Focusing his attention on the latter type of *jihad*, Roy is careful to point out the difference between the fundamentalist and the jihadist, both in *Globalised Islam* and in *The Politics of Chaos in the Middle East*. For Roy, fundamentalists focus more on the imagined *umma* and thus direct their energies towards conversion and missionary activities, *dawah*, to allow this *umma* to grow. It wishes to inscribe *sharia* as a code of law outside state influence, and is thus basically multicultural in vision (Roy 2008: 58). Jihadists, on the other hand, 'fight not to protect a territory but to re-create a community' (Roy 2004: 289). Al-Qaeda has developed, according to Roy, a 'two-pronged strategy' involving 'spectacular anti-Western attacks, but also the hijacking of local conflicts to bring them under the banner of global jihad' (2008: 154). For Roy, both fundamentalists and jihadists are intricately connected to the crisis of identity in the process of globalization, particularly as related to 'an explicit process of deculturation'. He argues:

> It [jihadism] looks at globalisation as a good opportunity to rebuild the Muslim *ummah* on a purely religious basis, not in the sense that religion is separated from culture and politics, but to the extent religion discards and even ignores other fields of symbolic practices. Neofundamentalism promotes the decontextualization of religious practices. In this sense it is perfectly adapted to the basic dimension of contemporary globaliation: that of turning human behavior into codes, and patterns of consumption and communication, delinked from any specific culture. (2004: 256)

Roy points to the documents left by 9/11 hijackers for a glimpse into this highly codified world. For example, they included a guidebook on which prayer or *sura* to utter at each step of the mission, the various codes of conduct, and twenty-six rules for eating and drinking (Roy 2004: 266). It is important to note, however, that the inscription of these codes is part of a process whereby identity is both deconstructed and reformulated. As Roy notes, faith itself is constructed:

> What is reconstructed here is not only religion: it is the self itself, in some sort of permanent representation and staging of the self. Believers (and especially converts and born-again Muslims) act in such a way as to stage their own faith: a sort of 'exhibitionism' is often manifested among neofundamentalists, who use deliberate markers of their own religious identity. (2004: 267)

In short, Roy argues that neofundamentalism, which includes *jihad*, appeals to youths because it involves a rupture with the religion of the elders, and fosters a cultural version of Islam that favours individualism, and a reconstruction of self. The codes of practice are adaptable to any culture, and in the process of reconstruction neofundamentalism borrows from different elements to rebuild the body and the daily life of a true Muslim, either from an imagined tradition or from Western sources. Furthermore, the world of the imagined *umma*, beyond ethnicity race, language and culture, and even traditional Islamic orthodoxy, no longer embedded in a specific territory, is imagined as being surrounded by a hostile or indifferent secular world (Roy 2004: 275).

These counter-narratives as articulated by Esposito, Rauf and Roy have been reproduced and recirculated in film and literature by Muslims, just as the neoconservative narrative has, as discussed in the previous chapter. Various works of fiction both highlight the socio-political reasons for *jihad* and document the process of acculturation, placing the debate on the intentionality of the jihadist outside the Orientalist argument. Perhaps this is why the film *Paradise Now* made such an impact, for it disrupted the consistency of the Orientalist narrative, prevalent in even America's heavyweight writers, with a fully humanized fictional account of the jihadist on the big screen. *Paradise Now*, directed by Hany Abu Asad and released in 2005, after the London bombings, winner of multiple prizes at the 2005 Berlin Film Festival and of the Oscar for Best Foreign Film of the year, played a seminal role in humanizing the intentionality of the jihadist. The film was condemned in some quarters in Hollywood as being pro-terrorist, while conversely, and typical of the way extreme reactions vie for attention in the popular imaginary, there were rumours that the culture minister in the Palestinian government considered banning the film for being too critical of the bombers (Bradshaw 2006).

Paradise Now problematizes the intentions of *jihad* through two friends, Said and Khaled, who are not particularly religious, not apparently very political (though politics turns out to be an important looming force in their background), but who accept a 'suicide bombing' mission in Tel Aviv. While the terrorist network propelling the young men forward is presented as cold, exploitative and bureaucratic, Said and Khaled are quite likeable; in fact, their lives are remarkably ordinary, as ordinary as they can be in the occupied West Bank, and both are motivated by factors outside the neoconservative debate. Said is motivated by a desire to prove himself, to repay the crime of his absent father, who was accused of being a collaborator with the Israelis. Khaled merely follows Said, out of despair, boredom and hopelessness, and the desire to make his family proud of him. What makes *Paradise Now* unusual and controversial is that it presents the political and religious landscapes as mere backdrops for the personal landscapes of despair and honour of the two central characters struggling to survive in occupied Palestine. The film succeeds in making the characters both human and exotic. The two young men are both well-realized characters, and thus seemingly familiar, though their action, 'suicide bombing', is foreign and unfamiliar.

A particularly illuminating achievement of the film is how it makes the life of the jihadist ordinary, even though it is set in the foreign landscape of occupied Palestine. For example, the sombre filming of the suicide bombers' last message is given a comic turn when both the audience watching the filming of the video, fellow radicals, and the cameraman, eating a sandwich as he films, are unmoved by the pre-written messages, which have become almost mundane to them. The construction of the video itself becomes the subject of commentary and humour, with its staging, non-working cameras and the disruptions of daily life, such as Khalid interrupting his video to mention to his mother the best place to buy water filters. The shock at the end of the movie occurs because the audience has become accustomed to seeing the jihadist as a normal person. Ironically, it is Said who turns away from the act and Khaled, who was never as committed to it as Said, who goes through with it – represented by a suddenly blank, black screen at the moment of the attack.

This same type of disjuncture occurs in Chris Morris's film *Four Lions*, where four familiar and comedic British Muslim characters plan a suicide attack on an undefined target. As in *Paradise Now*, the main characters are likeable and human: aspects of Omar's family life are shown in the film, as is Hassan's predisposition to pop music. In many ways, they are typical British young men, though ironically the 'convert' in the group, Barry, is the most radical and the one ultimately responsible for triggering a series of events that lead to the deaths of the others. Slapstick humour predominates as Omar, Waj, Faisal, Barry and, later, Hassan clumsily try to plot an attack by practising their bombing technique on crows and sheep. The tragic turn at the end of the film, as with *Paradise Now*, is not only the detonation itself but also the deaths of endearing and misguided characters whom the audience has come to perceive as familiar and likeable.

These cinematic attempts to explore the intentionality of the jihadist, outside of a purely religious and culturist narrative, to make him human, are indeed an effort to build a counter-narrative to the dominant discourse of *jihad* and of contemporary power relations. Similarly, novels such as Slimane Benaïssa's *The Last Night of a Damned Soul* (2004), and Orhan Pamuk's *Snow* (2004) achieve, with varying degrees of success, a continued articulation of this counter-narrative.

Slimane Benaïssa is best known for his plays. Following the eruption of the Algerian Civil War he exiled himself to France permanently. Benaïssa received the Grand Prix Francophone de la SACD in 1993 and his work has won the recognition of institutions such as the Commission Internationale des Francophonies, the Association Beaumarchais and the Maison du Théâtre et de la Danse d'Épinay-sur-Seine. In 2000, French president Jacques Chirac nominated him for membership of the Haut Conseil de la Francophonie,[6] firmly establishing him as an influential figure in the French culture industry. *Les fils de l'amertume* (*Sons of Bitterness*, 1996), staged at the Festival d'Avignon, narrates the parallel lives of a radical Islamist and a journalist whose life is under threat. At Avignon, Benaïssa himself played the character of journalist Youcef. His play *Prophètes sans dieu* (*Prophets without a God*), which depicts a conversation between Moses, Jesus and the author as they await the absent Muhammad, staged at the Théâtre International de Langue Français (TILF) in Paris, also met with worldwide acclaim.

Benaïssa's novel *La dernière nuit d'un damné* (*The Last Night of a Damned Soul*), written in 2003 in the aftermath of the 9/11 attacks and published in English in 2004, explores the psychological, spiritual and religious dimensions of *jihad*. It earned recognition in France, winning the Prix Méditerranée 2003. Perhaps even more critically valuable than the novel itself is how Benaïssa uses the value of his Muslimness to state his own position in the Foreword of the book, which reads like a personal manifesto. Here he positions himself firmly in the Western intellectual tradition, citing the influence of Victor Hugo's *The Last Day of a Condemned Man* and Solzhenitsyn's *One Day in the Life of Ivan Denisovich*. He writes:

> I feel connected to both these writers, first because they are my literary masters, but especially because of the present historical context. As in their case, I feel history forces me to speak out responsibly against certain unjust, inadmissible, and inconceivable deaths. My response as a Muslim is dictated by my personal experience with religious extremism, which forces me to speak out, and, like Tom Thumb, to place the third stone in the way of ogres in order to point the way toward humanity. (Benaïssa 2004: vi)

Benaïssa then goes on to speak of what he believes to be the predicament facing the Muslim: to live out 'an Islam that is expressed through all manner of violence' (2004: viii) or be silent, positioning himself as one of the rare few who refuse to be silent. No doubt, like his fellow Algerian Mohammed Moulessehoul, Benaïssa did suffer personal trauma, specifically self-imposed exile in France, where he, like Moulessehoul, became a literary star after writing about the Algerian Civil War. After assigning value to his literary talent and personal voice, Benaïssa continues to explain what he believes are the various reasons for terror, including those cited by Esposito and Roy: globalization, poverty and the need to belong, noting that in the global system of domination 'religions are becoming more political as a way to fill a vacuum and construct, each in their own way, an opposing position' (2004: viii). In this way, Benaïssa attempts to place his novel, though a work of fiction, within the dialogue of contemporary historical academic discourse, but he does not attribute Islam with the capacity to speak to any of these problems: 'The solution to all of these problems, admittedly significant, is, in my mind, to be found outside of the realm of religion' (2004: viii). He also makes a rather embarrassingly sentimental appeal as a Muslim, taking it upon himself to speak for all Muslims: 'Speaking as a Muslim, I ask for forgiveness from all the families who have been victims of religious extremism across the globe, regardless of their faith' (2004: ix). This rather unusual plea allows Benaïssa to position himself as a 'good' Muslim and distance himself from the 'bad' ones.

Though Benaïssa feels an affinity with Hugo, Hugo he most definitely is not. The novel is a cumbersome read, adapting a familiar and tired formula, not unlike Updike's: a symbolic, missing father, a sense of exile and dislocation, a process of deculturation, treatises on the process of political radicalization behind the jihadist, codification of faith, the emergence of a new ethics focused on righting present wrongs, symbolic impotence and an aborted act. *The Last Night of a Damned Soul* is heavily peppered with Quranic quotations, much like Updike's *Terrorist*, at times to justify *jihad* in the mouths of jihadist characters, at other times to discourage violence, as 'moderate' Muslims do. Benaïssa's characters are not Saidian metaphoric exiles, blending hybridity to locate a new culture of intellectual opposition in the cosmopolitan metropolis, a secular criticism. On the contrary, they are radicalized and dislocated individuals who are merely symbolic mouthpieces for various ideologies. The two central characters, Raouf and Athman, are software engineers living in the Bay area of California, who join a team of five, ready to hijack a Boeing plane and crash it into a building. The characters refer directly to what is now well known about the 9/11 bombers; like Atta et al., Raouf, the narrator, grew up in a comfortable middle-class Muslim household (both parents are professionals) and benefited from an education in the West (several of the 9/11 bombers seemed to be long-term graduate students in Germany). Athman himself has even completed his Ph.D. in Germany. It is under Athman's firm tutelage that Raouf begins his descent into *jihad*, involving an in-depth process of deconstruction. Raouf notes about Athman: 'He likes to say that by destroying logic, a new structure of meaning could result, and those new meanings could undermine the logical structure upon which they are based' (Benaïssa 2004: 10). Athman's objective is to strip Raouf of the adopted culture in which he had wrapped himself, by merging the historical past of the Quran with the present, a reproduction of Roy's process of deculturation and acculturation, as described above. As Raouf notes,

> Athman uncovered my true identity, the one I had always kept in check so I could finish my studies, not upset my parents, maintain a certain distance from the country of my roots, and question the country of my birth still in keeping with my parents' principles. (2004: 52)

The detailed description of Raouf's process of transformation through first-person narrative outlines a process of deculturation and acculturation. First, Raouf's engagement is an emotional and an intellectual one which requires separation from his past. In his repentance, he says: 'I give up my former life as I gave up the milk of my mother' (Benaïssa 2004: 80). Once he becomes a born-again Muslim, Raouf cannot remember how he had organized his world before: 'When I try to remember how I thought before and about what, I haven't the slightest idea, no memory whatsoever. I became an amnesiac of the void that used to be inside me' (2004: 93). The process of becoming a jihadist is equated to the process of being in exile: 'I had to exile myself by naming my country of origin, by inventing my adopted country' (2004: 136).

With this separation from his previous life, including his lover and his mother, the process of politicization takes hold and he intellectualizes the position of the middle-class Western jihadist: 'If real minds don't die for Islam, martyrdom will remain an idiotic idea for idiots. I think the fact that people like us agree to do it will change the scope of the problem' (2004: 108). By 'people like us' he means thinkers, Westerners: 'those trained in their universities' (2004: 109). The period of isolation leading to the event reads almost exactly like the letter of instruction from Atta, as fictionalized by both Updike and DeLillo. Raouf and his fellow jihadists live in a house, isolated, hooded when they are together, in a life of ritual, deprivation, purification of the body and prayer. During this time, the erasure of self is supposedly completed: 'They re-created me for another world. I was no longer the same, and in my eyes, the world was no longer the same either' (2004: 160). This period of purification through codification, as highlighted by Roy, is described in painstaking detail by Raouf, who outlines the supplications and codes required to guarantee a place in paradise, and the ritual of the event rather than the spiritual meaning behind it: shaving, ablutions, and the recitation of certain words at every step.

Athman, having made the transition from Marxist to Muslim, has his own Islam with its Machiavellian ethics. Noting that America needs to be attacked at the heart of its contradictions – 'You have to terrorize those who terrorize you' (Benaïssa 2004: 67) – Athman highlights the difference between the jihadists and the activists of the anti-globalization movement, who he believes lack a coherent intentionality because their ideas are based in worldly politics: 'like the anti-globalization militants who don't really know how to destroy the system. It's up to us to do it for them' (2004: 118). Athman philosophizes his own form of Islamic politics, outside Marxism and the anti-globalization movement: 'Politics is the art of creating a structure for your expansion. In order to live your religion fully you need this structure, and as long as you don't have it, you're just plain political, period. I am really a politicized believer' (2004: 119). The difference between the political activist and the jihadist, then, lies in utopian belief, not in changing the current system but in creating an entirely new one.

Despite the shortcomings of the novel as a literary work, it is worth exploring its awkward narrative strategies to elaborate upon how Benaïssa inventively employs the novelistic form to explore the issue of exile and its connection to the formation of the Western jihadist. Strangely enough, the quotations from the Quran are not taken from standard translations but from the author's own French translation from Arabic, which is then rendered into English. So it is that the original Quran is twice removed in the text, displaced and yet heavy with authority, as each verse is identified for easy access. The identification of the sections of these twice-removed Quranic references exemplify the plight of the exile, who is also twice removed from culture, the culture of his origin and the culture he has adopted. This is, of course, a central theme in the novel, and various narrative strategies are deployed to demonstrate this state of dislocation and to reflect on the location of *jihad*, perhaps as being in a deculturated zone of personal and exilic strife. Benaïssa emphasizes repetitively that as the Quran and Hadith are removed from their historical period and reinterpreted for political objectives, they too are exiled from their metaphysical roots, just as his character Raouf is exiled from his culture.

In addition to the twice-removed Quran, there are also twice-removed eulogies and letters, which the narrator recalls verbatim: the recalling of his mother's eulogy at his father's funeral, and a letter from his dead mother. Like the Quran in the text, these treatises, though unconvincing as literary strategies, function metaphorically to express exile itself. The location of the novel is the narrator's own consciousness, at the centre of which are his parents, symbolic of a distorted homelessness, removed, exiled and deformed in some way. The only description of Raouf's father is

of a dead body embalmed in his casket, against Muslim tradition,
so bloated and distorted that Raouf throws up when he sees him,
the object of a cross-cultural debate between Raouf's mother and
his father's relatives as to the proper mode of burial. The dead,
absent father is remembered only in relation to the exiled Lebanese
mother, who serves to deliver various speeches on exile, including
the unconvincing eulogy at her husband's death:

> I am in exile from a utopian country. I am exiled from a utopia
> which would be a fusion of my country of birth and my adopted
> country. But what saves true exiles is that they develop an extra-
> ordinary energy, and if they are talented, they will be exceptional.
> (Benaïssa 2004: 186)

The mother echoes Said's sentiments on the privileged position
of those between cultures, believing that exile leads to a kind
of universalism, a disinterested space: 'we become unfettered
observers of others, of ourselves' (2004: 186). This worldliness
allows the metaphorical exile, the intellectual, to escape both
filiative and affiliative connections to a certain degree. Her last
letter to her son after his arrest synthesizes her secular approach,
positioning her as a metaphor for a moderate and genuine Islam
which has given birth to a deformation, her son. Tellingly, she
feels as if she has had a miscarriage, drawing an analogy with
jihad as the miscarried offspring of Islam: 'I feel all of the changes
a woman's body feels in the beginning of a pregnancy as it
gets ready for a baby, except that in me they are occurring in
a vacuum. The baby is not there, and this absence compounds
the pain suffered by each function of the woman's body. This
absence is catastrophic for a mother, for a father' (2004: 239).
She hoped her son would be her father, the carrier of a new
vital Islam, and wonders 'Did our history transform us into
savages.... Are we capable of becoming adult Muslims?' (2004:
242). While it is hardly the letter a dying mother would write
to a son contemplating a suicidal act, it does convey a basic
premiss, upon which the novel ends: 'the solution is not to fight

violence, but to eradicate the causes that created this violence in the first place' (2004: 252).

Perhaps one of the most interesting aspects of the novel, besides the close correlations made between *jihad* and exile, is that Raouf remains both guilty and innocent of the act itself. The event does occur and he watches it on television screens among many other spectators; however, although his calculations led to the event, he did not board the plane. Again, as in Khadra's *The Sirens of Baghdad* and in Updike's *Terrorist*, the logic of the failed jihadist is never really made clear. When asked why he had chosen martyrdom, Raouf connects his reason to the death of his symbolic father, which had left him spiritually alone, and with a need to redeem his father's sins, which he suffered due to exile, and to right the wrongs done against him. The father, at once a real and personal figure, representative of the failed Muslim community, becomes Raouf's major reason for *jihad*. However, the reader is never quite sure why Raouf deserts his fellow jihadists and his role in the act of terror, other than that he aborts his act after he stops taking his pills and finds clarity. For Benaïssa, then, the codification of the jihadist experience is a kind of hypnotic and drug-induced state, from which his character emerges, if not totally. The conflicted Raouf is remorseful, but as he watches the event on television, as a member of an unsuspecting audience, he is also proud of his contribution: 'The rapidity, precision, and acrobatics of the maneuver intensified the violence of the act to the extreme. Maybe that's the one divine aspect of it all – I'm really proud of my calculations' (Benaïssa 2004: 224). If the character of Raouf is conflicted and neurotic, he is at least human. Raouf's reasons for not going through with the act become, like his mother's letter, a mantra for a new-found moderate Islam. The moment of illumination is left open, as if it is unexplainable, except for the knowledge that God 'is fundamentally against all extremes and immoderation' (2004: 232).

If Benaïssa's counter-discourse reproduces Roy's narrative on the role of exile and dislocation in producing the Western jihadist, and presents various arguments for placing the phenomenon of the jihadist in the exilic experience of globalization, accentuating the urgency for reclaiming a more authentic and non-violent Islam as advocated by moderate Muslims, Orhan Pamuk's *Snow* (2004) recycles Esposito's counter-narrative in a political landscape where the boundaries between the 'Middle East' and 'Europe' are purposefully blurred. With the sometimes Islamophobic debates on the possible inclusion of Turkey in the European Union,[7] Pamuk's post-9/11 novel provides an example of critical intervention into the concerns regarding the jihadist among *us*, or, in other words, the possibility of Turkey with a population of over 70 million Muslims and the second largest military in NATO becoming officially European. The worldliness of Pamuk's texts became obvious in 2005 when he complained in a series of interviews that Turkey had been responsible for the massacre of a million Armenians and 30,000 Kurds and, as a result, Turkish prosecutors charged him with 'insulting Turkishness'. The charge was eventually dropped following an international outcry, but had hit international headlines just weeks before due talks on Turkey's entry into the EU. Pamuk, who has always argued for Turkey's place in the EU, was cited in order to demonstrate that Turkey, with its human rights violations, was not ready to join the democratic EU. Pamuk comments directly on this scenario: 'in Europe, conservative people who do not want to see Turkey in Europe tried to abuse my situation. They wanted to show that this country [Turkey] does not deserve Europe, which put me in an awfully awkward situation' (Edemariam 2006).

Pamuk's work has come under even more scrutiny since he won the Nobel Prize for Literature in 2006. Since then, Pamuk, who writes in Turkish, has become known to a larger international audience, and his work positioned within the framework of the debate over Turkey's negotiations for EU membership. Pamuk, commenting on his Nobel award, acknowledges his own value in this situation: 'Well, unfortunately, that makes the thing very precious in Turkey, which is good for Turkey of course, getting this prize, but makes it more extra sensitive and political and it somehow tends to make it as a sort of a burden' (Pamuk 2006). It is in this context, read against the ongoing debate on Turkey's entry into the EU, that *Snow* offers a direct commentary on the jihadist among us, and on the political tensions in Turkey, notably among secular nationalists and Islamist political movements. Although Margaret Atwood's 2004 *New York Times* review places *Snow* firmly in the tradition of post-9/11 literature, it is more than a post-9/11 novel – it is also an articulation of the debate on the potential increasing Muslimness of Europe.

Pamuk has commented that *Snow* was intentionally written as 'a political novel in which I explored my own spiritual dilemmas – coming from an upper-middle-class family and feeling responsible for those who had no political representation' (Gurría-Quintana 2005). *Snow* becomes an exploration of the political conflict between secularism and Islam in Turkey, as well as a philosophical commentary of the mediation of the novelist and poet in representing others. Pamuk notes that neither the secularists nor the Islamists were happy with the novel:

> The secularists were upset because I wrote that the cost of being a secular radical in Turkey is that you forget that you also have to be a democrat. The power of the secularists in Turkey comes from the army. This destroys Turkey's democracy and culture of tolerance... They also didn't like that I portrayed Islamists as human beings.
>
> The political Islamists were upset because I wrote about an Islamist who had enjoyed sex before marriage. It was that kind of simplistic thing. Islamists are always suspicious of me because I don't come from their culture, and because I have the language, attitude, and even gestures of a more Westernized and privileged person. They have their own problems of representation and ask: How can he write about us anyway? He doesn't understand. This I also included in parts of the novel. (Gurría-Quintana 2005)

Of course, it is this debate on the secular-versus-Muslim nature of Turkey that permeates many of the debates over Turkey's entry into the European Union.

In *Snow*, Orhan, a novelist, goes to Kars, 'snow' in Turkish, in Anatolia years after his now departed friend Ka, short for Kafka, had returned there after a decade abroad in Germany (Stoda 2007). Orhan wishes to retrace Ka's journey to find out why girls were committing suicide and to rekindle his lost love with Ipek, who has recently divorced her Islamist husband. The conflict between the Islamists and the secularists provides the political argument of the novel and Pamuk problematizes the binaries of Islam and secularism, often making the Islamists the victims rather than the perpetrators of violence. Pamuk's art in this novel is ultimately to destabilize the image of the potential jihadist and the modern secularist, the religious and the secular, as two separate and self-contained entities. For example, even the motives of the girls who are committing suicide, supposedly out of religious conviction, are not what they appear: there are rumours that the first girl killed herself not as a political statement about her right to wear the hijab, but because her father was planning her marriage to an older man, not allowing her to marry for love. Kadife, ringleader of the headscarf movement, is having an affair with the Islamist leader Blue, and her sister Ipek, a secularist, divorced her husband not on account of his new-found fundamentalism, but because of a love affair, like her sister's with Blue. These contradictions destabilize the world of appearances: nothing is as it appears; private acts are politicized and compete with ideology for the identity and allegiance of the individual.

Pamuk's Islamists are multifaceted, articulate and aware of their contradictions. Every character is shown wrestling with belief and all characters go through believable transformations in their thinking about God and the roles of Islamic and secular symbols in society. Blue, the potential and suspected jihadist, is a rich and complex character, fully aware of and articulate about his complexities. When Blue is first introduced, Ka (and the reader) is aware of his mythological status, as a shadowy figure in hiding whose history has been mythologized. He is immediately positioned as a performer and activist who has taken the opportunity of numerous media appearances: 'he was such a hit as the "wild eyed scimitar-wielding Islamist" that he was invited to repeat the performance on other channels' (Pamuk 2004: 69). Yet when Ka meets Blue, he is amazed at his grace and handsomeness and how different he is in reality compared to the image presented in the media: 'In his manner, expression and appearance there was nothing of the truculent, bearded, provincial fundamentalist whom the secular press had depicted with a gun in one hand and a string of prayer beads in the other' (2004: 72). Blue is interested in Ka because he sees him as a link to the West, as a possible journalist and mediator. In order to convince Blue of his false status as journalist, Ka invents a German who, he assures Blue, will publish his 'Statement to the West', reminiscent of bin Laden's various statements. The conversation between the two becomes a fine example of the ironic stance of mediation between the scribe and the jihadist. For example, as Ka edits Blue's statement he focuses on the role of language in winning sympathy from a Western audience. It begins when Ka attempts to explain the discomfort the fictional editor might feel at the term 'the West' itself:

> 'He takes offense when people discuss the West as if it's a single person with a single point of view,' Ka said carefully.
> 'But that's how it is' Blue said, after another pause. 'There is, after all, only one West and only one Western point of view. And we take the opposite point of view.'
> 'The fact remains that they don't live that way in the West,' said Ka. 'It's not as if it is here; they don't want everyone thinking alike. Everyone, even the most ordinary grocer, feels compelled to boast of having one's own personal views. If we used the term *Western democrats* instead of *the West*, you'd have a better chance of pricking people's consciences.' (Pamuk 2004: 228)

Blue concedes to Ka's analysis and recognizes the power of language and articulation in representing oneself. In short, he plays the game. This is evident later, when Blue asserts his exhibitionistic and individualistic stance and chooses to be executed rather than compromise:

> There is a a word Europhiles very commonly use when they deni-grate our people: to be a true Westerner, a person must first become an *individual*, and then they go on to say that, in Turkey, there are no individuals! Well, that's how I see my execution. I'm standing up against the Westerners as an individual; it's because I *am* an individual that I refuse to imitate them (Pamuk 2004: 324).

Blue is capable of using the language of his enemies to turn it back on them in his performance, and he is aware of the role of journalism in creating and sustaining his mythological status. Blue notes the inability of the Islamists to represent themselves under their own terms and notes the reason for it: 'now because we've fallen under the spell of the West, we've forgotten our own stories. They've removed all the old stories from our children's textbooks' (Pamuk 2004: 78). The only way to reach the Turkish public, he admits ruefully, is via the Western press. At the same time, the journalist himself becomes responsible for the articulation of the message. Blue, similarly, notes the complicit role of the writer, as one responsible in articulating the jihadist's message: 'But having heard it from me, you can't claim to be innocent from now on' (2004: 237).

The role of journalism and theatre in mediating violence is explored further by Pamuk through various conversations be-tween Ka and Serday Bey, the owner of the *Border City Gazette*, and through two plays staged in the theatre. Bey writes stories before they happen, ironically noting that the writing itself makes the event real, that papers print what sells, are purely commercial enterprises run by commercial interests and that if people wanted the truth papers would sell it: 'They even come to believe the lies we print about them' (Pamuk 2004: 302). The fact that all the pre-written articles come true in the novel suggests that the audience is prepared for the violent enactment of the real violence produced and performed in the symbolic system.

The first play enacted in the novel, 'My Fatherland or My Head Scarf', tells a tale of religious fanatics who plot a conspiracy and are gunned down by the protectors of the Turkish state. However, the absurdity occurs when the actors, who are real police agents, gun down the boys from the religious school who are members of the audience. A massacre results, which is written into Kars' history as a coup, blamed on Kurdish nationalists and supported by Ka. Therefore history is reversed as the actors perpetrate violence on the audience, a metaphoric commentary on the nature of the *jihad* which attacks its audience. However, ironically, here the attackers are the secularists and the audience, or victims, the Islamists.

In the second act of violence, a play titled 'The Spanish Tragedy', Kadife, who is supposed to remove her headscarf in submission to secularism, instead makes a deal with the actor Sunay, a secularist, to shoot him, theatrically and in reality, and then kill herself. Hence, in the second play, one performer commits violence, accepted and agreed upon, on the other, and the audience participates in witnessing and even willing this death, since the murder–suicide has already been predicted in the paper before the act itself has occurred. In both performances, the audience has become so disconnected from the real that it is unable to recognize it when it sees it. In Pamuk's world, the theatre does the very thing it seems to be representing, and as such confuses the audience, which has come to expect performance to be fictional.

The audience of 'My Fatherland, My Headscarf' is baffled and unsure if the violence is actual or merely part of the performance: 'A number of Kars residents – out of touch as they were with modern theatrical conventions – took it for yet another bit of experimental staging' (Pamuk 2004: 156). Even the admirers of theatre rise to clap for the 'beauty of the theatrical effects' (2004: 157). When someone utters that the guns are loaded, 'His words gave utterance to what everyone in the hall knew in his heart but still could not bring his mind to accept' (2004: 157).

Even if the real is too real to accept, the play continues after the murders, with an uncertainty between what is theatre and what is real. Even though the audience sees the actions on stage, they only really believe Sunay's death has occurred when they read it in the paper. This savvy audience is so suspicious of the real that when it is performed in front of them, murder becomes mere performance; it needs to be mediated to be accepted as reality. Pamuk insinuates, therefore, that the audience is responsible, in part, for the death of the performer. As the colonel who investigated the act concludes, 'if the people of Kars were so eager to see him kill himself onstage, if they were still prepared to enjoy the drama, telling themselves it was just a play, they too were complicit' (2004: 407).

Pamuk's destabilization of the binary of secular and jihadist motives and his comments on the mediation of violence send a strong message to European audiences regarding their perceptions of a fearful Muslim Turkey. His reflections on identity, the European and Turkish nature of his main characters, Ka, Orhan and Blue, also imply that the Turkey is already part of Europe, and always has been, involved in the same metaphysical battles with the nature of identity and politics. His comments on the role of theatre and journalism in creating reality also send a strong message regarding the diabolical image of Turkey, its politics and people, one which is held by many Europeans, and which, at times, becomes a self-fulfilling prophecy.

Necip is a young Islamist, caught between his world of political Islam and his desire to be a poet, who sees in writing the ability to exert control over existence: 'We could be the poets of our own lives if we could first write about what shall be and later enjoy the marvels of what we have written' (Pamuk 2004: 141). It is worth nothing that though Necip and Ka both die, the soul of Necip supposedly lives on in Fazil, an Islamist science-fiction writer, who himself has a few direct words of warning to the novelist, Orhan, about representation. Fazil, Necip's double, warns

Orhan, Ka's double, that he refuses to be represented unfairly in his novel and will only agree to be represented if he can speak directly to his Western audience:

> your Western readers would be so caught up in pitying me for being poor that they wouldn't ... have a chance to see my life. For example, if you said I was writing an Islamist science-fiction novel, they'd just laugh. I don't want to be described as someone people smile at out of pity and compassion. (2004: 410)

He continues, 'I'd like to tell your readers not to believe anything you say about me, anything you say about any of us. No one could understand us from so far away' (2004: 426). Fazil warns Orhan that he must insert this disclaimer into his novel, making an important point about the nature of mediation. The reason he asks for this disclaimer is not because Fazil does not respect art, but the opposite: because he knows it often constructs a reality that is difficult to change. Pamuk seems to be suggesting that the power of mediation in constructing reality, particularly in the case of understanding the jihadist, requires significant attention in order to explore the latter's intentionality, both outside of a purely religious and culturist narrative and outside an exclusive secularist narrative. In this way his narrative is truly anti-Orientalist.

As I have noted in this and the previous chapter, the line between fiction and nonfiction is consistently blurred in this process of construction, as popular knowledge of actual jihadists finds its way into the fictionalization of jihadist characters. Similarly, fictionalized jihadists actively construct the dominant narratives of mass culture regarding *jihad* and, in fact, reproduce the figure of the jihadist as a highly unstable sign. I have argued that mediation of the jihadist has become a major thematic for Muslim interlocutors who navigate around accepted narratives of Orientalism and anti-Orientalism, through the forms of cultural criticism, film and fiction. In doing so, a consistent descriptive and multi-faceted genealogy of the jihadist is constructed. Bobby Sayyid has noted an interesting paradox in Orientalist and anti-

Orientalist studies: that, as anti-Orientalists deconstruct how Orientalists misrepresent Islam, they never actually affirm that Islam actually exists and therefore can be represented. Sayyid argues that such a negation of Orientalism turns into a negation of Islam itself (2004: 35). While anti-essentialist understandings of Islam conclude that there is, in fact, no Islam, only Islams (see Chapter 3), neoconservatives (see Chapter 2) perceive *jihad* as an irreducible kernel of violence at the heart of Islam. It seems to me, therefore, that the differentiation between Orientalism and anti-Orientalism is not particularly productive, and it is perhaps more beneficial to see the field of Orientalism, or writing about Islam, as both discontinuous and continuous, with the same field that Said himself critiqued. Like humanism, to which it belongs, and to which Said pledged his allegiance, Orientalism is duplicitous and connects itself to both the essentializing of *jihad* and the secularization and universalization of *jihad*, sometimes, as the next chapter will argue, at the expense of careful attention to the articulations of the jihadists themselves.

CHAPTER 4

Ree(a)l jihadists:
the media-tion of intentions

The blank screen at the end of the film *Paradise Now*, signifying the act of terror, comes as a shock to the viewer: the process of humanizing Khalid, the unlikely jihadist, leads the viewer to believe that he will not go through with the act. In some ways the plot should be predictable: Khalid does what he says he will do throughout the film, yet the audience, like the theatre audience in Pamuk's *Snow*, cannot distinguish reality from performance, and the disjuncture occurs when the actual act and the performance of it collide. In *Welcome to the Desert of the Real* Slavoj Žižek argues that people have become so accustomed to seeing images of the Real that they are unable to recognize it when it is in front of them, often mistaking reality for fiction (2002: 19). In short, viewers have come to expect the unreal not the Real, and when they witness it, they don't recognize it. The unique thing about the bomber is not whether he is certain or not about his belief or cause, as in Khalid's case, but that he believes in the '"performative force" of the ideological illusion itself' (2002: 72). In this way the cause and its performance become conflated. Viewers receive the mediation of the jihadist, half-believing he is an actor, shocked that he actually is what he claims to be, a jihadist, not quite believing that he is willing to annihilate himself and others for a cause he may not even be certain of. In *Reality TV: The Work of Being Watched*, Mark Andrejevic (2004) refers to Žižek's description of the savvy audience and applies it to reality television by recounting Žižek's interpretation of a Lacanian joke: travellers meet each other on a street, one man asks the other 'why do you lie to me saying you're going to Cracow so I should believe you're going to Lemberg, when in reality you *are* going to Cracow' (2004: 16–17). Andrejevic notes that the same applies to reality television, which pretends to be real so that we can believe it is phony, while it 'accurately portrays the reality of contrivance in contemporary society' (2004: 17). This observation of the savvy watcher can be applied to the situation of the jihadist as performer. Why do you convince me you are a jihadist, when I should believe you are only a performer, when in reality you *are* a jihadist? In this case, both the performance (of the actor) and the actual action (death) occur.

This reflection on the process of mediation is eerily present in the video of Mohamed Siddique Khan, one of the London bombers:

> I'm going to keep this short and to the point because it's all been said before by far more eloquent people than me. And our words have no impact upon you, therefore I'm going to talk to you in a language that you understand. Our words are dead until we give them life with our blood. I'm sure by now the media's painted a suitable picture of me, this predictable propaganda machine will naturally try to put a spin on things to suit the government and to scare the masses into conforming to their power and wealth-obsessed agendas. I and thousands like me are forsaking everything for what we believe. Our driving motivation doesn't come from tangible commodities that this world has to offer. Our religion is Islam – obedience to the one true God, Allah, and following the footsteps of the final prophet and mes-senger Muhammad.... This is how our ethical stances are dictated. Your democratically elected governments continuously perpetuate atrocities against my people all over the world. And your support of them makes you directly responsible, just as I am directly responsible

for protecting and avenging my Muslim brothers and sisters. Until we feel security, you will be our targets. And until you stop the bombing, gassing, imprisonment and torture of my people we will not stop this fight. We are at war and I am a soldier. Now you too will taste the reality of this situation. (Khan 2005)

Khan's audience is clear: the community to which Khan, with his Northern English accent, clearly belongs, but, as a Muslim, feels no part of. The appeal to 'you' not only makes the audience the witness to his act after the event, but also puts them in a position of responsibility for it, since Khan informs them clearly why he decided to act on his 'ethical stance'. Further, Khan is deeply cognizant of media representation, commenting on how the media will represent him and how people will blindly follow this interpretation, serving 'power and wealth-obsessed agendas', and he notes that it is these agendas which cause the fear, not his act. Finally, his use of the pronoun 'our' puts him in the position of mediator for oppressed Muslim communities: he speaks as a Muslim, for 'my people', disassociating himself from the community of victims to which he speaks. He clearly states that his goals are political as well as other-worldly, focusing on his 'responsibility' as a Muslim to obey only God and institute these principles on earth because he is a 'soldier'. Interestingly, his use of the words 'by now' directly draws attention to the fact that his message will be received after his death and after the media image and spectacle of him have been constructed. In his recording Khan is aware of the delay with which his message will be received and he intends it as a counter-narrative to the media's construction of his intentions. Khan is intent on representing himself as an ordinary man withan extraordinary ethical stance.

The desire to relate the ordinariness of his life and death is accentuated by the release of a second video, showing Khan as a father (Khan 2008). Here we see Khan holding his daughter and talking to her while recording himself. The viewer focuses on his message to his toddler, obviously too young to understand what he is saying and not the real audience for the video; he tells her that he is 'doing this for the sake of Islam, not for materialistic or worldly benefits'. The effect is to present himself as a loving father, explaining his motives in the mode of reality television. However, the video also shows Khan recording himself and his daughter, holding the camera in front of him, which means that a second camera is present. The audience can assume that this second camera is somehow connected to the other three bombers, who appear on screen to flex their muscles and make other playful gestures. Thus the viewer is watching the jihadist (Khan) enact a staged performance while he is willingly being *viewed* and recorded. This playful home video, then, comments directly on his role as mediator, and makes obvious the act of recording, thereby showing the synoptic and panoptic nature of the event. The audience, like that in Pamuk's theatre, is spectator to an act of violence about which it has been warned, according to Khan, making the audience, as in Bey's formulation in *Snow*, complicit in the act of violence. Further, the audience (many) is watching the jihadist (few), enacting a synoptic relationship, while at the same time both the jihadist and the audience are aware that not only is the performance of the jihadist being watched by intelligence agencies, government security networks and so on, but so are the viewers, who are enthralled or even disgusted by the jihadist, enacting a panoptic relationship of the few viewing the many. Therefore the viewers are aware that they are also being viewed, as are the muscle-flexing jihadists who appear in Khan's video.

Because the jihadist is deeply cognizant of the panoptic and synoptic nature of viewing, he openly reflects on this relationship. Shehzad Tanweer's video, released on 6 July 2006 and broadcast by Al Jazeera (Tanweer 2006), is shot in the form of a documentary with accompanying commentary by Ayman al-Zawhiri and Adam Gadahn, maps of London, and a description of the bomb-making process, as well as a message from Tanweer. In this way, Tanweer manages both to document the process of his own death and return to comment on it a year later. His death has been viewed, but it is as if he too were viewing the result of this death, as the observant and ever-present *shahid*, offering answers one year on as to the meaning of the event. In this way, he acts as both viewed and viewer.

It is evident from Khan and Tanweer's videos that through the media of reality television and documentaries they wish to deconstruct the very realities that these media claim to make transparent. The spectacle of violence is actual violence: victims actually died. Unlike reality television shows, where real people become unreal characters, the jihadists' performances have actual and political repercussions which cannot be accounted for by seeing their role as merely performative. The jihadist is not merely a simulation in the sense that Baudrillard would explain it, for while 'Representation stems from the principle of the equivalence of the sign and of the real. ... Simulation, on the contrary, stems from the utopia of the principle of equivalence, from *the radical negation of the sign as value*' (Baudrillard 1994: 6). Khan and Tanweer do not negate the sign, but attempt to assign new value to the jihadist, outside the value already assigned by the society they are addressing and critiquing. In fact, it can be argued that the jihadist engages in a metanarrative, commenting on his role as mediator, openly reflecting on his simultaneously exhibitionistic and voyeuristic role. He simulates the spectacle of *jihad* which his audience has already constructed in their hyperreality, play-fully reproducing images and adding new ones that familiarize the jihadist and thus disrupt the consistency of this hyperreality. He observes his own simulation and in this way objectifies his actions, asserting himself into the narrative regarding his own representation. The videos discussed here, with Khan acting as loving jihadist father, and Tanweer as panoptic *shahid*, seduce the audience with performance, but, in the end, the viewer is shocked by the crisp reality of transparency. The video is in fact what it says it is: despite its performative value, it is a testament to an act of violence, not a simulation, which results in actual deaths. For an audience accustomed to hyperreality, and seduced by familiar simulations, reality is a shock, a testament to Baudrillard's assertion that 'Terrorism is always that of the real' (Baudrillard 1994: 47).

A similar kind of Lacanian transparency occurs in beheading videos. These start out as crude enactments, or simulations, of barbaric scenes, but actual beheading does occur. While it is true that the videos play up to a fearful and barbaric image of Muslims, such performances do have measurable political effects. Commenting on this spectacle, Giroux notes that 'the political overshadows the aesthetic' and that 'the representation of politics has not disappeared into the vortex of the simulacra' (Giroux 2006: 65). However, he interprets the videos as a way to 'sanction a renewed commitment to authoritarianism, … to promoting a view of the social defined almost exclusively through shared apprehension and distrust' (2006: 65). This notion of the social, he argues, used to promote threatening religious orthodoxies, functions by 'prohibiting the exercise of critical thought and transforming citizens into automatons' (2006: 66). Though this may be true, it is important to add that these videos had real *political* value: for example, the threatened beheading of Filipino workers in Iraq resulted in that government withdrawing all Filipino contractors as per the jihadist demands. This 'spectacle of terror', Giroux argues, refers to a new kind of politics wherein terrorism is marketed and politicized through fear and shock, and is not about illusion but the thrill of the real (2006: 30–31). This 'thrill of the real' occurs at the point of transparency, where simulations of hyperreality, as discussed above, tantalize and seduce, but in the end represent rather than simulate a reality, not hyperreality. According to Giroux this spectacle manipulates a small-screen culture, constructs a subject and a public in a state of permanent fear in a chaotic world, and creates 'a new type of politics organized around the modalities of death, hysteria, panic and violence' (2006: 31). For Giroux, 'the public interest has been largely fashioned as a giant Reality TV show where notions of collectivity register as a conglomeration of private concerns' (2006: 3). Likewise, it privatizes discourse:

> In the post-9/11 world, the space of shared responsibility has given way to the space of private fears; the social obligations of citizenship are now reduced to the highly individualized imperatives of consumerism, and militarism has become a central motif of national identity. (2006: 1)

Giroux is right to notice that the 'spectacle of terror' has a political motive as well as symbolic value, but he is not completely correct in assuming that it has privatized public space, since in many instances this spectacle has served as an invitation to public engagement rather than a withdrawal into the private realm. To be fair, Giroux focuses on the effects of the *jihad* on Western society, arguing that the language of the social has been sacrificed for state protection, translated into the suspension of civil liberties, the expansion of government surveillance and the proliferation of the view that dissent is anti-American (Giroux 2006: 3). In this he is correct; since citizens are terrified for their safety, they respond as powerless individuals, clinging to a perverted sense of patriotism that justifies the torture of others. However, the 'spectacle of terror' has also had a series of both intended and unintended effects that, instead of privatizing public space, have allowed for new calls to public engagement. For example, the spectacle has been a critical part of al-Qaeda's recruitment strategy and served the intended goal of publicly engaging more jihadists in *jihad*; this is not privatization of the public realm. The spectacle has also had an enormous public impact on American and European Muslims in particular. In this sense the spectacle itself has had a series of perhaps unintentional consequences, including the mobilization of Muslims internationally to counteract the images circulated by the spectacle itself; increased public interest in Islam; and higher rates of conversion to Islam across America and Europe.

This is hardly a withdrawal into the private sphere, at least not for Muslim communities. It can even be noted that the spectacle of the jihadist, as I will argue in the following chapters, has re-politicized theory, acting as an impetus for an urgent social engagement between the intellectual and society, particularly in postcolonial and post-secular theory. Although Giroux notes that the spectacle of the insurgent videos 'ties us to a retrograde notion of the social that is organized around a culture of shared fears rather than shared responsibilities' (2006: 50), I argue that, in fact, while the jihadist's goal *is* to instil fear, he does not wish to privatize it; instead he hopes that this fear will become a call for a genuine social engagement.

It is obvious that the American government recognizes the potential political impact of such videos, their appeal to a real audience, not merely their performative value. The videos are hosted on websites that are regularly monitored and shut down.[1] The debate around what is allowed to be shown in the 'war on terror' reached a pinnacle in 2006 when it became evident that the American government had plans to bomb the Al Jazeera headquarters in Qatar, a friendly and pro-American state, accusing Al Jazeera of supporting terror because it aired various jihadist messages. This debate over access to the Internet and particularly access to Al Jazeera raises the pertinent question as to why access is denied to some violent materials and yet others are widely televised. For example, the disturbing content of torture in Abu Ghraib was circulated freely on television and the Internet, while horrific content of beheadings by jihadists was banned. Kellner positions Abu Ghraib as a depiction of the 'brutal colonial mentality' (Kellner 2005: 82) and notes that the archive, which was the work of young US soldiers, included over a hundred photos, not only of the torture but also of daily life in Iraq: pictures of camels, and scenes in Iraq were side by side with the photos of abuse, as if it were a document of travel literature (80). This spectacle lasted for a few weeks and, though much discussed in human rights circles, then faded from television screens. This was immediately followed by the 11 May 2004 beheading of Nick Berg. The actual act of beheading was not shown on television. Why was it that the Abu Ghraib photos were so widely circulated but the Nick Berg beheading remained unseen? Giroux would perhaps answer this by arguing that in today's global network images cannot be stopped; this is true, but it does not mean they must be shown on major television networks. Why was Al Jazeera's airing of jihadist speeches and beheadings of such concern to the American administration while the major network broadcasts of the abuse conducted by this very administration were not? Did audiences really identify themselves with the Abu Ghraib prisoners as they did with Nick Berg? Perhaps images of such colonialist abuse evidenced in the Abu Ghraib archive intentionally serve as a warning to the jihadist that this can happen to anyone; perhaps the American administration had its finger on the pulse of society when it assumed the Abu Ghraib images would be less bothersome than the Nick Berg beheading because Muslim victims remain less important and identifiable than American ones. It is easier to see *Homo islamicus* denigrated, as the object of degradation and sexual abuse, and perhaps even advantageous in the 'spectacle of terror', than it is to see a fully human American body.

It appears evident, then, that the American government, at least, is cognizant of the fact that spectacles have direct political implications both for the recruitment of potential followers and for the American public's general perception of their own government. While governments state that they will not negotiate with terrorists, it is common knowledge that secret negotiations take place, and there is ample evidence that terrorism works. Gould and Klor (2010), for example, after examining attacks in Israel from 1988 to 2006, conclude that local attacks cause Israelis to be more willing to grant territorial concessions to the Palestinians, and that terrorism appears to be an effective strategy in terms of shifting the entire political landscape to the left. Robert Pape (2005) claims that terrorists achieved significant policy changes in six of the eleven terrorist campaigns that he analysed and argues that terrorism is particularly effective against democracies because the electorate typically is highly sensitive to civilian casualties from terrorist acts. Karol and Miguel (2007) provide empirical support regarding voters' sensitivity by showing that American casualties in Iraq caused George W. Bush to receive significantly fewer votes in several key states in the 2004 elections. The 11 March 2004 Madrid train bombings made a direct intervention by installing a party in power that might not otherwise have been elected. Indeed, just three days after the bombings, a government that was a strong supporter of America's global war on terror and a participant in the war in Iraq was replaced with a government determined to pull Spanish troops out (Jenkins 2004).

The obvious connection between violence and achieving political goals allows us to return to the instance of disjuncture created by the Lacanian joke when the audience actually realizes that the jihadist is an actual jihadist and that his intentions are exactly what he says they are. The evidence seems to suggest that the jihadist has directly inserted himself into both the Symbolic and the Real, raising serious questions about the nature of mediation and performance and the possibility of political action. The jihadist is now speaking for himself directly. He operates in the same field as his Muslim interlocutors, often employing the same kind of engagement and language to assert a voice. Though he competes with them for his performance, he is capable of political action. Further, he is a sophisticated and savvy performer, who, however, does not perform for the sake of performing, but does so to institute a political result and change. However, in the process of 'translating' the intentions of the jihadist, interlocutors, including Muslims, transform this message into an ethical rather than political message, abstracting the *jihad* from its Islamic intention.

In general, the debate over the intentionality of *jihad* focuses on worldly and other-worldly motives, the latter a thoroughly underdiscussed issue. The dominant practice in accentuating secular and religious motives is to emphasize that religious violence is more fanatical, fearful and unmanageable, with its perpetrators referred to as 'new terrorists'. Walter Laqueur, in *No End to War*, explains that 'the "new" terrorism has increasingly become indiscriminate in the choice of its victims. Its aim is no longer to conduct propaganda but to effect maximum destruction, especially in terrorism inspired by religious fanaticism' (2003: 9). Simon and Benjamin also note the difference between secular and religious-inspired violence and the consequent paradigm shift:

> the old paradigm of predominantly state-sponsored terrorism has been joined by a new, religiously motivated terrorism that neither relies on the support of sovereign states nor is constrained by the limits on violence that the state sponsors have observed themselves or placed on their proxies. (2000: 59)

As Bruce Hoffman likewise elaborates, 'whereas secular terrorists attempt to appeal to a constituency of actual supporters or potential sympathizers, religious terrorists are at once activists and constituents engaged in what they regard as a total war. They seek to appeal to no other constituency than themselves' (1998: 95). Central to this division between the new (religious) and old (secular) binary is the view that the practitioners of this new form of terrorism are more fanatical, radical and, perhaps, irrational than the secular organizations of old terrorism, their paranoia and fanaticism distancing them from the political and rational motives of their predecessors. Thus the new terrorists engage in 'performances of violence that symbolize a cosmic war' and their acts are framed as largely symbolic and transformative (Juergensmeyer 2000: 162). This assertion is dominant in interpretations of jihadist discourse, particularly in the works of Jean Baudrillard, Slavoj Žižek and Faisal Devji.

Clarke has convincingly argued in *Oriental Enlightenment: The Encounter between Asian and Western Thought* that Orientalism has had various oppositional strains, sometimes collaborating with power and often going against it:

> Orientalism … cannot simply be identified with the ruling imperialist ideology, for in the Western context it represents a countermovement, a subversive entelechy, albeit not a unified or consciously organised one, which in various ways has often tended to subvert rather than to confirm the discursive structures of imperial power. (Clarke 1997: 9)

These 'oppositional strains' are particularly evident in Baudrillard's and Žižek's configurations of *jihad*. In *The New Orientalists: Postmodern Representations of Islam from Foucault to Baudrillard*, Ian Almond critiques both, along with others, particularly those who have offered a critique of modernity and capitalism in French culture and often make recourse to Islam as a way of 'obtaining some kind of critical distance from one's own society' (Almond 2007: 2). Tracing the Islamic references in the works of Nietzsche, Foucault, Derrida, Kristeva, Baudrillard, Žižek and others, Almond notes that many of these writers employ the Islamic Orient to relocate Western modernity and critique it; they want to re-evaluate many of modernity's central tenets but also invoke an Islamic/Arab Other in doing so (2007: 2). In this way, postmodernity inherits, in a more subtle manner, 'the Orientalist/imperialist tropes that had been so prevalent in modernity' (2007: 4). On Nietzsche, for example, whom Almond posits as the progenitor of Žižek, he notes that 'Islam forever hovers in the background of Nietzsche's writing, both published and unpublished. … Nietzsche's interest in Christianity's combative Other appears to increase as the years pass by' (2007: 8). Foucault, Almond argues, after conducting a review of references in Foucault's work of his time in Tunisia and to half a dozen articles on Iran, employs Islam to critique the Eurocentric view, in the process positing Islam as the Other and reaffirming this Otherness (2007: 22–3). The idea of the Iranian

Revolution allowed Foucault to focus on the madness of Islam: as an energy that resists the control and containment of the West and reverses history. Almond concludes that 'the Islamic Orient Foucault finds in Iran is the same Islam we find in *The Antichrist* and the *Genealogy of Morals*' (2007: 41).

In an interesting extension, Almond connects the works of Jean Baudrillard and Slavoj Žižek to the Nietzsche/Foucault tradition. For example, Baudrillard's admiration for Saddam Hussein was based on seeing in him the transparency of power of an Oriental despot, and like Nietzsche and Foucault he connects the Oriental to a 'more authentic premodern understanding of power' (Almond 2007: 161). For Baudrillard, 'Arabs appear to have no problem with being playthings in the order of something larger than themselves' (2007: 161); they can accept the role of object. Baudrillard admires the object status, an understanding of our place in the world of things, which he believes is superior in the Oriental rather than the Occidental viewpoint (162). Almond argues that in this sense *The Gulf War Did Not Take Place* is the 'postmodern Orientalist text *par excellence*' (2007: 163), in which Baudrillard produces a discourse about the Iraqis but never includes them in his discussion (2007: 164). Almond cogently points out that Baudrillard erases the reality of the Arab perspective and experience, and adds that it is difficult to imagine what would have happened if Baudrillard had written a book called *9/11 Did Not Take Place* (2007: 165). Although Almond's critiques are justifiable and well-argued, he does not elaborate carefully enough the difference between the Orientalism of Baudrillard and that of Lewis, Huntington and Friedman, for example. While the Orientalism of such neoconservatives is used to justify the 'war on terror' and particularly the attack on Iraq, Baudrillard's perspective is oppositional to the dominant political discourse; for example, he occupied an adversarial position on the Iraq War. While he does not engage with *jihad* itself as a specifically Muslim response and uses Islam symbolically in his discourse, Baudrillard does show sympathy for Muslim victims.

It is necessary to emphasize the double track of Baudrillard's engagement with Islam by noting his comments on *jihad* in *The Spirit of Terrorism* (2002), along with his thoughts on the Abu Ghraib scandal.

Clearly, in *The Spirit of Terrorism*, as Almond argues, Islam is merely a metaphor for the implosion of globalization's excess, a metaphor of 'anti-power', a substitute for communism, a 'ghostly enemy ... infiltrating itself ... from all the interstices of power' (Baudrillard 2002: 15). According to Baudrillard, the superpower fomented the violence itself and bred the 'terroristic imagination' (2002: 5), and so the attack on the towers was a symbolic destruction of the epicentre of capitalism which always contained within itself the catalyst of its own destruction. In fact, Baudrillard argues, 'we can say that they did it, but we wished for it' (2002: 5), positing the jihadists as the agents who instigated the common dream of humanity for the self-destruction of power. For Baudrillard, the rhetoric of evil has been attached to the event, because without our complicity the event could not have happened, since it is human nature that 'the increase in the power of power heightens the will to destroy it' (2002: 7). The metaphysical terms of good and evil are misunderstood as opposites, while, in fact, they advance together as part of the same movement; neither conquers the other, but they are irreducible and interrelated. With the only objective being to radicalize the world by sacrifice, viewing death as symbolic and sacrificial, the *jihad* functions by believing that the system itself commits suicide in response to multiple changes posed by deaths and suicide (2002: 17). As such, terrorism does not seek the elimination of the Other, but rather an engagement with the Other, contrary to what Giroux has argued. In this it can be argued that Baudrillard had indeed grasped some of bin Laden's intentions. However, since the purpose of the *jihad* for Baudrillard is destruction only, its function is 'to substitute for a real and formidable, unique and unforeseeable event, a repetitive, rehashed pseudo-event' (2002: 34). Without ideology, the *jihad* can offer no utopian vision for replacement of global capitalism; it can only be part of its destruction. Later, in *The Intelligence of Evil*, Baudrillard makes the same point:

> Terrorism operates at a higher level of radicalism: it is not a subject of history; it is an elusive enemy. And if the class struggle generated historical events, terrorism generates another type of event. Global power (which is no longer quite the same as capital) finds itself here in direct confrontation with itself. It is now left to deal not with the specter of communism, but with its own specter. (2007: 128)

After 9/11, Baudrillard was forced into a position where he had to defend himself from accusations that such reflections constituted anti-Americanism or the legitimation of terrorism.

> I have glorified nothing, accused nobody, justified nothing.
> One should not confuse the messenger with his message. I have endeavoured to analyze the process through which the unbounded expansion of globalization creates the conditions for its own destruction. (Baudrillard 2004)

Therefore Baudrillard does not place hope in *jihad* to radically transform the trend of globalization, but merely sees it as a disruptive force contained in globalization, an excess. It can be argued that Baudrillard too flippantly employs *jihad* to make a point, but his position is not a case of Oriental enchantment or romanticism. He employs *jihad* as a self-reflexive mechanism to theorize the nature of globalization, not the nature of *jihad* itself. This, when coupled with his article on the images of Abu Ghraib, gives us a clearer idea of Baudrillard's stance. As Kellner observes, Baudrillard argues in 'The Violence of the Global' that the Abu Ghraib images were 'a parody of violence and the Iraq war itself in which the "reality show" of the "the liberation of Iraq" became an "Ubesque and infantile" farcical spectacle of the impotency of American power' (Kellner n.d. e). As Kellner observes, Baudrillard notes the racist and colonial degradation evident in the images, for which the entire West was responsible: 'it is the whole of the

West that is present in the sadistic smiles of the American soldiers, just as it is the whole of the West that is behind the building of the Israeli wall' (Baudrillard quoted in Kellndr n.d. e).

Žižek's case is slightly more contentious. For Almond, Žižek's post-9/11 work is a continuation of Baudrillard's argument. He argues that for Žižek, Islam has a fanatical revolutionary energy and also serves a transitional function towards an unactualized socialism (Almond 2007: 179). Žižek's Iraq, as shown in *Iraq: The Borrowed Kettle* (2004), which the author admits is not a book about Iraq, is reminiscent of Baudrillard's *The Gulf War Did Not Take Place*. In fact, Iraq is used to elaborate his Lacanian theories and argue for a Eurocentrism which will challenge the notion of American multiculturalism and reposition the war as 'the first war between the USA and Europe' (Almond 2007: 180–81). Žižek's call for Eurocentrism is not an apology for imperialistic arrogance, but a desire for social justice and an expression of frustration at the way capital has used identity politics to distract and manipulate that desire; at the same time, it pushes Iraq to the margins of his book (Almond 2007: 181).

Besides the marginalization of the socio-political reality of Iraq, Almond contends that Žižek celebrates what he perceives as the violence of Islam, which he describes in *Welcome to the Desert of the Real* as primarily an explosion of lethal *jouissance* (Almond: 185). Žižek hopes that Islam can be articulated into a socialist project because of its irreducible characteristics, which are the exact features that make it the Other: its anti-modernity, its sense of collectivity and its resort to radical violence. Islam lies in an intermediary stage as something to be used. Almond concludes that Žižek's Muslims are not real Muslims but 'beings-for-others – other countries, other causes, other projects' and his Islam has a kind of 'dehumanized functionality' (Almond 2007: 192).

Certainly, it is true that Žižek's positioning of *jihad* as an instrument to be used as a way out of the paralysis of postmodernism and post-politics is evident in many of his works. For Žižek, the jihadist is a challenge to the Nietzschean deadened last man who is consumed by post-political society:

> Is not this antagonism the one between what Nietzsche called 'passive' and active nihilism? We in the West are the Nietzschean Last Men, immersed in stupid daily pleasures, while the Muslim radicals are ready to risk everything, engaged in the struggle even up to their own self-destruction. (Žižek 2002: 40)

Thus, for Žižek, the jihadist, in his excessiveness, may serve as a hope for an alternate position. He provocatively romanticizes:

> What if we are 'really alive' only if we commit ourselves with an excessive intensity which puts us beyond 'mere life'? What if, when we focus on mere survival, even if it is qualified as 'having a good time', what we ultimately lose is life itself? What if the Palestinian suicide bomber on the point of blowing him- or herself (and others) up is, in an emphatic sense, 'more alive' than the American soldier engaged in a war in front of a computer screen…? (Žižek 2002: 88)

This romanticism is the core of Almond's concern in regard to Žižek's approach to Islam and specifically *jihad*. The important point is that Žižek is disappointed in the Western response to the excess of the jihadist, which he sees reflected in two ways: a reassertion of conservative dialogue about the Other, and a restriction on the expression of dissidence by accommodating it to liberal multiculturalism in naive gestures of superficial inclusion. Nevertheless, Muslims basically remain on the fringes of Žižek's formulations; so does the entire Third World. Žižek's call for Eurocentrism posits Europe as a site of resistance to American hegemony. For him the real catastrophe of 9/11 was that of Europe, since America's hegemony was strengthened while Europe lost power:

> It is a unified Europe, not Third World resistance to American imperialism, that is the only feasible counterpoint to the USA and China as two global superpowers. The Left should unashamedly appropriate the slogan of a unified Europe as a counterweight to Americanized globalism. (Žižek 2002: 145)

At times, however, Žižek's understanding of *jihad* runs danger-ously close to the Lewis/Huntington/Friedman school. In *Violence*, Žižek argues that the 'fundamentalists', whether Christian or Muslim, are not strong enough believers, because if they were they would not be threatened by the 'sinful life of the non-believers' (Žižek 2008: 85). He then presents a wholly culturalist argument to explain the anger of Muslims during the Danish cartoon crisis:

> How fragile the belief of a Muslim must be, if he feels threatened by a stupid caricature in a low-circulation Danish newspaper. The fundamentalist Islamic terror is *not* grounded in the terrorists' conviction of their superiority and in their desire to safeguard their cultural-religious identity from the onslaught of global consumer-ist civilization. The problem with fundamentalists is not that we consider them inferior to us, but rather that *they themselves* secretly consider themselves inferior. This is why our condescending, politi-cally correct assurances that we feel no superiority towards them only make them more furious and feeds their resentment. The problem is not cultural difference (their effort to preserve their identity) but the opposite fact that the fundamentalists are already like us, that secretly they have internalised our standards and measure themselves by them. (Žižek 2008: 86)

Žižek does not attempt to place the cartoon crisis in the socio-political circumstances in which it was generated: the occupation of Iraq and Afghanistan, a recent Israeli attack on Lebanon, the ongoing siege of Gaza, the continuing persecution of Muslims in Abu Ghraib and Guantánamo Bay, and a rapidly rising right in Europe. Instead, he uses a cultural argument of envy and inferiority to posit *Homo islamicus* as a pathetic figure in a liberal multicultural Europe. However, such posturing often appears as a dramatic flourish in Žižek's work, along with his occasionally provocative bad taste.[2] As in *Iraq: The Borrowed Kettle*, Žižek seems interested mainly in employing Muslims to support a point, this time regarding the paralysis of multiculturalism. For example, the debate over the Danish cartoon crisis is 'patronizing', Žižek argues:

What, however, about submitting Islam – together with all religions – to a respectful, but for that reason no less ruthless, critical analysis? This, and only this, is the way to show true respect for Muslims: to treat them as serious adults responsible for their beliefs. (Žižek 2008: 139)

At the same time, Žižek does not give up hope that the destructive energy of *Homo islamicus* can be channelled into a significant challenge to global capitalism and multiculturalism, and on occasion he turns to an investigation of Islamic terminology for support. For example, *ijtihad* becomes a means to 'reinvent eternity': '*Ijtihad* is a properly dialectical notion: neither a spontaneous immersion in old traditions nor the need to 'adapt to new conditions' and compromise, but the urge to *reinvent eternity itself* in new historical conditions (Žižek 2002: 52–3). In *jihad*, too, he sees a similar kind of hope:

> The basic meaning of *jihad* in Islam is not a war against the external enemy, but the effort of inner purification. The struggle is against one's own moral failure and weakness. So perhaps Muslims should more actively practice the passage from the publicly best-known meaning to the true meaning of *jihad*. (Žižek 2008: 126)

Žižek's appropriation of *ijtihad* and *jihad* are not unique to him, of course, but serve as a means to universalize *jihad*. Similar appropriations are made by Faisal Devji, Zanibari/Canadian historian, inserts himself as an intimate commentator hailing from the peripheral areas of which bin Laden, in particular, spoke. In the preface to his *Landscapes of the Jihad*, Devji positions himself as a viable spokesperson, a Muslim of Indian ethnicity born in Dar es Salaam, an inhabitant of the deterrioralized zones of which Olivier Roy has written. Devji's choice to position his own history in the introduction – 'I was in Dar-es-Salaam, the town of my birth, on August 7, 1998, when the American embassy was blown up' (Devji 2005: viii) – allows him to insert a personal element into the debate on the nature of the *jihad* which had struck at the heart of the community with which he was familiar. He also directly comments, as do all of the Muslim writers discussed in this book, upon the new role for interpreters, such as himself, to play in the discourse on Islam and *jihad*:

> When the Quran is on the *New York Times* bestseller list, are we not justified in saying that Islam has become an American phenomenon, to the degree that Americans might be even more interested in and informed about it than are Muslims? This is demonstrated by the fact that Islam no longer remains the preserve of academic or religious specialists but has become a subject upon which anybody can pronounce – because it has indeed become part of not just of American but also of global culture. (2005: xiii)

Similarly, in *The Terrorist in Search of Humanity*, Devji personalizes his position as a Muslim as both a potential victim and a suspect in the *jihad*:

> On July 7, 2005, as I was going through the airport security in New Delhi, en route to Mumbai, four bombs ripped through London's mass transit network. Just before being herded onto the plane, I saw images of the carnage on a television monitor in a departure lounge. Among these were shots of the bus that Hasib Hussain had blown up in Tavistock Square, directly in front of the pedestrian walkway that led to my flat … I was left thinking not only how close I had come to being one of its victims, but also of how I had equally become a potential suspect in the process. (Devji 2008: 57)

In both books, Devji uses his status as a Western Muslim from a peripheral area of Islam to comment, as an insider, that the *jihad*'s intentions do not arise from Middle Eastern geopolitical issues, or even from a coherent Islamic vision. Instead, as a supranational movement the current *jihad* can be interpreted as part of what he sees as a central trend of the post-Cold War era, namely the replacement of territorial politics with ethical issues. He argues that jihadists tend to view the West as a negative mirror image of Islam, but asserts that this is not enough to understand the nature of the *jihad*, which is a 'series of global events that have assumed a universality of their own beyond such particularities' (Devji 2005: 87).

Since intentionality cannot fully explain the nature of the *jihad*, the symbiotic relationship between the media and 'martyrdom' can offer some insight: 'As a series of global effects the *jihad* is more a product of the media than it is of any local tradition or situation and school or lineage of Muslim authority' (Devji 2005: 87). Devji further argues that the media are a means of both exhibitionism and recruitment and allow Islam to become a global spectacle, for both Muslims and non-Muslims, not as a 'religious universality expressed in the vision of converting the world' but as a 'conversion of vision itself' (2005: 93). For Devji, this is Islam devoid of real intentionality, and therefore of political objective, replaced with ethical objectives displayed through spectacular and symbolic performances as acts of martyrdom:

> Islam comes to exist universally in the places where its particularity is destroyed, the presence of its ruins on television screens bearing witness to the Muslim's universality as martyr and militant. What makes Islam universal, then, is the forging of a generic Muslim, one who loses all cultural and historical particularity by his or her own destruction in an act of martyrdom. (2005: 94)

Thus for Devji the jihadist emerges as universal mediator, although speaking from within a Muslim context, representing grand causes and the victims of global capitalism, a similar perspective to that of Žižek and Baudrillard.

As if in anticipation of such wide assertions, in *Literature and Terrorism* Alex Houen questions whether terrorism is primarily discursive or figurative. Houen reminds us of Said's warning that there is a danger of attaching political abstractions to the act of terror, focusing only on the figurative practice, and concludes that 'the performative aspects of discourse affect the nature of material events' (Houen 2002: 6). I want to argue that just because the intentionality of the *jihad* cannot be explained by secular or religious binaries alone, *and* because its claims are ethical and universal, *and* because the media are critical to its articulation and recruitment, it does not follow that the *jihad* is emptied of its Islamic motives, assigning it a performative and nonpolitical status. Devji, for example, sees the rhetoric and actions of the jihadist as spectacular in the sense that they cannot propel political action, but attain a similar status to globalization and environmentalist movements. To do this, however, he often ignores the direct interventions of the jihadists in relation to their audiences and the manner in which they present Islam as an alternative to the audience's current mode of victimization, instead claiming that the *jihad* is a 'set of ethical performances' and as such free from a 'utopian politics of intentionality' (Devji 2005: 110). On bin Laden, for example, he states:

> His full list includes the following accusations against America: attacks on Muslims, support of dictatorial client regimes, theft of wealth and natural resources which are bought at negligible prices, occupation and corruption of Muslim lands, spread of immorality and debauchery in the forms of sex, usury and intoxicants, exploitation of women, environmental degradation, racism, deploying weapons of mass destruction, war crimes and violations of human rights.... It is on this level, then, that the jihad joins movements like environmentalism or anti-globalization.... at the forefront of ethical life today.
> (Devji 2005: 129–30)

For Devji, this signals a shift from geopolitics to metaphysics, and the acts themselves are encoded as part of a highly metaphysical act only. Again, this is only *partially* true, as part of the jihadist's objective is to create a just community on earth, which is a worldly rather than a metaphysical act. In short, the *jihad* is not only a response to globalization but, in itself, is founded on a global vision to begin with, since Islam is a global vision for jihadists.

The jihadist's list of demands and the audiences to which they are addressed tend to be transparent. The jihadist consistently addresses a community of victims and often subverts the form of reality television for his oppositional politics, as we have already discussed. In addition, various speeches, especially those of bin Laden, Adam Gadahn and Anwar al-Awlaki, interpret and clarify the performance of the bombers, making their deaths public spectacles that require political deliberation. The speeches hold no significance without the spectacle of the media, since bin Laden, Gadahn and al-Awlaki are not statesmen in the ordinary sense and the deaths of the bombers are significant only by the fact that they kill others, but the commentary upon them position these deaths as political acts, witnessed by a community. The ideologues of the *jihad*, bin Laden and his American frontmen al-Awlaki and Gadahn, repeatedly articulated the claim that social engagement and public action were their objectives. If we consider the audience – for example, the community of responsible victims to which each of them spoke, the implied and sometimes directly implied viewer/reader – it is evident that it was specific, not abstract.

Bin Laden, for example, was very clear about his multiple audiences and addressed both Muslims and non-Muslims. In an early interview with CNN, in 1997, bin Laden speaks to an obviously Western audience. When asked what message he would have for then President Clinton, he retorts none, but he does have one for the mothers of the American troops stationed on the Arabian Peninsula:

> To these mothers I say if they are concerned for their sons, then let them then object to the American government's policy and to the American president. Do not let themselves be cheated by his standing before the bodies of the killed soldiers describing the freedom fighters in Saudi Arabia as terrorists. It is he who is a terrorist who pushed their sons into this for the sake of Isr[ae]li interest. (bin Laden 2008: 52)

There are a two points of interest here: first, the call to American mothers to witness the deception of the government and their responsibility to stand against it; and, second, a belief in their ability to understand the objectives of power. Bin Laden appeals directly to this community of women, as one who is compassionate regarding their loss, for they have been deceived by their president and his war machine. He therefore attempts to create a bond of identification between himself and these victims. Note that he is careful not to call the American soldiers 'terrorists', but instead positions them as misguided victims, with President Clinton as the real terrorist. Therefore he re-creates a new community of victims of the American administration. Similarly, over a year later, in an interview with Al Jazeera, bin Laden appeals to the responsibility of a Muslim audience:

> We believe very strongly ... that they want to deprive us of our manhood. We see ourselves as men, Muslim men, committed to defend the greatest house in this universe, the holy Kaaba, which is an honor to die for and defend. (bin Laden 2008: 58–9)

Here, bin Laden evokes the concept of honour and religious obligation to inspire the Muslim masses to stimulate their support and action. In this way he tries to appeal to and activate both an American and a Muslim audience, shifting registers to address the different groups.

In his speech 'Nineteen Students' bin Laden praises the 9/11 bombers by reciting poetry for them as 'heroes, these true men, these great giants who erased the shame from the forehead of our *umma*' (bin Laden 2005a: 155). Bin Laden notes that their battle was partly to fight oppression on earth as it was they who 'shook America's throne, struck its economy right in the heart, and dealt the biggest military power a mighty blow' (2005a: 149), but their largest impact was in the affirmation of their faith, their testimony to their faith:

> With their actions they provided a very great sign, showing that it was this faith in their hearts that urged them to do these things, to give their soul to 'There is no god but God'. By these deeds they opened a great door for good and truth. (2005a: 153)

It is clear that for bin Laden the 9/11 bombers, as jihadists, achieved the ultimate in human experience, the testimony to faith exemplified in crossing over to the immortal realm, inspired only by faith. For certain, *jihad* it also a political and worldly struggle for the existence of an earthly *umma* at a specific historical moment, but it is not *only* that – above all it is a testimony of faith.

Bin Laden could not be more transparent than in his message 'To The Americans' in 2002, in which he explicitly describes the nation of the *umma* in an attempt to clearly answer 'Why are we fighting and opposing you?' and 'What are we calling you to and what do we want from you?' (bin Laden 2005b: 162). In answer to the first question, bin Laden replies 'because you attacked us and continue to attack us' (2005b: 162), directly affirming the cause of foreign occupation, as documented by anti-Orientalists such as Esposito. Yet he also puts his response in an Islamic context: 'It is commanded by our religion and our intellect that the oppressed have a right to respond to aggression. Do not expect anything from us except *jihad*, resistance and revenge' (2005b: 164). In answer to the second question, 'What do we want from you', number one on bin Laden's list was 'The first thing that we are calling you to is Islam'; after that his request is 'to stop your oppression, lies, immorality and debauchery that has spread among you' (2005b: 166), followed by a list of demands such as withdrawal of support for Israel, leaving Muslim lands and 'to deal with us and interact with us on the basis of mutual interests and benefits, rather than the policies of subjugation, theft and occupation'. It is interesting to note that bin Laden's first intention is a call to Islam and the call to an Islamic nation, which he describes as 'the Nation of Monotheism, which puts complete trust on God and fears none other than Him' (2005b: 171).

Perhaps one of bin Laden's most interesting addresses is 'The Towers of Lebanon', released days before the 2004 American presidential election. This was a bin Laden intervention into the American electoral process, acting as an equal statesman for the 'sovereign-less' State of Islam, a stance he repeated in years to come, using America's own rhetoric of 'we have been fighting you because we are free men who cannot acquiesce in injustice' (bin Laden 2005c: 238). Bin Laden chastises his American audience for their mental lethargy with the personalized affront, 'I am amazed at you' – amazed because the American audience continue to believe the lies they are told. He makes an emotional and personal appeal to them, explaining his motivations as spokesperson for the *jihad*: 'the events that made a direct impression on me were during and after 1982' (2005c: 239). As Devji notes, bin Laden is here describing Lebanon; although his account of the Israeli invasion is accurate, bin Laden was never in Lebanon in 1982, and so the personal way he presents Lebanon is as a representative of the Muslims, the eyes of their collective vision of the event (Devji 2005: 96). He describes Lebanon in a graphic manner as if he were present, with the goal of describing what 1982 in Lebanon meant for Muslims, directly relating what he saw in Lebanon to the plot to bring down the Twin Towers, tracing a line of cause and effect, and tells his American audience that 'we have no other option' (bin Laden 2005c: 240). He argues that he had no choice but to commit a spectacular and violent act because all other forms of mediation had failed:

> This is the message that we have repeatedly tried to convey to you in words and deeds, years before September 11th. You could see this, if you were so inclined, in the interview with Scott MacLeod in *Time* magazine in 1996, as well as the one with Peter Arnett on CNN in 1997, and with John Weiner in 1998. You could see it in the events in Nairobi, Tanzania and Aden; you could see it in my interviews with Abdul Bari Atwan, and with Robert Fisk, who is a fellow [Westerner] and a coreligionist of yours, but one whom I consider unbiased. (240)

Here bin Laden clearly expresses his sense of disappointment at the failure of his interventions, through actions (the Nairobi, Kenya and Aden bombings) and mediation (the various news sources that he used in an attempt to make the public responsible witnesses to current events), directly mentioning the familiar names of journalists whom he believed were also ignored. Since the American audience had ignored all these attempts at communication, they were now responsible for their own victimhood. Bin Laden assures them that their security is in their own hands, not those of their leaders, giving them direct responsibility for the acts their politicians are perpetuating in Muslim countries. In this way, he grants his audience the power to change the system which he is attacking, with the assurance that if they were to use that power they would be safe from his attacks. Bin Laden wished to transform his audience of victims into a community of responsible citizens who could actively challenge the unjust system they are living under.

This message is also consistently clear in bin Laden's 'The Solution' (2007), which again addressed the American people, but this time on the occasion of the sixth anniversary of 9/11. As discussed in Chapter 1, in 'The Solution' he expresses his surprise at the lethargy of American people, whom he further presents as powerless not only on account of their political leaders, but also due to the corrupt aims of corporations and capitalists: 'you permitted Bush to complete his first term, and stranger still, chose him for a second term, which gave him a clear mandate from you – with your full knowledge and consent to continue to murder our people in Iraq and Afghanistan' (bin Laden 2007). Bin Laden speaks at length about American failure in Iraq, but uses it to focus on his main point, the problem to which he later provides a 'solution': capitalism and its effect on the globe. He argues that the war in Iraq, despite the American people appearing to repudiate the Bush administration and its foreign policy by electing the Democrats to Congress in 2006, was doomed to continue because of the greed of capitalists and corporations, the 'real tyrannical terrorists', controlling American interests through corrupt government officials. He declares that capitalism and democracy have detrimentally affected not only the people of

Iraq and Afghanistan through war, but also the people in Africa through displacement, and mankind in general through global warming. The 'solution', bin Laden argues, is for the American people to embrace and join Islam:

> However, there are two solutions for stopping it. The first is from our side, and it is to continue to escalate the killing and fighting against you. This is our duty, and our brothers are carrying it out, and I ask Allah to grant them resolve and victory. And the second solution is from your side. It has now become clear to you and the entire world the impotence of the democratic system and how it plays with the interests of the peoples and their blood by sacrificing soldiers and populations to achieve the interests of the major corporations.
>
> And with that, it has become clear to all that they are the real tyrannical terrorists. ...
>
> And despite this brazen attack on the people, the leaders of the West – especially Bush, Blair, Sarkozy and Brown – still talk about freedom and human rights with a flagrant disregard for the intellects of human beings. So is there a form of terrorism stronger, clearer and more dangerous than this? This is why I tell you: as you liberated yourselves before from the slavery of monks, kings, and feudalism, you should liberate yourselves from the deception, shackles and attrition of the capitalist system. ...
>
> The capitalist system seeks to turn the entire world into a fiefdom of the major corporations under the label of 'globalization' in order to protect democracy. (bin Laden 2007)

Here, bin Laden positions Western populations as victims of their political leaders and capitalism, living in a state of false consciousness. Interestingly, he assures his Western audience that as they managed to free themselves from the false consciousness of their religion through secularism, they could now transcend secular capitalism to engage in a greater morality by sharing in the utopian vision of Islam. He points to the *mujahidin*, jihadists, as an example: 'There is a message for you in the *Mujahideen*: the entire world is in pursuit of them, yet their hearts, by the grace of Allah, are satisfied and tranquil' (bin Laden 2007). Even the *mujahidin*, the jihadists, are not victims as they are living by the laws of truth as opposed to the materialistic laws of capitalism.

In Islam, for bin Laden, there are no victims, and he asks his audience to transcend their status as victims by embracing Islam: 'The true religion also puts people's lives in order with its laws; protects their needs and interests; refines their morals; protects them from evils; and guarantees for them entrance into Paradise'. If they accept Islam, bin Laden, argues, the wars will end, for people will see the truth and no longer agree to be governed by their rulers, 'because as soon as the war-mongering owners of the major corporations realize that you have lost confidence in your democratic system and begun to search for an alternative, and that this alternative is Islam, they will run after you to please you and achieve what you want to steer you away from Islam'. Because people's new-found faith will deprive the capitalist of 'the opportunity to defraud the peoples and take their money under numerous pretexts, like arms deals and so on', the war will stop (bin Laden 2007).

For bin Laden, the objective is not to stop the war and then hope that people will join Islam. His objective is for people to join Islam, which he is certain would stop the war. In this way his intentions are clearly both secular and other-worldly, since only by living by divine injunctions could worldly life be just. He even provides an example of the advantage of such divine laws, arguing they are worldly, practical and just: 'There are no taxes in Islam, but rather there is a limited *zakaat*[3] totaling only 2.5%' (2007). This entire excerpt is quite remarkable because it is evident that bin Laden clearly wishes to convince his audience that the solution is Islam, which does not allow victimhood or sovereignty to anything but God, and he asserts that after embracing Islam there will be no more victimhood.

It is therefore evident that bin Laden was keenly interested in communicating his messages to American audiences; he claimed consistently that he was attempting to free them from the intellectual terrorism of their leaders and open their minds to a critical discussion. This is hardly the authoritarian closing of discourse of which Giroux writes. It is also clear that bin Laden spoke as an insider, from inside their own cultural heritage, referencing the texts and the analysis of political events that could aid in their critical reconstruction and propel them into public life. Devji compares bin Laden to a ventriloquist when he refers to the works of dissenting figures such as Chomsky:

> His own critique of the West is therefore an immanent or internal one, but more than that it is a form of ventriloquism in which the prince of terrorists speaks through one or more dummies rather than in his own name. In itself this adoption of ready-made positions is not strange, marking in fact the language of most politicians in Europe and America, but in the case of Osama bin Laden it illustrates additionally the fact that he possesses no position outside the world of his enemies. (Devji 2008: 204)

The point here is not whether bin Laden was particularly innovative in his messages, but that he did attempt to persuade his American audience to engage in public life, contrary to Giroux's claim, and he did call for critical thinking. He was more than a ventriloquist; rather, he engaged in an intertextual debate with sources in the target culture that he obviously admired.

Similar persistent messages can also be divined in the speeches of two American al-Qaeda operatives, Adam (al-Amriki – the American) Gadahn and Anwar al-Awlaki, in their cases to intercede in the discourse of Americans in general and American Muslims specifically. Gadahn first appeared on ABC television in October 2004, on a videotape in which he identified himself as 'Adam the American', speaking in American English and directly addressing his fellow Americans; another videotaped message was broadcast on the fourth anniversary of the 9/11 attacks in 2005, on *Good Morning America*, in which he attacked US foreign policy and military activity, particularly in Iraq and Afghanistan, predicting there would be future attacks in Los Angeles and Melbourne, Australia. There have been numerous other interventions by Gadahn, enough to have him listed on the FBI's most-wanted list.

The appearance of Gadahn, the fact that his identity was uncertain, and the various false reports of his capture, have allowed him to occupy a prominent position as the jihadist within. This spokesperson is an American, speaking in English, making cultural references an American would make, but dressed in Arab clothes and arguing for *jihad* to be understood within a socio-political context. On 2 September 2006, in a video titled 'Invitation to Islam', Gadahn directly reflects on the importance of mediation in the *jihad*, and invites a number of Orientalists to join Islam, including Daniel Pipes, Robert Spencer, Michael Scheuer, Steven Emerson and George W. Bush. In the same recording, Gadahn praises British politician George Galloway and journalist Robert Fisk for expressing their respect and admiration for Islam and for 'demonstrating their sympathy for Muslims and their causes', and he urges American soldiers to 'surrender to the truth', 'escape from the unbelieving Army', and 'join the winning side' (Gadahn 2006). The diversity of this projected audience is interesting: American opponents who construct neoconservative views of Islam, the leftist politicians and journalists who try to contextualize the geopolitical nature of the *jihad*, and the American soldiers in occupied lands. The text addresses multiple audiences, echoing bin Laden's 'Message to the American People', and calls on them to convert to Islam. Similarly, on 4 October 2008, Gadahn released a video primarily focused on Pakistan, but with reference to economic woes in the USA, arguing, again like bin Laden, that the capitalist system is the cause of the world's ailments and urging its victims to find truth and justice in Islam and the sovereignty of God, the only sovereign who should be obeyed (CNN 2008). Throughout 2009–11, Gadahn appeared in various recruitment videos for English-speaking converts, voicing support for the Fort Hood shooter, criticizing Pakistani politics and calling for American Muslims to arm themselves.[4]

Anwar al-Awlaki, another English-speaking American, who was assassinated in a September 2011 drone attack in Yemen, played an even larger role than Gadahn in addressing Western Muslims. In 2010 he was the subject of a major civil rights incident when he became the first American citizen to be openly put on the CIA hit list. After spending over twenty-one years in America and Britain as a student and then imam, al-Awlaki's call to a jihad for justice became more militant, which put him into direct confrontation with moderate Muslim mediators, upon whom he remarks:

> They reject the principle of pride and demanding justice, they want to promote the principle of humiliation and compliance. They want to market the democratic and peaceful U.S. Islam that calls for obeying the superiors even if they were traitors and collaborators, they want an Islam that recognizes the occupation and deals with it, they want an Islam that has no sharia ruling, no jihad and no Islamic caliphate. (al-Awlaki 2010b)

In another message, al-Awlaki clearly articulates the difference between the mediators, many of whom are discussed in this book, and the jihadists, and directly intercedes to contradict them and speak to Muslims in America:

> To the Muslims in America, I have this to say; how can your conscience allow you to live in peaceful co-existence with the nation that is responsible for the tyranny and crimes committed against your own brothers and sisters? How can you have your loyalty to a government that is leading the war against Islamic Muslims? The Muslim community in American has been witnessing a gradual erosion and decline in core Islamic principals so today many of your Scholars and Islamic organizations are openly approving of Muslims serving in the US Army to kill Muslims, joining the FBI to spy against Muslims, and are standing between you and your duty of jihad. Slowly but surely your situation is becoming similar to that of the embattled Muslim community of Spain after the fall of Granada. Muslims of the West, take heed and learn from the lessons of history. There are ominous clouds gathering on your horizon. Yesterday America was the land of slavery, segregation, lynching and Klu Klux Klan and tomorrow it will be a land of religious discrimination and concentration camps. Don't be deceived by the promises of preserving your rights from a government that is right now killing your own brothers and sisters.

> Today with the war between Muslims and the West escalating you
> cannot count on the message of solidarity you may get from a civic
> group or political party or the words of support you hear from a kind
> neighbor or nice co-worker. The West will eventually turn against its
> Muslim citizens. (al-Awlaki 2010a)

This message is intriguing because it focuses upon a very specific
audience in the 'spectacle of terror'. Western Muslims are not
threatened, but they are warned not to have faith in the American
system to protect their rights, for 'The West will eventually turn
against its Muslim citizens.' This is an open attempt to radicalize Western Muslims into developing a critical consciousness, a
violent one, perhaps, with which Giroux may not agree, but a
critical consciousness nonetheless. This is an effort to mobilize the
Muslim minority into rejecting their government's policies, and
to persuade them to act not as private individuals, but publicly,
as members of a collectivity – as Muslim Americans.

From this analysis of the audiences and the explicitly stated
intentions of bin Laden, Gadahn and al-Awlaki's speeches, we
can readily discern a concerted effort to shift the Western public
from a private to a public stance. This is contrary to Devji's claim
that the audience remains abstract and intentions universalized;
to Giroux's notion that public space is becoming increasingly
privatized; and to Baudrillard's and Žižek's tendencies to see in
jihad only a mad pool of irreducible Islamic violence, incapable
of addressing real politics. In fact, it appears that the messages
of the jihadist are clearly political and intended to elicit political
responses from a range of audiences. The role the media play in
forming and disseminating these messages is indeed critical, but
we should be careful to heed Chomsky's warning when assigning
globalization and spectacle as the sole cause of the *jihad*, as it
is evident that 'bin Laden is quite clear about what he wants'
(Chomsky 2001: 60). In this case, by positioning the jihadists
as abstract, spectacular and barbaric, we situate ourselves in the
position of perpetual audience, surprised at the irruption of the

Real, even though we are aware of its existence. In fact, the mediation of the jihadist's articulations demonstrates that the environment for hearing his transparent messages is cluttered with interlocutors and prone to misinterpretation. In the process of mediation, his intentions, which I have argued are both worldly and other-worldly, spectacular and performative, are emptied and recirculated as a cacophonous reflection on globalization in which Islam disappears at the very point where it inserts itself.

CHAPTER 5

Recovering invisible traces:
jihad and postcolonialism

In her seminal essay 'Can the Subaltern Speak?' (1988), Gayatri Spivak[1] raises two points that are directly relevant to the discourse on *jihad*, particularly the issue of representation. Although Spivak acknowledges the violence done to Indian subalterns, she suggests that any attempt from the outside to ameliorate their condition by granting them collective speech would invariably encounter both a logocentric assumption of cultural solidarity among a heterogeneous people and a dependence upon Western intellectuals to 'speak for' the subaltern condition rather than allowing them to speak for themselves. As Spivak argues, by speaking out and reclaiming a collective cultural identity, subalterns would re-inscribe their subordinate position in society. The second point of interest in Spivak's article is the discussion on the suicide of a young Bengali woman that indicated a failed attempt at self-representation. Because her attempt at speaking outside normal patriarchal channels, through suicide, was not understood, Spivak concludes that the subaltern cannot speak. Spivak's point about the widow is not that the subaltern does not cry out in various ways, but that she is incapable of dialogue because she has been excluded from the political economy. Spivak posits the subaltern as a silent, unrepresentable excess outside the labour relations: 'Between patriarchy and imperialism, subject-constitution and object-formation, the figure of the woman disappears, not into a pristine nothingness, but into a violent shuttling which is the displaced figuration of the "third-world woman" caught between tradition and modernization' (Spivak 1988: 306). Therefore, Spivak concludes 'the subaltern cannot speak' (308). Spivak's victim of suttee, who becomes representative of oppressed peoples, presents her suicide as her only act of rebellion, which ends in silencing herself.

The case of the jihadist is different. As this book argues, the jihadists are engaging in the very discourse they are committing violence upon: directly addressing their victims, while refusing to see themselves as victims. They use spectacular media performances to display their death, and they violently reassert that through their deaths, and the deaths of others, they are inscribing a message, which they hope will convince the community of victims to join them in their revolutionary, if perhaps anarchic, project. Unlike Spivak's subaltern, the jihadists are in fact speaking, and are aware of the difficulty of having their message heard. However, their ability to articulate a new discourse is severely limited by their insistence on Islamic terminologies and the elaboration of historical particularities that are not understandable or taken seriously by the secular-biased West. At the same time, the ability of 'good' Muslims to articulate a new discourse and mediate that of the jihadists is severely limited by the lack of familiarity with their own texts, which serve as the core of this point of articulation. Further, the 'good' Muslim cannot appear as if he is actively supporting the radical violence of the jihadists, so he must maintain a certain disengagement from them, or else risk becoming the target of Campus Watch. At the same time, he must assert his Muslimness as a real value, balancing his need to maintain credibility in a First World intellectual discourse and his need to claim credibility in a separate discourse that directly and violently challenges his position. In short, there is a cacophony of speaking, but is anyone listening, or, better still, why is hearing not taking place? The question that has dominated postcolonial studies, 'Can the Subaltern Speak?', displaces the more pressing question: what are the historical, material and ideological conditions required for hearing?

I want to argue that the conditions for hearing in postcolonial criticism have been severely restricted because of its secular biases and its reticence at recognizing the violent roots of its inception in anti-imperialist struggles. While there is some evidence that valuable attempts are being made to understand the contributions of Islam to postcolonialism, the foundational framework of postcolonial criticism has not been designed to provide such a space. For example, the 2010 publication of the essay collection *Terror and the Postcolonial* attempts to theorize various types of contemporary terror as inflicted with the postcolonial condition. In a particularly captivating essay in this collection, 'Sacrificial Militancy and the Wars around Terror', Alec Houen asserts: 'we need a theory of sacrificial militancy that focuses less on religious underpinnings and more on the complicated exchanges it establishes between disparate regions and different realms of social life' (Houen 2010: 115) and argues that a postcolonial *jihad* has evolved through the work of intellectuals such as Qutb and Shariati that use 'Marxist theory and theories of colonialism to posit new forms of revolutionary and nationalist Islamic ideology' (2010: 119). Though Houen no doubt has a point (as I have argued in the previous chapter the jihadist seeks to transform the community and simultaneously cross over to a transcendent one), he does not question why postcolonial theory has been reticent to examine the issue of *jihad* in the first place, why the dialogue between Shariati's and Fanon's work, for example, has been left unexamined, or why Fanon's theory of violence has often been treated with an embarrassed shrug by postcolonial critics. In this chapter, I argue that there seem to be two poignant reasons why postcolonial critics have not heard the jihadist: the first is the acquiescence to 'secular criticism', popularized through the work of Edward Said, which has been critical in formulating the canon of postcolonial studies; the second is the reserve and ambiguity that postcoloniality displays when confronted with utopian post-colonial visions that require violent transformations.

Certainly, Said's legacy is colossal. Zachary Lockman rightly notes that *Orientalism* significantly influenced the future of Orien-talist and area studies, particularly Middle Eastern studies, result-ing in an entire generation of new Orientalists who deconstruct colonial discourse on the Orient and produce numerous case studies validating Said's thesis.[2] He also contends that *Orientalism* gave birth to the field of postcolonial studies, particularly by shifting the pre-Saidian emphasis on political economy to the issue of representation (Lockman 2005: 210). In posthumous tributes to Said, the giants of postcolonial theory, Homi Bhabha and Gayatri Spivak, both write about the effect of Said on the field of post-colonialism and on their own development (Bhabha 2005; Spivak 2005). Though Said often demonstrated impatience with the obtuse language of postcolonial theory,[3] his work on representation, particularly the role of the intellectual in taking oppositional stances, became a foundation for theorization on the postcolonial subject and the complexities faced by Third World intellectuals in representing peripheral communities. Said's questions, more than those of his contemporaries and predecessors, raised episte-mological concerns about the issue of essence, and hence about the entire humanist tradition, the nature of representation and anthropological research, and the institutional functions of the intellectual and theory. In this regard, we can position Said as both a 'founder of discursivity' and an 'enunciative modality' in the Foucauldian sense.

Foucault used the term 'enunciative modality' to represent 'the various subject positions [one can] occupy or be assigned when speaking' (Hart 2000: 66). Said, though he offered a sustained critique of humanism, was also an avid supporter of the bases of the secular humanist tradition, and so he occupied various subject positions. His final work, *Humanism and Democratic Criticism* (2004), attempted to clarify his multiple positions as an 'enunciative modality' whose critique is from inside humanist discourse. Foucault's notion of the 'founders of discursivity' recognized that authors are both produced by and produce knowledge, speaking 'within the archives of their times' (Hart 2000: 67), but also reshaping these archives to produce new possibilities for discourse. In short, 'founders of discursivity' operate within a certain discursive tradition, occupy various subject positions within this tradition, and transform the tradition itself (Foucault 1984: 130). Said was produced within the humanist tradition and in turn produced knowledge which led to the growth of the field of postcolonialism, which critiques humanism. I want to argue here that as a 'founder of discursivity', Said set up new binaries for understanding Islam and the West which form the central metaphor of all of his work, up to the latest works before his death. The perceived battle between progressive secularism and backward Islam, the debate on the role of good and bad Muslims, and the role of Muslim reformers, are rooted in Said's work on the role of the secular intellectual. The disdain for Islamic political radicalism and *jihad* is evident in many of Said's interviews and overtly political texts. The positing of a multicultural solution to the issue of Muslimness, especially in Europe, is also foreshadowed in Said's work on the cosmopolitan intellectual and the role of exiles in a global world. In this chapter, I argue that the very shape of the current debate exists because of the framework already staged for this newly formed discourse, a displaced Orientalism that became rooted in postcolonialism, contained within the work of Said himself. By means of a close reading of several of Said's works, this chapter argues that the legacy of Said's secular humanism and cosmopolitanism formed the framework for both how Islam is studied in a post-Orientalist world and the development of postcolonial theory's engagement, or lack of engagement, with Islam – particularly when *jihad*, with its global demands and ethics, presents a radical critique to imperialism and global capitalism.

Said's critique of humanism developed through his notion of secular criticism, and its functions. Therefore, he often left out discussions of intellectuals who did not fit his categorizations of secular critic. When he wrote *Orientalism*, Said simply did not recognize the rich body of work already under way by various Arab and Muslim writers such as A.L. Tibawi, S.H. Alatas, Anouar Abdel-Malek and Abdallah Laroui, who had all made valuable contributions to the assault on Orientalism. This curious fact invites the question as to why Said did not engage with the already existing anticolonialist critique, which broadly fell into two camps: leftist or Marxist criticism from a political economy point of view, and Islamic scholarship. It appears that Said felt equally uncomfortable in both camps,[4] considering both 'religious' or dogmatic criticism. The issue as to the intentionality of Orientalism for the Marxist camp was quite clear – ideological 'covering' of reality to sustain the aims of capitalism. For faith-based Islamic scholarship, the intentions of the Orientalists were to discredit Islam and replace it with a deformed version of Christianity, secularized and reformed. Said could accept neither. Aijaz Ahmad usefully observes that Said placed representation over all forms of human activity and never really said why representation *must* interiorize the Other. Ahmad asks if this representation of Orientalism is representation in the postmodernist sense, having no connection with the actual Orient, outside of how it is represented, or is it wilful misrepresentation produced in the West in the pursuit of power and imperialism (Ahmad 1994: 292). He notes that a theory of intentionality was not developed in Said's work because, from a discursive point of view, representation is regulated by the power of discourse, and so does not correspond to an external truth, subjectivity or purpose, but only to the regularity of discourse itself. It may be fairer to say that while Said did not evade the issue of intentionality, connecting it directly to colonialism and Orientalism in *Culture and Imperialism*, the overt intentionality of Marxists such as Abdel-Malek and the Islamist Tibawi ran against Said's conceptual framework of secular criticism.

Anouar Abdel-Malek, an Egyptian who studied sociology at the Sorbonne and taught at the Centre National de la Récherche Scientifique, situated his work in the leftist tradition of Third World resistance literature. He argues that after the Second World War, the resurgence of African, Asian and Latin American national liberation movements made a new understanding of the Orient necessary. The intention of Orientalism for Abdel-Malek is clear; in fact, there was a transparent relationship of

> university dons, businessmen, military men, colonial officials, missionaries, publicists and adventurers, whose only objective was to garner intelligence information in the area to be occupied, to penetrate the consciousness of the people in order to better assure its enslavement to European powers. (Abdel-Malek 2000: 49)

Unlike Abdel-Malek, Said was much more conscious about drawing a direct line of intentionality: for him, Orientalism remained 'a certain *will* or *intention* to understand, in some cases to control, manipulate, even to incorporate, what is a manifestly different (or alternative and novel) world' (Said 1979: 12). For Said, Orientalism operated as cultural hegemony, not as a capitalist or imperialist plot to control the Orient. However, Said and Abdel-Malek agreed on the nature of Orientalism itself as a humanist failure. Both agreed, in other words, the rational, progressive, democratic West was constituted on the existence of an essential Other, the irrational, regressive totalitarian East. This point, of course, would form the basis of Said's theory that the West was constituted on the Othering of the Orient and that the Orient only existed as a construct of the West, and Said quotes Abdel-Malek's description of Orientalism at length (Said 1979: 96). Abdel-Malek also describes at some length the methods of the Orientalists, particularly the dehistoricization and the exoticization of the Orient. He claims that in order to sustain the discourse of essence, the history of the Orient had to be erased and rewritten. Instead, the Orient was positioned as static and fixed, and so study and research focused on the past as the preferred period, especially in cultural aspects of language and religion as 'detached from social evolution' (Abdel-Malek 2000: 51). As a result, everything that happened in the present reappeared as the emergence of a static history, unable to adapt to the dynamics of modern life: 'That which re-emerged appeared as a prolongation of the past, grandiose but extinct. From historicizing, history became exotic' 2000: 52). Said develops this same point in *Orientalism*, as well as in *Covering Islam* (1997) and *The Question of Palestine* (1992), works that he considered a trilogy.

The second intellectual of interest in this argument is A.L. Tibawi, a fellow Palestinian, who in a series of three articles written between 1964 and 1980 engaged in a debate with English-speaking Orientalists who, he claimed, essentialized, Otherized and dehistoricized the Orient. As a Muslim, Tibawi targets Islamic Orientalism. His work focuses on the relationship between Orientalists and missionaries, noting that the hope of the early Orientalists was that 'Islam might be transformed through "Westernization" or "modernization" or "reformation"' (Tibawi 1980: 60). He notes specifically that two techniques were deployed to discredit Islam. First, its doctrines, specifically the Quran, were held up as inauthentic, actually a refashioning of Hebrew documents and pre-Islamic literature; second, the authenticity of the Prophet Muhammad was questioned by assigning to him profit-oriented rather than spiritual-centred goals (62–5). Tibawi, in fact, asserts that the failure of Orientalists was an inability to understand the role Islam plays in the lives of Muslims. He speaks harshly of token Muslims, who are used by Orientalists to validate their views of the Orient and Islam in particular:

Encounters between different cultures did and do produce alienated individuals, denationalized and deculturalized, who try to live in both worlds at the same time but are at peace in neither: some of the persons named do not write in Arabic, others avoid speaking it, and some are neutral or silent on Arab or Islamic questions. (Tibawi 1980: 176)

For Tibawi, the Muslim exiled from his culture is no Saidian 'specular intellectual', the exile on the margins of society, interpreting both, but a conflicted and pathetic individual, robbed of his heritage and stripped of his identity, engaged in a discourse that the Orientalists want to hear or else remaining silent. Far from Said's utopian border intellectual, Tibawi predicted the rise of the figure of Ibn Warraq, interpreting Islam for the world, intent and insistent on its reform, perhaps on its destruction.

Various critics have noted Said's conspicuous decision to ignore Tibawi's work, which he relegates to a footnote in *Orientalism*. MacFie, for example, notes that

> Said's evident unwillingness to incorporate Tibaw's critique of orientalism into his study of the subject arises, perhaps, from the fact that he feels uncomfortable with Tibawi's deep sense of personal commitment to the Islamic faith ... and also from the fact that Tibawi, a Palestinian Arab, succeeds in breaking the orientalist rule, identified by Said, that since the Orient is incapable of representing itself, it must be represented. Far from being intimidated by the West, in his two critiques of English-speaking Orientalists, Tibawi, writing from an Islamic point of view, succeeds in mounting a devastating critique of English-speaking orientalism, identifying in considerable detail what he believes to be its major faults. (MacFie 2002: 99–100)

Or could it be that Tibawi represents an Islamic point of view with which Said did not wish to engage, a point of view mocked by his contemporaries who considered the assertion of Islamic belief as contradictory to a critical stance on Orientalism? These biases can be seen in the responses of Said's contemporaries to Arab and Muslim critiques of Orientalism. For example, in his review of the literature, Donald Little argues that he will ignore the vast

body of work written in 'Islamic languages' as the more important
work is directed at a foreign audience and that Arabs writing
in Western languages 'have embraced Western methodology
and a Western approach to the Arabs and Islam which is virtually indistinguishable from that of non Arabs' (Little 2000: 134).
Even MacFie, in an otherwise balanced account of the assault on
Orientalism, commenting on the argument between Little and
Tibawi, notes that Tibawi's work 'betrays a strength of feeling out
of place perhaps in an academic debate' (108) and concludes that
'the argument illustrates all too clearly the difficulties inherent
in any attempt made to bridge the gap between a Muslim and
a Christian/secular view of knowledge, religion and the world'
(MacFie 2002: 108). It is clear that the assertion of Islamic beliefs
is considered by reviewers, and was perhaps by Said himself, as
contradictory to a judicious debate on Orientalism.

The discomfort Said felt with the certainties of Abdel-Malek
and Tibawi is evident in his response to the Arab criticism and
translation of *Orientalism*, in the 'Afterword' appended from the
1995 edition onwards. Said commends the translation into Arabic
and expresses particular satisfaction with the translation of words
such as 'discourse, simulacrum, paradigm or code' into the 'classical
rhetoric of the Arab tradition', noting that the translator attempts
to place Said's books 'inside one fully formed tradition, as if it
were addressing another from a perspective of cultural adequacy
and equality' (338). Yet he noted that despite this, the book was
experienced as 'an affirmation of warring and hopelessly antithetical identities' (Said 1995a: 338). He explains that he had intended his
book to launch a study of Otherness, as had happened in Europe,
the United States, Australia, India, Ireland, Latin America and
Africa. The Arab world, however, appeared to be the exception
in responding to Said's challenge in *Orientalism*:

> That does not seem to be the case (insofar as I can judge it) in the
> Arab world, where, partly because my work is correctly perceived as
> Eurocentric in its texts, and partly because ... the battle for cultural

survival is too engrossing, books like mine are interpreted less usefully, productively speaking, and more as defensive gestures either for or against the 'West.' (Said 1995a: 339)

And so, according to Said, the Arab rejection of his book was due to the fact that 'decades of loss, frustration and the absence of democracy have affected intellectual and cultural life in the Arab region' (Said 1995a: 339): his homeland was basically devoid of the type of secular intellectual he could credit as influencing his ideas While defending himself against the accusation that he was a defender of Islam, Said clarified again that he was not interested in a true Islam or true Orient: 'I have no interest in, much less capacity for, showing what the true Orient or Islam actually are' (331).

The above discussion about Said's engagement with Arab sources serves as a useful point of departure to assess the impact of Said's secular humanism on his choice of intellectual heroes. Tibawi notes that

> The first essential prerequisite for any successful change (or reform) is therefore native initiative, independent of foreign control or suggestion. The second prerequisite is that all change must be acceptable to learned orthodox authority. (Tibawi 2000: 73)

Said would definitely have disagreed with the second condition; in fact, he would have asserted that an intellectual must remain oppositional and defiant in the face of authority, in other words maintain a 'secular' stance. For Said, the kind of critical distance necessary to be a critic and intellectual can only be obtained if one maintains a distance from religion and ideology, which he considers inherently doctrinal.

Various critics have noted the two very diverse hero/intellectuals Said chose in constructing his 'secular critic': Antonio Gramsci and Julien Benda. Saree Makdisi notes,

> From Gramsci, Said accepts the notion that intellectuals compose a large and variegated social body, connected to classes, movements

and traditions and fulfilling all kinds of social roles, including the production and reproduction of official ideologies and worldviews. But at the same time he finds deeply compelling Benda's much more restricted notion of the intellectual as a member of a small, embattled, morally driven group speaking out against prevailing opinions regardless of the consequence to themselves. (Makdisi 2008: 53–4)

Said defines the role of the intellectual both in the Gramsci-style collective actor and in the lonely stance of the heterodox cleric like Benda: 'The proper role of the intellectual, then, according to Said, is to maintain intellectual and political integrity, and to speak out, like one of Benda's lonely clerics, against all the odds, and despite all costs to oneself' (Makdisi 2008: 57).

In *Representations of the Intellectual*, his 1993 Reith lectures, Said wrote directly of his intellectual heroes, and outlined how the figure of the intellectual has been represented by various thinkers. In the introduction to this series of lectures, Said clearly connects intellectual vocation to the secular tradition, which for him 'is a spirit in opposition, rather than in accommodation' (1996: xvii). It is evident that for Said the secular is a metaphor for independence and freedom rather than merely acquiescence to secularism itself, and that the secular critic has to stand apart from his society and apply a single standard of humanity to all. None of the heroes in his pages espouses a particularly 'religious' point of view. In fact, in the lecture 'Holding Nations and Traditions at Bay' he argues that just as Arab intellectuals must reject nationalism, they must also reject Islamic dogma. He postulates as the type of Arab-Islamic intellectual that might be considered eligible for entry into his flock of secular critics Adonis, the Syrian poet and intellectual, who is involved in 'a revival of *ijtihad*, personal interpretation, and not a sheeplike abdication to politically ambitious *'ulema* or charismatic demagogues' (1996: 40).

For Said, then, the exemplary Muslim intellectual is Adonis, who refers to himself in a 2002 *New York Times* interview as 'a pagan prophet', self-identified as a 'renegade and anti-Muslim'

(Shatz 2002). In 'Intellectual Exiles: Expatriates and Marginals', another of the Reith lectures, Said turns again to the example of a Muslim intellectual to demonstrate the adversarial stance. Taking V.S. Naipaul as a starting point – another interesting choice, since his book *Among the Believers* was hailed as a shallow and derogatory account of Muslim societies, even in Salman Rushdie's estimation in *Imaginary Homelands* – Said strikes the critical stance of the metaphorical exile, where one remains attached to but stands outside one's own cultural bounds. In the lecture 'Speaking Truth to Power', Said identifies Rushdie himself as the prototype of his secular intellectual:

> In the secular world – our world, the historical and social world made by human effort – the intellectual has only secular means to work with; revelation and inspiration, while perfectly feasible as modes for understanding in private life, are disasters and even barbaric when put to use by theoretically minded men and women. Indeed I would go so far as saying that the intellectual must be involved in a lifelong dispute with all the guardians of sacred vision or text, whose depredations are legion and whose heavy hand brooks no disagreement and certainly no diversity.... That is why the defense of Salman Rushdie's *Satanic Verses* has been so absolutely central an issue. (Said 1996: 88–9)

And so Rushdie joins Vico, Gramsci, Auerbach and Adonis on Said's list of admirable secular intellectuals.

Said's support for Rushdie as a metaphoric exile, the ultimate example of a secular intellectual, demonstrated an unwillingness to discuss the Rushdie affair in the context of the worldliness of the event surrounding his exile.[5] Said's defence of Rushdie remained squarely based on the freedom-of-speech argument, one used frequently since to discredit Islam and prove its barbarity.[6] By asserting a universal, cosmopolitan existence for the metaphoric exile, Said had become dangerously disconnected from the worldliness of the debate. In a rather disappointing gesture, Said did not employ the incident to reflect on the rhetoric of freedom of speech as an example of the type of hypocritical double standards of which he often wrote; nor did he use the moment to reflect upon the positioning of the Muslim intellectual in today's world, particularly focusing on the relationship between Islam, Empire and globalization. In his final words on the value of the intellectual, in the last chapter in *Humanism and Democratic Criticism*, Said notes that in the post-9/11 world there has been an increasing need for, and a reaching out to, intellectuals, in both the American and the Muslim world: 'the special symbolic role of the writer as an intellectual testifying to a country's or region's experience, thereby giving that experience a public identity forever inscribed in the global discursive agenda', and again he cites Salman Rushdie as a living example of speaking truth to power (Said 2004a: 127).

The example of Said's stubborn allegiance to Rushdie, in the face of complex political and historical circumstances, surely highlights the limits of Said's theory. Especially since 9/11, when the relationship between Islam and the West was radically inserted into articulations of the present, the general public and intellectuals alike have been struggling to understand the emergence of 'radical' Islam, the challenge of *jihad*, the nature of Muslimness in a global world, and the mediating role of Muslim intellectuals, the questions Said articulated over a quarter of a century ago have been given a new urgency. Who are *they* and who are *we*? What defines *them* and *us*? What do *they* want? How can *they* be understood? Who has the authority to interpret *them*? Who is the mediator between the jihadists and *us*? Is mediation possible? Or, simply put, why do *they* hate *us*?[7] In fact, the question as to who speaks for Islam has become so pressing that conferences are arranged internationally and annually to consider it.[8] Said's theorization cannot provide a framework for exploring these issues. Said remained a secularist but he never tried to explain the many meanings of secularism, certainly not the relationship between secularity and Islam throughout the rich tradition of Islamic philosophy. For Said, the object of radical criticism is religious criticism, which necessarily contains both religion and nationalism, as well as other professional allegiances.

Said's inability to give up the secular–religious dichotomy that formed the basis of his own imaginative limits prevented him from engaging with the richness of Islamic tradition in anything more than a cursory fashion.

In this regard, perhaps the most thoroughgoing assessment of Said's relationship with religion and ideology is William D. Hart's *Edward Said and the Religious Effects of Culture* (2000). Commenting upon the strong secular/religious thematic in Said's work, Hart notes that Said was not indifferent to religion, nor did he want to avoid engaging with religion, but he was in fact antagonistic to it. For Said, an antagonism to religious criticism was necessary to being a genuine intellectual who spoke truth to power; in fact, it was essential to resist the 'quasi-religious authority of being comfortably at home among one's people, supported by known powers and acceptable values, protected against the outside world' (Said 1983: 16). Hart critiques Said's views concisely:

> Said is not a religious thinker. But this does not mean that he is indifferent. On the contrary, religion is something that he can neither tolerate easily nor leave alone. Religion is an issue for him unlike those who are indifferent, whom we mistakenly call secular. Secularism, in this respect, is a particular kind of relationship with religion. It is a skeptical, wary, or hostile interest. Secular thinkers are pre-occupied with boundary-drawing and boundary-maintenance, with where secularism ends and religion begins. (Hart 2000: 11–12)

Hart observes that for Said secular criticism is, in this sense, the 'Other' of religious criticism: 'Without the counterpoint of religious criticism, it has no point' (Hart 2000: 12). To illuminate this, he examines two of Said's central concepts, first developed in *The World, the Text, and the Critic*: filiation/affiliation and worldliness. Filiation is natural or cultural relations (family), and affiliation contains those relations which compensate for filiation failures, such as professional associations. For Said, an intellectual must resist the systems of culture to which he is bound filiatively and the systems he acquired affiliatively; only

then can he avoid 'religious criticism' in order to speak truth to
power. According to Said, religious criticism blocks the road to
inquiry and is irrational, organized, collective, vague, esoteric and
secret. On the other hand, the secular intellectual is sceptical of
cultural filiation and systems affiliation. Hart notes that for Said
nationalism and religion deter secular criticism, as does any kind
of sense of belonging to a professional cult. In short, Said believes
that religiosity has returned under a secular guise and that criticism itself has become religious; hence his criticism of criticism,
particularly nationalist discourse and deconstructionism. Second,
Hart notes that Said's concept of worldliness was developed in
counterpoint to what he perceived as the other-worldliness of
religion. In religious discourse, worldliness is a profane preoc-
cupation with the here and now while other-worldliness deals
with the more noble goals of the imagined future. Hart notes
that Said appropriates and reverses these terms. Worldliness becomes a desired goal and other-worldliness becomes obscure. Hart
makes the astute observation that, particularly in *Orientalism*,
Said reproduces the Orientalists' distinctions between East and
West as applied to secular/religious: 'Said rejects the Orientalist
distinction between Western rationality and Eastern mysticism
only to readmit and valorize this distinction under the rubrics of
secularism and religion' (Hart 2000: 86). It is ironic that secularism displaces Orientalism in Said's terminology – as Hart notes,
'Religion and secularism are East and West in Said's imaginative
geography' (2000: 86).

Said's secular/religious distinctions have been noted by a
number of critics besides Hart, though not all agree that this
new binary re-creates a kind of displaced Orientalism.[9] Peter van
der Veer points out that 'the very distinction between secular
and religious is a product of the Enlightenment that was used
in Orientalism to draw a sharp opposition between irrational,
religious behavior of the Oriental and the rational secularism
which enabled the Westerner to rule the Oriental' (quoted in

Robbins 1997: 74–5). Others in the subaltern studies group connect secularism to postcolonial nation-building, with Guha linking Western Orientalism to the growth of secular indigenous elites and Chakrabarty claiming secularism as an act of appropriation of the colonizer's government, particularly in India (Robbins 1997: 75). On the other hand, Robbins argues that Said uses the term 'secular criticism' not to oppose religion but to oppose nationalism, and the actual subject of critique is nationalism itself, as evidenced in Said's anti-American stance as an American intellectual during the Gulf War and his critical stance as a Palestinian on the Palestinian issue (1997: 74). W.J.T. Mitchell insightfully points out that the secular limit in Said's work can be directly traced to Vico's assertion that we cannot know things that we have not made (Mitchell 2005: 102). This prevents Said engaging with any kind of sacred knowledge or recognizing 'that sphere of the uncontrollable and inexplicable that, at the same time, has an immense power over human thought and action' (2005: 104). Mitchell directly links this view of the sacred to Said's 'blind spot' to mystery and the 'frequently baffled or panicky' feeling Said confessed to when engaging with the domain of the visual arts (Mitchell 2005: 104–5). Viswanathan, on the other hand, argues that Said's secularism has been interpreted too narrowly and that it is intended to demonstrate the competing affiliations faced by the intellectual:

> So that while Said seems to be polarizing terms like secular/religious, critic/cleric, human history/sacred time, worldly/mystical, his insistence that culture is a site for hegemonising tendencies, open to co-optation by the state for its own purposes ... places dissent in a much more complex adversarial relation, not only to religious orthodoxy but also to state hegemony. (Viswanathan 1997: 153)

In a later article, Viswanathan argues against Hart's observations of Said's hostility to religion and asserts that if one considers religion to include orthodox and heterodox elements, Said was sympathetic to heterodox elements of Islam (Viswanathan 2008:

164). However, Viswanathan does not provide a close reading of Said's texts to support this claim.

In short, Said's use of 'secular' has not been left uninvestigated: Said has been accused of using inappropriate Enlightenment terminology (van der Veer), reinventing the meanings of secularism and nationalism (Robbins and Viswanathan), holding secularism as a blind spot (Mitchell), and presenting theoretical inconsistencies (Hart). Two points are clear. First, for Said religious criticism was a metaphor – for any system that binds an individual to it and compromises his or her critical distance. Above all, Said argues for a critical distance for the intellectual, in line with Vico's 'rational civil theology' (Mitchell 2005: 107). Religious affiliations, which may include actual religion but are not limited to it, do not allow such distance, according to Said. Second, even if Said intends the term 'religious criticism' as an all-encompassing one, including but not limited to religion, he surely was aware of the consequence of his usage of 'secular' terminology, particularly when describing Muslim societies. Yet he insistently employs such terms throughout his work – until his last book, that is, in which the term 'secular criticism' is replaced with the term 'democratic criticism'.

There are ample occasions where Said directly connects 'religious' criticism to both religion and nationalism, which he views as unproductive and debilitating. For example, In *Power, Politics and Culture* Said clarifies his notion of religious criticism as nationalism, a response to imperialism, 'an emphasis upon forging a self-identity as a nation or people that resists but has its own integrity' (Said 2002a: 129), which, he adds, leads to the 'fetishization of the national identity', producing a 'kind of desperate religious sentiment' (2002a: 129). This is the 'religious' criticism that refers to nationalism. Further, Said notes that this sentiment is a component of Islamic radicalism as it is opposed to what he defines as secularism, evoking Ibn Khaldun as support: 'therefore it must be possible to interpret that history in secular terms, under which religions are seen, you might say, as a token of submerged feelings of identity, of tribal solidarity, *'asabiyyah*, in Ibn Khaldun's phrase. But religion has its limits in the secular world. Possibilities are extremely curtailed by the presence of other communities' (2002a: 129–30). Said goes on to argue that while 'To fight around the slogans provided by nationalist, religious, or cultural identity is a much quicker thing', it does not exemplify 'a certain interpretive sophistication' which is contained in secular interpretation (2002a: 130). Interestingly, he notes that secularism's advantage is that it argues for 'the potential of a community that is political, cultural, intellectual, and is not geographically and homogeneously defined' (2002a: 130), while supposing that all 'religious criticism' is confined to geography (such as nationalism) and is homogeneous. The community of resistance Said envisions 'takes place in many different places', and, he says, 'I suppose those places taken all together could be considered international' (2002a: 132). In this regard, Said's 'blind spot' (Mitchell 2005: 104) prevents him from considering the *umma* a transnational and heterogeneous community of Muslims that shares a common faith, and as such a potential community of resistance. Said remains silent on the possibility of the *umma* as a global community with universal principles and vision, perhaps not antithetical to his concept of a secular community. It is unclear if Islam can play any role at all in Said's reinvigorated humanism, which is best laid out in his last book, *Humanism and Democratic Criticism* (2004), and its intellectual predecessor *The World, the Text, and the Critic* (1983), published over twenty years earlier.

Said's language is more nuanced in *Humanism and Democratic Criticism*; clearly, the post-9/11 world changed his terminology but not his central position, that of defending Islam from a secular point of view, but not engaging deeply with the contribution it could make to scholarship. Indeed, there are occasions when Said makes a considered effort to inject Islamic discourse into his theory, but these instances remain superficial examples to prove a point about the necessity of a decentred humanism. For example, in *The World, the Text, and the Critic*, to explain his concept of worldliness Said uses the example of the linguistic interpretative theory of a group of Andalusian linguists called the Zahirites (Said 1983: 36–9). In fact, he drastically simplifies the work of a group of obscure medieval Arabic linguists to make the point that the meaning of the text is not in the text itself, but is the product of a time, an author and a reader:

> I have very quickly summarized an enormously complex theory, for which I cannot claim any particular influence in Western European literature since the Renaissance, and perhaps not even in Arabic literature since the Middle Ages. But what ought to strike us forcibly about the whole theory is that it represents a considerably articulated thesis for dealing with a text as a significant form, in which – and I put this as carefully as I can – worldliness, circumstantiality, the text's status as an event having sensuous particularity as well as historical contingency, are considered as being incorporated in the text, an infrangible part of its capacity for conveying and producing meaning. (1983: 39)

Revealingly, Said's recourse to Ibn Hazm, an Adalusian jurist, theologian and philosopher, and the Zahirites, is followed later in the same book by a critique of the 'dramatic increase in the number of appeals to the extra-human, the vague abstraction, the divine, the esoteric and secret' (1983: 291). Certainly, scholarship such as Ibn Hazm's appealed to the divine, and yet Said, a couple of hundred years before, praises it as a 'considerably articulated thesis' (1983: 39). Still, he laments the fact that 'religion has returned in other ways, most explicitly in the works of formerly militant secularists … for whom it now seems that the historical social world of real men and women is in need of religious assuagement' (1983: 291). Thus, while at the beginning of *The World, the Text, and the Critic*, Said credits Islamic scholarship with a contribution to interpretation, by the end he is exasperated at the impossibility of religious criticism and its lack of contribution to critique.

A similar contradiction emerges in *Humanism and Democratic Criticism*, though here Said distances himself from his earlier terminology of secular and religious criticism. Instead, he begins by clarifying his humanism by commenting upon what Clifford (1988) has interpreted as a methodological weakness or inconsistency in *Orientalism*, that of combining Foucauldian and humanist analysis. In *Humanism and Democratic Criticism*, Said defends his position as a purposeful extension of humanism:

> Although I was one of the first critics to engage with and discuss French theory in the American university, Clifford correctly saw that I somehow remained unaffected by that theory's ideological antihumanism, mainly, I think, because I did not (and still do not) see in humanism only the kind of totalizing and essentializing trends that Clifford identified. (Said 2004a: 10)

Said clarifies that his work was always intended as a critique, but not the abandonment, of humanism and defines cogently what humanism means for him: 'the core of humanism is the secular notion that the historical world is made by men and women, and not by God, and that it can be understood rationally' (2004: 11). By making this connection, Said reinserts secularism into his definition of humanism; in fact, they are inseparable. Throughout *Humanism and Democratic Criticism* Said reasserts that 'Humanism is the achievement of form by human will and agency', and that the humanities concern 'secular history' (2004a: 15). However, rather than set secular and religious criticism as binaries, Said examines the tendency within humanism to align itself to ideologies such as Orientalism and nationalism. Rather than refer to these trends as religious, as he had in his earlier work, he places these oppositions within a transformed humanist tradition: 'a varied and complex world with many contradictory, even antinomiam and antithetical currents running within it' (2004a: 45), which, instead of collapsing under the strain of postmodernism, is being transformed by critiques which are 'non-European, genderized, decolonized, and decentered' (2004a: 47). This view posits hope for a democratic criticism as a replacement for secular criticism, since Eurocentric or nationalistic humanism, of the kind Said previously had equated with religious criticism, could not be sustained in the postcolonial world where new spaces for democratic dissent had opened up.

The question remains, however, whether this democratic criticism can contain religious criticism, of all sorts, considering that the binary between orthodoxy and heresy is so unstable, as we have noted. Unfortunately, Said did not explore this issue in depth in *Humanism and Democratic Criticism*. For example, when writing there about philology, Said turns to the Islamic tradition and introduces his readers to the Islamic interpretive system of interdependent readings, *isnad*, personal effort and creativity (Said 2004a: 68). Indeed, he asserts that the Islamic tradition has much to offer interpretation, but registers that it is 'little known amongst Eurocentric scholars all too busy extolling some supposedly exclusive humanistic Western ideal' (2004a: 68). He had made this same argument over twenty years before, in reference to the Zaharite interpretive community in *The World, the Text, and the Critic*. Like its progenitor, *Humanism and Democratic Criticism* praises Islamic scholarship and then quickly condemns 'religious enthusiasm' as a dogma entirely separate from this scholarship:

> Religious enthusiasm is perhaps the most dangerous of threats
> to the humanistic enterprise, since it is patently anti-secular and
> antidemocratic in nature, and in its monotheistic forms as a kind of
> politics, is about as intolerably inhumane and downright unarguable as
> can be. Invidious commentary about the world of Islam after 9/11 has
> made it popular wisdom that Islam is by nature a violent, intolerant
> religion, much given to raving fundamentalism and suicidal terrorism.
> There have been no end of experts and evangelists repeating the same
> rubbish, aided and abetted by discredited Orientalists like Bernard
> Lewis. It is a sign of the intellectual and humanistic poverty of the
> times that such patent propaganda (in the literal sense of the word) has
> gained such currency and, even more disastrously, that it is carried
> on without the slightest reference to Christian, Jewish and Hindu
> fundamentalism, which, as extremist political ideologies, have been at

least as bloody and disastrous as Islam. All these enthusiasms belong essentially to the same world, feed off one another, emulate and war against one another schizophrenically, and – most seriously – are as ahistorical and as intolerant as one another. (Said 2004a: 51)

This passage serves to clarify Said's late position on religion and particularly Islam, which often seems contradictory. There remains a dichotomy in Said's work, perhaps an elitist one, between the productive contribution of Islamic scholarship to democratic criticism and the destructive effect of 'enthusiasm' or radical political thought and action, which is inspired by Islamic doctrine.[10]

Post-Said, there have been noted contributions by Muslim postcolonial critics to envision what a universal Islam might offer criticism. Anouar Majid, for example, argues that the notion of hybridity presented by Said, Spivak and Bhahba as the best alternative to polarizations does little for the cause of seriously questioning the relations of global capital. He positions Said, 'the prototypical "specular border intellectual"', as an embodiment of the predicament of Palestinians themselves, 'who have been condemned to be at home their homelessness' (Majid 2000: 27). He is particularly critical of the status Said 'confers on the migrant or the exile as the best-situated intellectual and contrapuntal reader of culture in the age of global capitalism' and accuses him of 'utopian cosmopolitanism unachievable in the present capitalist system' (2000: 28). Majid asserts that although Said questions Orientalism he does not outline an alternative that takes into account the secular premises upon which Orientalism is based. Majid argues that the secularist bias of the hybridity project, indeed of postcoloniality itself, has excluded religious traditions, including Islam, from the debate, and disallowed grand causes and utopian projects. This postcolonial substitution of theoretical playfulness for anti-imperial causes has resulted in an inability to mount a significant resistance, particularly among Western intellectuals. Arguing, for example, that Islamic discourse on human rights focuses on the right to freedom from economic exploitation, Majid extends the cultural debate to economic territory, and places the issue of resistance in the context of a Third World narrative of the reclaiming of economic and political rights from foreign occupiers (2000: 39–42). Thus, for Majid, the challenge to postcoloniality, as represented by the jihadist (though he does not refer to the jihadist specifically), is not only a response to military occupation by a foreign power, but a Third World expression of dissidence in relation to economic exploitation. Majid posits as a solution a 'polycentric' world that can accept various cultures, including Islamic ones. However, an integral part of this process involves a strengthening of Islamic cultures as alternatives to homogeneous world capitalist culture:

> if delinking the Islamic social imaginary from the capitalist driven process of Westernization could help maintain, expand or even reclaim noncapitalist spaces of social relations, then Islam could be (re)imagined in more utopian terms and become a founding bloc in a multicultural world governed by a strong ethic of reciprocity. (Majid 2000: 63)

Therefore Majid's interest is in the urgent need for Muslims to develop an understandable and coherent vocabulary that would posit Islam as a leader in this 'polycentric' bloc of multicultural communities.

A favourite strategy of Majid to demonstrate this creative imagining of 'polycentricity' is the contrapuntality that Said argues for in *Humanism and Democratic Criticism*. Majid indicates how contrapuntality might lead to new alliances and communities of resistance in *A Call for Heresy* (2007), where he maintains that Islamic impetus for equality and progress complements the revolutionary ethics upon which America has been founded. In an attempt to produce a truly contrapuntal discourse, Majid traces the religious beginnings of American society, drawing correlations between its founding documents and the documents of the Islamists. He compares the rhetoric of the founding fathers of America to the voices of various Islamist thinkers to highlight the radical nature of their founding vision, privileging the thoughts of heretical thinkers such as Jefferson, Washington, Paine and Whitman, and the Mu'tazilites, the poet Abu al-Ala Maarri and scholars Muhammad al-Warraq and Ibn al-Rawandi. Such a contrapuntal reading allows Majid to universalize the Muslim message for freedom of critical thought and freedom from oppression, which he maintains has always been part of the Western tradition as well. In a truly creative refiguring of history, in *Freedom and Orthodoxy* (2004) Majid maps a post-Andalusian world where, after the collapse of Muslim Spain, the colonization of the world began, with a complex process of erasing Arabs and Muslims from the history of the West and constructing a new lineage for Europeans with direct links to Ancient Greeks, bypassing historical connections with Arabs. Noting that the construction of such an ancestry of white Eurocentricism was convenient for colonization, Majid also connects the erasure of Muslimness to a direct capitalist agenda of exploitation of the New World in which all Others were necessarily seen as the Muslim Other, as inferior in the process of capitalist exploitation. Majid's goal echoes Said's interest in *The World, the Text, and the Critic* and *Humanism and Democratic Criticism* in reviving the ideas of Muslim free thinkers, but his purpose is not a rejuvenated humanism per se, but a rejuvenated Islamic terminology, history and discourse that will lead towards strong Islamic cultures, able to coexist with others in a 'polycentric' world.

To elaborate upon this idea, Majid extrapolates a system of Islamic ethics that is opposed to global capitalism. Arguing that capitalism has polarized the world and created various peripheries, he hypothesizes how these peripheries can strengthen their indigenous economic, social and cultural systems to confront a homogenizing global capitalism. These peripheries, including such communities as Native Americans, South Americans, Asian farmers, Muslims, and so on, need to develop their own indigenous systems, many based on tradition and faith, to challenge global capital. Yet Majid believes that Islam still lacks the universalistic view necessary for the project of polycentricity. While he notes that the Islamists are right in their arguments about Western hegemony, he argues that they have been unable to articulate a world-view that meets global challenges. For Majid, this is the critical role of *ijtihad*, or creative reinterpretation of texts, which he argues must expand outside a purely textual and theological framework to encompass a cultural practice to revitalize Islam, to delink it from the capitalist system, and to launch a new dialogue based on reciprocity, not hegemony, similar to the way liberation theory in Latin America has developed. Majid argues that 'liberation theory and a progressively defined Islam could address the injustices of the modern capitalist system and provide alternatives to failed Eurocentric models for social, economic and political arrangements' (Majid 2000: 150). In this way, the Islamic revival Majid envisions is connected to Third World resistance, an alliance of peripheries, where Islam serves as critical leader. To realize such polycentricity, he argues, secular academics must include religious world-views, and Islamic thinkers must rethink their attachment to texts that veil the liberationary role of Islam (2000: 153). The goal of *ijtihad* for Majid is not to reclaim an authentic Islam, and to build Muslim neoliberal societies that are compatible with American values, but to offer Islamic alternatives for a serious Third World challenge to global capital.

Similarly, the migration to *ijtihad* in discussing issues of representation and Islamic resistances to capitalism is especially evident in the work of Ziauddin Sardar, who positions himself as a cultural theorist.[11] In *The A–Z of Postmodern Life* (Sardar 2002) and *Why Do People Hate America* (Sardar and Davies 2002), Sardar develops his cultural analysis of postmodern life and imperialism, while in his two collections of essays *How Do You Know?* (2006) and *Islam, Postmodernism and Other Futures* (2003) he examines epistemology, multiculturalism and future ethics. In the latter he calls for *ijtihad* and places the responsibility on Muslims, as does Majid, to transform their internal systems, arguing that ethical statements need to be translated into policy statements to produce Islamic alternatives that are complete models (Sardar 2003: 107). In this act of *ijtihad*, Sardar authoritatively rejects *jihad* and opts for reform over revolution, claiming that 'the zeal of the righteous and the fanaticism of the revolutionary end in tyranny' and asserting that 'A reformist is not a revolutionary; he or she is not foolish enough to believe that the world can be put right by a single act of political violence' (2003: 108). Change, for Sardar, has to be systematically implemented to achieve the goal of a multi-civilizational world, not unlike Majid's polycentric world. Sardar's solution is found in Christian–Muslim cooperation focused on 'a God-centred ethics' (Sardar 2003: 179). These thoughts are developed further in *How Do You Know?* (2006), in which Sardar argues that, rather than harmonizing Islamic thought with Western norms and values, Muslim intellectuals should scrutinize all modern scientific culture through the discriminatory eye. Thus, as Majid divides his world into First and Third, Sardar divides his into West and non-West, secular and non-secular, both advocating for serious challenges to the Western mode of scientific rationalism and the neoliberal market economy. For both, Islam provides a direction, a way out of the crisis of modernism and postmodernism.

Like Majid, Sardar also critiques Said, though perhaps more vehemently, writing an entire book also titled *Orientalism* (1999), where he has sections on Islamic Orientalism, Orientalism in popular culture and art, and analysis of works by Tibawi and Abdel Malek which Said had virtually ignored. Sardar argues that 'An alternative to Orientalism is not possible for Said, I would argue, because for him there is no option beyond secular humanism and its high culture' (Sardar 1999: 74). Interestingly, Majid voices a similar complaint:

> Thus Edward Said's diagnosis of a self-perpetuating Orientalist tradition of distortion and prejudice is being applied to the Western culture at large, since Muslims' inability to represent themselves – partly

because of their passive participation in their own Orientalizing – is
not only related to repressive regimes and inadequate facilities in the
Islamic world, it is also actually hindered by the pervasive proliferation
of a few theories ... that have now become the standards against which
all postcolonial theories are tested. (Majid 2000: 25–6)

Contrary to Said's faith in a reinvigorated humanism, for Sardar
and Majid it is Islam and other faith-based systems – not a secular
humanism incapable of recognizing the contributions of other
traditions and religions to its own construction – that point the
way forward.

Although Sardar and Majid insist on the importance of a universal contribution from Islam through a rejuvenation of Islamic
terminology and discourse that is capable of offering a sustained
challenge to secular humanism, neither spends much time reflecting on *jihad* as a viable intervention, both preferring instead *ijtihad*
or *zanadaqa* ('heresy' in Majid's *A Call for Heresy*), which privileges
discussion over overt physical resistance or violence. While both
Majid and Sardar recognize the contribution of *ijtihad* to the
deconstruction of multiculturalism and liberalism, they situate
this contribution not only in a socialist project, but in a Third
World approach to development, with Majid actively arguing
for a 'polycentric' approach, and Sardar for a 'mutually assured
diversity', where Islam is part of a Third World project of reform.
They both distance themselves from *jihad*, either avoiding an in-
depth discussion of its means or focusing instead on its intellectual
companion *ijtihad*, which results in a twofold process of, on the
one hand, deconstructing liberalism, secularism and capitalism,
and, on the other, reconstructing strong Islamic alternatives.
Since *jihad* and *ijtihad* are so closely related, we might ask why
it is that contemporary Western Muslim thinkers concentrate on
ijtihad, or even the greater *jihad*, and devote so little attention to
the lesser *jihad*?[12]

The answer possibly lies in the dangerous climate for dissent
in the post-9/11 academy. In order to have their works published

and to maintain or be granted tenure, one of the first steps a
Muslim writer has to take is to disassociate him- or herself from
the lesser *jihad*. This closing down of criticism is discussed at
length by Henry Giroux in *The Terror of Neo-liberalism* (2004). He
relates it to 'proto-fascist' tendencies in the USA. 'Fascism', Giroux
elucidates, should not be considered to be 'an ideological apparatus
frozen in a particular historical period' but seen as 'a theoretical
and political signpost for understanding how democracy can be
subverted' (Giroux 2004: 18). Democracy, and therefore the space
for terminologies that compete with the dominant discourse,
withers not only when dissent is suppressed and police-state tactics
are employed, but also when people lack the means, ideological
and material (including resources of time and space), to exercise
their rights collectively in meaningful and effective ways to make
vital popular forms of democracy possible (2004: 20). It can be
argued that Muslim writers in the West are particularly sensitive to these conditions as they constantly have to prove their
adherence to perceived American or European values to maintain
intellectual credibility and even their sources of livelihood. Giroux
also argues that the construction and proliferation of a culture
of fear, exacerbated by the war on terrorism where 'all citizens
and noncitizens are viewed as potential terrorists', create an anti-
intellectual atmosphere grounded in simplified moral absolutes
around 'good and evil' and accompanied by notions of 'patriotic
correctness' (2004: 22, 24). Giroux contends that public space,
including the spaces of public education, is being increasingly
militarized through the 'logic of fear, surveillance, and control'
(2004: 41). One can extend Giroux's argument to the examples
of Campus Watch and the lists of America's most dangerous
intellectuals.[13] In such a battle for good, evil and tenure, it can be
argued, it is wiser to stick to the theorization of *ijtihad* – which
is in itself not without risk – than theorize about the universal
applicability of *jihad*. It may even be necessary to identify *jihad* as
the misunderstood rhetoric of 'bad' Muslims in order to sustain

one's position as a 'good' Muslim. Therefore the migration of Muslim reformers such as Majid and Sardar from the terminology of *jihad* to *ijtihad* needs to be understood within the context of the institutionalization of neoliberalism and the culture of fear that accompany the war on terror in Europe and America. As Giroux has argued, 'neoliberalism is more than an economic theory'; it is also a 'corporate public pedagogy ... an all-encompassing cultural horizon for producing market identities, values and practices' which operates by grossly constraining the available 'range of identities, ideologies and subject positions' (2004: 113).

Certainly Said himself was often the victim of the 'corporate public pedagogy' of which Giroux writes. Notwithstanding Majid's and Sardar's accusations of political paralysis, which I consider unfair, Said always insisted that theory could not be separated from practice, as was evidenced in his own involvement with the Palestinian cause about which he wrote and was actively involved. Indeed, the Palestinian issue was for Said foundational as a case study in formulating his theories of power and of the role of the intellectual and his insistence on a secular criticism. As Ilan Pappé notes,

> Once you read Said writing specifically on Palestine, you realize that his theoretical deconstruction of power bases of knowledge and exposure of the more sinister interests behind Western knowledge production on the Orient would have lacked impetus and zeal had they not been motivated by his struggle for the Palestinian cause. (Pappé 2008: 84)

There is also ample evidence that Said, as an independent Palestinian activist, reflected deeply on the role of violence in general in political transformation. For example, in *Power, Politics and Culture*, Said discusses the Palestinian intifada and notes that Fanon's process of conversion, 'the transformation of national consciousness into political and social consciousness, hasn't yet taken place. It's an unfinished project, and that's where I think my work has begun' (Said 2002a: 134). He argues that the intifada has been commodified for television and presented as mindless and discrete acts of violence which can be turned off, adding that the stone-throwing of the intifada is 'an alternative, an emergent formation, by which on the simplest level Palestinians under occupation have decided to declare their independence from the occupation by providing different, not so much models, but different forms for their lives which they themselves administer, develop and have in fact created' (2002a: 135). While Said watched with admiration the emergence of various Palestinian communities taking control of their own schools, hospitals and so on, outside of Israeli authority, he made no mention of Hamas in this. In the midst of the second intifada, Said made a devastating critique of Hamas, chiding Arafat for allowing them to wreak havoc with the cause:

> He [Arafat] never really reined in Hamas and Islamic Jihad, which suited Israel perfectly so that it would have a ready-made excuse to use the so-called martyrs' (mindless) suicide bombings to further diminish and punish the whole people. If there is one thing that has done us more harm as a cause than Arafat's ruinous regime, it is this calamitous policy of killing Israeli civilians, which further proves to the world that we are indeed terrorists and an immoral movement. For what gain, no one has been able to say. (Said 2004b: 185)

Thus, while Said admired the energy of the intifada, he did not approve of its methods, or of its close association to Islamist politics. In fact Said had never been unambiguous about his position on Hamas. Consider his first written reference to Hamas:

> In 1992 when I was there, I briefly met a few of the student leaders who represent Hamas: I was impressed by their sense of political commitment but not at all by their ideas.... I found them quite moderate when it came to accepting the truths of modern science ... their leaders neither especially visible nor impressive, their writings rehashes of old nationalist tracts, now couched in an 'Islamic' idiom. (Said 1994b: 403)

It is clear Said had little faith in Hamas's intellectuals; his comment 'I found them quite moderate when it came to accepting the truths of modern science' reveals his surprise that young Islamic activists are able to accept contemporary scientific realities. As Hamas gained in momentum throughout the 1990s, Said warned: 'I know that the organization is one of the only ones expressing resistance. ... Yet for any secular intellectual to make a devil's pact with a religious movement is, I think, to substitute convenience for principle' (Said 1995b: 111). In *Power, Politics and Culture* he refers to Hamas as practising 'violent and primitive forms of resistance. You know, what Hobsbawn calls pre-capital, trying to get back to communal forms, to regulate personal conduct with simpler and simpler reductive ideas' (Said 2002a: 416). Said goes on to connect the rise of Islamism, the resurgence of communal and religious identities, as the 'legacy of imperialism' (2002a: 417), and identifies them as narrow, negative and constricting. In another interview, also published *in Power, Politics and Culture*, Said responds to the question of whether or not it bothers him that his work is often cited by Islamists:

> Certainly, and I have frequently expressed my concern on this subject. I find my opinions misinterpreted, especially where they include substantial criticism of Islamic movements. First, I am secular; second, I do not trust religious movements; and third, I disagree with these movements' methods, means, analyses, values, and visions. (2002a: 437)

Said could not have been clearer: he critiqued Islamist movements, didn't trust them and disagreed with their methods. As early as *Covering Islam* Said's criticism was direct as he portrayed a dreary history of political Islam: in Algeria, 'thousands of intellectuals, journalists, artists and writers have been killed'; in Sudan, Hassan al-Turabi is referred to as 'a brilliantly malevolent individual, a Svengali and Savonarola clothed in Islamic robes'; in Egypt, the Muslim Brotherhood and the Jamaat Islamiya are described as as 'one more violent and more uncompromising than the other'; Palestine, 'Hamas and with it Islamic Jihad have metamorphosed into the most feared and journalistically covered examples of Islamic extremism' (Said 1997: xiii). All in all, Said's list of Islamists was not that promising a group of activists in terms of effecting real social change. In fact, Said didn't recognize the notion of a religious intellectual, and so held no hope that resistance could arise from religion itself. He reconfirmed this in *Politics, Power and Culture*, where he comments on

> a very important struggle taking place between the forces, broadly speaking, of what one would want to call *secularism*, to which I attach myself, and the forces that could be broadly described as *religious*.... There is a debate going on, and I think we are now at a point in the Arab world where the religious alternative has shown to be a failure. You can be a Muslim, but what does it mean to have Muslim economics, Muslim chemistry? In other words, there's a universal norm when it comes to running a modern state. But the question is, what of those people who represent another side of Islam, which is Islamic resistance to the West. On the West Bank, in Gaza, people consider themselves Islamic militants fighting Israeli occupation, because that's the last area of their lives that the Israelis have not been able to penetrate, as was the case with Algeria during the French occupation. So there are different kinds of Islam, there are different kinds of secularism. (Said 2002a: 389)

This statement is interesting on two counts. First, Said directly asserts that there is an active struggle going on between secularism and religion, and he aligns himself unequivocally with secularism. At the same time, he notes that secularism can have various meanings, as does Islam. Second, he secularizes Islamic motifs: the Islamic militants of Gaza are fighting for the secular goal of nationalism, as were the Algerians, not a particularly other-worldly goal or a vision that is global and universal in nature. This directly differentiates the Islamists, such as Hamas, from the global jihadists, such as al-Qaeda. Said no doubt viewed both Islamist nationalists and Islamic universalists as equally impotent.

To be fair, however, Said's attitude towards Islamism and *jihad*, in particular, is not dramatically different from that of Sardar and Majid. For example, in writing about the hope for a unified Arab (not Muslim) revolution Said speaks of a 'necessary coalition' and 'serious discussions between secular and Islamic forces'; and calls for a 'critique [of] power in the Arab world' (Said 2002a: 364) He notes that 'We also need a language of appreciation based not on dogmatic orthodoxy or reverence to Quranic and authoritative ideas, but rather one that develops out of this critique of power' (2002a: 364), noting that 'Authority is not God-given. It's secular' (2002a: 367). And such a stance he applies to the Palestinian situation, which he believes could be resolved through political and diplomatic activity not violence (2002a: 347). Thus, Said's problem with political Islamists is not merely their religious stance, but their violent means. His discomfort with violence is shared by Sardar, who in his foreword to *Black Skin, White Masks*, calls Fanon's violence 'problematic'; indeed, he notes, in an interview with *Naked Punch*, that 'Violence is where I depart from Fanon. Fanon thought violence was necessary to resist imperialism. Gandhi proved him wrong' (Sardar 2010). This shared discomfort is also evident in Said's reworking of Fanon.

In his essay 'Traveling Theory', in *The World, the Text, and the Critic* (1983), Said considers what happens to a theory or idea when it 'travels' from place to place, from person to person, from situation to situation, from one period to another. In 'Traveling Theory Reconsidered', published in *Reflections on Exile* (2000), Said develops his argument by proposing that ideas and theories can be reinvigorated and made to speak to whole new political situations when they travel from one location to another. A major example to support this hypothesis is how Frantz Fanon revolutionized Lukács's concept of reification to apply it to Algeria. In a close reading of Fanon's *The Wretched of the Earth* (1963), Said shows how Fanon employs Lukács's subject–object dialectic to discuss the process of decolonialization and the inheritance of colonial traditions: 'Lukács's dialectic is grounded in *The Wretched of the Earth*, actualized, given a kind of harsh presence nowhere to be found in his agonized rethinking of the classical philosophical antinomies' (Said 2000: 446). According to Said, Fanon adapts

Lukács's theory to the relationship between the colonizer and the colonized, recognizing that violence is but one component in the decolonization process that does not necessarily resolve these antinomies. Said notes: 'No one needs to be reminded that Fanon's recommended antidote for the cruelties of colonialism is violence' (2000: 447); yet he also asks, 'But does Fanon, like Lukács, suggest that the subject–object dialectic can be consummated, transcended, synthesized, and that violence in and of itself is that fulfilment, the dialectical tension resolved by violent upheaval into peace and harmony (2000: 447)? Said's response to the question he poses is clearly no, and he reads Fanon as saying that liberation doesn't consist only of the violence of nationalism, for nationalism will necessarily be followed by more oppression and violence: 'Thereafter Fanon is at pains to show that the tensions between colonizer and colonized will not end, since in effect the new nation will produce a new set of policemen, bureaucrats, merchants to replace the departed Europeans' (2000: 450). Said argues that according to Fanon neither violence nor nationalism and its consciousness is a sufficient emancipatory goal, and that, rather, the essential point of *The Wretched of the Earth* is to note how anticolonial struggle must necessarily take on a broader, and more radical, global human emancipatory dimension in order to succeed. And this is a revolution of consciousness: 'an entirely new consciousness – that of liberation – is struggling to be born' (2000: 450). Said also notes that Fanon's ideas were ahead of the Algerian struggle within which they were generated: 'Fanon's radicalism, I think, is and has been since his death too strenuous for the new postcolonial states, Algeria included' (2000: 450). Mohammed Tamdgidi has commented with insight on Said's engagement with Fanon:

> Fanon in particular has come to be known for his more explicit advocacy of revolutionary *physical* violence in reaction to global racism and colonialism particularly in the Algerian and African contexts. Said, more ambivalent on the use of physical violence in the

context of the Palestinian nationalist struggles amidst the Arab/Israeli conflict, seems to have been inspired in part by a more intimate (not cruder and caricatured) reading of Fanon's discourse on revolutionary violence in historical context, while dedicating his life to waging more of an intellectual struggle against the underlying ideological, especially Orientalist, structures of knowledge fueling the West's global violence of colonialism and racism. (Tamdgidi 2007: 115)

It is no accident that Said viewed Fanon as an intellectual hero, even though he was not as enthusiastic about the role of violence in revolution. As a forefather of postcolonial theory, Fanon has a great deal in common with Said. Bhabha notes that the similarities between the two thinkers are striking:

> Committing himself to the 'undocumented turbulence' of the wretched of the earth of our times, Said echoes Frantz Fanon's descriptions of the 'occult instability' of the decolonizing conscious-ness in the mid-twentieth century wars of independence. Both Fanon and Said died of leukemia, almost half a century apart, in hospital beds on the East Coast of the United States, only a few hundred miles from each other. Both of them produced last books beckoning the world towards an aspirational 'new' humanism. Fanon, however, wrote (or so he thought) with his foot on the threshold of a Third World of nations, on the verge of 'start[ing] over a new history of man.' Said could be persuaded of no such humanist haven. The 'unsettled energy' of the times, or what he describes elsewhere as 'the implacable energy of place and displacement,' provides him with a double vision of history in which tragedy and transition, incarcera-tion and emancipation seem to be part of the same unraveling thread of events. (Bhabha 2005: 14)

Interestingly, Fanon, like Said, one of the founders of post-colonial theory, had a similar relationship to Islam and Islamic thinkers. The indigenous culture in Algeria was seminal to Fanon's work on revolutionary violence, as Palestine was to Said. As Fouzi Slisli (2008) notes, 'There is an elephant in *The Wretched of the Earth*. It is Islam and its anticolonial tradition in Algeria.' Slisli argues that while Fanon continuously cites and exalts this tradition, he defines it as an indigenous culture, not a Muslim one; in other words, Fanon explains Algerian acts of resistance and applauds the culture of Algerian peasants, but he does not name this resistance for what it is – the tradition of Islamic resistance to colonialism. Slisli examines the work of the Sufi brotherhoods and the Association of Muslim Scholars, as well as Algerian responses to Fanon, and argues that because Fanon is writing for a primarily atheistic and Western audience, he reshapes any references to Islam to refer to tradition and culture, rather than to Islam itself, and uses Marxist terminology of spontaneity and organization as a substitute for a distinctly Islamic anticolonial tradition that, by the time Fanon was writing, had been in existence for over a century. Though Fanon was a secular revolutionary, Slisli notes, he edited the FLN's paper *El Moudjahid*, thereby basically championing a revolution that was articulated as *jihad*. In a letter to Ali Shariati, the intellectual whose thought inspired the Iranian Revolution and translator of Che Guevara and Fanon, Fanon expresses concerns that religion could become an obstacle to Third World unification but also encourages Shariati to exploit the resources of Islam for the creation of a new egalitarian society: 'breathe this spirit into the body of the Muslim Orient' (quoted in Slisli 2008).

Fanon himself comments directly on his struggle with Islam and *jihad* in one of his lesser known books, *A Dying Colonialism*, first published as *L'an cinq de la révolution algérienne* in 1959. It is in this book that Fanon writes directly of his 'Moslem comrades' (1965: 165) and recounts an interesting meeting he had with Muslims and Jews in Algeria which provoked the development of his ideas on violence as an 'excess made possible by the excess of colonialism' (1965: 165). Fanon writes about his inner struggle to accept violence as a necessary part of the Algerian struggle and how, in the end, he was convinced by a Jewish speaker at the meeting who seduced him with a 'profession of faith' that was 'patriotic, lyrical and passionate' (1965: 165). Interestingly, Fanon also reflects on his own biases and the fact that he was more easily convinced by a Jew than a Muslim, noting 'I still had too much unconscious anti-Arab feeling in me to be convinced by a Moslem Arab' (1965: 165). Throughout *A Dying Colonialism*, Fanon elaborates on how his theory of the necessity of violence deepened through his discussions with Muslims, and refers to their 'conscientiousness and moderation', noting that 'Little by little, I was coming to understand the meaning of the armed struggle and its necessity' (1965: 167). The most convincing evidence for Fanon came from the *fellaheen* (peasants), whom the media had branded 'extremists and highway bandits' (1965: 167). Reflecting on his confusion in becoming a member of the FLN, Fanon wrote,

> My leftist leanings drove me toward the same goal as the Muslim nationalists. Yet I was too conscious of the different roads by which we had reached the same aspiration. Independence, yes. I agreed wholeheartedly. But *what* independence? Were we going to fight to build a feudal, theocratic, Moslem state that [was] frowned on by foreigners? Who could claim that we had a place in such an Algeria? (1965: 168)

The answer to this question came from a comrade in the FLN, who retorted that 'it was up to the Algerian people' to decide (169). Interestingly, that same answer is being heard throughout the Arab world today as Western nations struggle to catch up with revolutions for which they were not prepared.

In the end, Fanon's analysis of colonialism begins and ends with the question of violence, which he developed through his engagement with the Islamist FLN. Through violence, as Said notes, Fanon was looking for a way to break completely from the past and seek a new humanity, not only to overthrow the colonizers but to establish a new consciousness based on equality and justice. For Fanon violence played a critical role in the reconstruction of self and nation, but it accompanied an epistemological revolution that pitted the colonizer directly against the colonized. In *The Wretched of the Earth*, Fanon argues that an entirely new world must come into being. This utopian desire, to be absolutely free of the past, requires total revolution, 'absolute violence' (1963: 37), and this true revolution could only come from the peasants, or *fellaheen*, who must also overthrow the bourgeoisie in their own society who cooperate with the colonizers. In *A Dying Colonialism* the fight which he documents is instrumental – violence for a specific end, decolonization. But for Fanon, violence is both 'instrumental' and 'absolute'. Samira Kawash notes that 'These are not two different kinds of violence. … Rather, instrumental violence and absolute violence are two ways in which violence emerges into and operates on a reality' (Kawash 1999: 239). She argues that instrumental violence in Fanon's text is

> the violence of revolt and of reversal, the violence whereby the colonized challenge and attempt to upend the domination that has oppressed them. At the same time, another violence (perhaps alongside or unleashed by instrumental acts of violence) emerges as the world-shattering violence of decolonization. Decolonization destroys both colonizer and colonized; in its wake, something altogether different and unknown, a 'new humanity,' will rise up. (Kawash 1999: 239)

The absolute violence of decolonization can only be 'symbolic violence,' 'violence that threatens the symbolic order, violence that bursts through history' (Kawash 1999: 243).

This concept of violence as serving a creative role to revive indigenous thought and throw off the chains of colonialism and occupation resonates well with contemporary *jihad* theory, particularly the notion that that *jihad* has both inner and outer dimensions, for individuals and societies. The inner dimensions, on a societal level, involve a restructuring of knowledge and a creative challenging and reclaiming of tradition; this is the greater *jihad, al-jihad al-akbar*, the fight against the desires of oneself and the desires of greed inside one's own society. The outer dimension involves translating this ethics into action in the form of engagement with global issues, and, if necessary, defending oneself, through violence, from occupation and colonization; this is the lesser *jihad, al-jihad al-asghar*. It is easy to see the transformation of these ideas in Fanon's thought. Instrumental and absolute violence refer to the reciprocal relationship between the greater *jihad* and the lesser *jihad* in the process of decolonization and reconstruction. And for Fanon, as for the jihadists, both processes are important. For example, bin Laden employed both instrumental and absolute violence: attacks on the bourgeoisie of predominantly Muslim countries in Saudi Arabia and Iraq, for example, as well as spectacular attacks on the neo-colonizers in America and Europe. The symbolic role of bin Laden's absolute violence was due to the enormity of the rupture in epistemologies that he was trying to achieve, asking citizens to transform themselves from being subjects of capitalist nation-states to being subjects of God only. While Fanon placed hope in the *fellaheen* as leaders of his revolution, bin Laden willed the masses of Muslim countries, *Homo islamicus*, Muslims in Western countries, and even oppressed non-Muslims to become the imagined *umma*. Bin Laden's vision was of a completely new society that had broken from secular Western liberalism and capitalism, similar to the complete break referred to directly in Fanon's text.

The new man that Fanon envisioned, free from the shackles of colonial oppression and without limitations on his desire for equality and justice, is similar to the reconstructed *Homo islamicus*, the true Muslim, in the utopian Muslim state envisioned by Ali Shariati, with whom Fanon engaged in dialogue. For example, Fanon argued: 'Let us decide not to imitate Europe. Let us combine our muscles and our brains in a new direction. Let us try to create the whole man, whom Europe has been incapable of bringing to triumphant birth' (Fanon 1963: 313). But Ali Shariati, who also collaborated with the Algerian FLN and translated an anthology of Fanon's work into Persian, asked how this 'whole man' would come about, why Europe had not been able to create him and what is the real impetus of change. This dialogue that Shariati conducted with Fanon's ideas on the formation of the new man, the nature of revolution, the role of intellectuals, and the duality of decolonization, away from both colonizers and the bourgeoisie of national societies, is present in all of Shariati's writings. For Shariati the answers are contained in Islam:

> There is only one religion and its name is Sub-mission 'Islam'. Through this announcement, the Prophet universalizes it and gives the idea of Submission a universal, historical viewpoint. He relates the Islamic movement to other movements which have, throughout history[,] been fought to free people. They have stood up, risen against the powerful, the wealthy and the deceivers. In this way, they have shown their unity of vision: one spiritual struggle, one religion, one spirit and one slogan throughout the whole of humanity's history in all domains, all times and all generations. (Shariati n.d. c)

For Shariati a just society would not be a new postcolonial configuration of an abstract rediscovered freedom, Said's reinvigorated humanism, Sardar's 'mutually assured diversity', or Majid's 'polycentricity'; justice could only be found in a universal Islamic community that balanced the ascetic and worldly needs in man, whom he saw as 'a two-dimensional being [who] needs a religion which can protect him from swinging to either asceticism or worldliness, and continually keep him at an equilibrium' (Shariati n.d. b). Further, though Shariati, like Fanon, studied Sartre and Marx, for him the impetus for change would not be accidental, spontaneous, or even based on a class struggle, but would be founded in the example of the Prophets, who arose from the masses but based their visions of a new society on Divine guidance, and this vision was carried forward by 'enlightened souls' who are 'a mixture of faith, idealism and spirituality and yet full of life and energy with a dominant spirit of equality and justice' (n.d. d).

Continuing the argument that the aim of revolution is to attain God's justice, he presents the examples of Prophet Muhammad and Ali to show how *jihad* in its dual struggle (intellectual and physical) against decolonization confronts both an 'external foe' and the 'internal foe':

> The Prophet is the manifestation of the struggle of an age in which, on the one hand, true, believing Moslems confronted foreign enemies who were known to be anti-Moslem, while Ali is the manifestation

of an age in which an internecine struggle took place between the
loyal, faithful and anti-movement elements who had donned the
masks of faith. (Shariati n.d. c)

Shariati's positing of the 'external foe' as the colonizer outside the
community, and the 'internal foe' as representative of the power
structures inside the society against which the revolutionary
must strive, echoes Fanon's configuration of the dual struggle
against colonialism and the postcolonial bourgeois. Success for
Shariati, however, can only be attained if the goals of the new
society are mandated by the vision of an Islamic community. He
directly refers to Fanon's stance as 'pessimistic about the positive
contribution of religion to social movement' and argued that
he has convinced Fanon of the positive role religion can play
to 'help the enlightened person to lead his society toward the
same destination which Fanon was taking on his own through
non-religious means' (n.d. d).

Perhaps, then, it can be argued that the engagement between
Muslim intellectuals and anti-imperialist revolutionaries, and the
concept of *jihad*, are the very essence of Fanon's theory of liberation, and as such the cornerstone of postcolonial theory itself.
Although Fanon's works were written from within and about Arab
and Muslim experiences, they do not put Islam at the centre of the
postcolonial experience. Perhaps it can even be argued that this
very absence of Islam was a necessary condition to the canoniza-
tion of Fanon, and Said, after him, as the progenitors of postcolonial theory. Is Islam, then, an invisible 'trace' in postcolonial
theory? Since the major forebears of postcolonialism, Fanon and
Said, theorized using examples from Muslim cultures, it can be
argued that Islam has been key to the formation of postcolonialism. By extension, perhaps Edward Said's 'democratic criticism' is
not Western at all, but has been formed through the encounter of
the West with the Islamic tradition, which to this day the West
is unable to recognize. Today, postcolonial intellectuals look with
hope to the Arab region because its revolutions are articulated in

a language with which they can identify. Will these revolutions remain in favour once Islamist and even jihadist elements enter the formations of these new societies? The response of postcolonial thinkers to the formation of governments across the region that contain Islamist and jihadist components will show us whether or not postcolonialism has already forgotten that its father, Frantz Fanon, was buried in Algeria under the name Ibrahim Fanon in a graveyard for *shuhada*. If true 'democratic criticism' is ever to take root, postcolonial critics also need to engage in a process of self-reflection concerning the limits of the discipline they have created. In this regard, there must be serious questioning of the avoidance of 'religious' criticism and its exclusion from the humanist tradition – the subject of the next chapter.

CHAPTER 6

Humanism and Islam:
jihad and postsecularism

In the previous chapter, I queried whether the type of humanism advocated by Said in *Humanism and Democratic Criticism* (2004) can accommodate religious traditions and criticism, considering Said's antagonism to 'religious enthusiasm', even if, on occasion, his recourse to 'heterodoxical' representatives of the Muslim tradition allowed him to employ various Islamic discourses in his decentring of traditional humanism. Said's reconfiguration of humanism works with a classical notion of the humanities, which would no doubt include the philosophical movements of China and India, classical Greece and Rome, which survived in the Muslim world into the European Middle Ages and were introduced to Europe in the Renaissance; this would take in Muslim philosophers such as the Zaharites and Ibn Hazm, to whom he refers in his work, as well as the scientific and humanist thought of the eighteenth century. Said's main argument echoes Fanon's similar critique that humanism had deviated from its liberationary objectives to become the rhetoric of colonization. Said and Fanon both argue for a new humanism that would be inclusive enough to embrace non-Europeans – for, in effect, the universalization of humanism. Both, however, also linked their humanism to notions of the secular. It can be argued that the spectacular attacks by the jihadists, as well as the 'Muslim problem' in Europe, have made arguments about the return of religion more pertinent and strengthened the growing discipline of postsecular theory in response to secular humanist discourse.

In *Formations of the Secular* Talal Asad argues that '"the secular" is conceptually prior to the political doctrine of "secularism"' (2003: 16), positing 'the secular' as a basic universal and inclusive stance that investigates how knowledge is made:

> The secular, I argue, is neither continuous with the religious that supposedly preceded it (that is, it is not the latest phase of a sacred origin) nor a simple break from it (that is, it is not the opposite, an essence that excludes the sacred). I take the secular to be a concept that brings together certain behaviors, knowledges, and sensibilities in modern life. To appreciate this it is not enough to show what appears to be necessary is really contingent – that in certain respects 'the secular' obviously overlaps with 'the religious.' It is a matter of showing how contingencies relate to changes in the grammar of concepts – that is, how the changes in concepts articulate changes in practices. (Asad 2003: 25)

On the other hand, *secularism* is a 'political doctrine' (2003: 1) that 'redefines and transcends particular and differentiating practices of the self that are articulated through class, gender, and religion' (2003: 5), and as such carries with it the doctrine of the universality of human rights and freedoms. But what happens when humanism, particularly secular humanism of the Saidian variety, confronts another universal vision, such as Islam? Can humanism accept an Islamic system of universal values outside the paradigm of secularism? In other words, does humanism have to be secular?

Asad's argument that Islamism cannot be treated as nationalism contains a useful insight. Outlining the common goals of anti-imperialism shared by Islamism and Arab nationalism, Asad turns to the concept of the *umma* for clarification: 'The Islamic *umma* in the classical theological view is thus not an imagined community on a par with the Arab nation waiting to be politically unified but a theologically defined space enabling Muslims to practice the disciplines of *din* [religion] in the world' (Asad 2003: 197). He notes that the use of the term *umma 'arabiyya* (Arab *umma*) by nationalists today is a conceptual transformation by which the *umma* 'is cut off from the theological predicates that gave it its universalizing power, and is made to stand for an imagined community that is equivalent to a total political society, limited and sovereign like other limited and sovereign nations in a secular (social) world' (2003: 197). In contrast, he notes that the *'ummatu-l-muslimīn'* (the Islamic *umma*) is 'not a "society" onto which state, economy and religion can be mapped' but 'eventually should embrace all of humanity' (2003: 197–8). Asad argues that although Islamists seek to work through the nation-state due to the socio-political configurations of the modern world, its theological grounding in the *umma* is not the same as the secular premises that underlie nationalism. Therefore the Islamic *umma* is conceptual and exists outside political order, much like 'the secular', while the Arab *umma* is a political configuration that operates in a manner similar to 'secularization' in mapping a political community.

Asad continues this line of inquiry into the differentiation between a political society based on the nation-state and the theological society of the *umma*, albeit indirectly, in *Is Critique Secular: Blasphemy, Injury and Free Speech*, a dialogue between Asad, Wendy Brown and Judith Butler and Sabah Mahmood, in response to the Danish cartoon crisis of 2005. Asad argues that in Western societies different vocabularies are used to place limits on individuals' self-ownership, and asks:

> What would happen if religious language were to be taken more seriously in secular Europe and the preventable deaths in the global South of millions from hunger and war was to be denounced as 'blasphemy', as the flouting of ethical limits for the sake of what is claimed to be freedom? What if this were done without any

declarations of 'belief', and yet done in all seriousness as a way of rejecting passionately the aspiration to totalized global control? Of course Europe's proscription of theological language in the political domain makes such a use of the word 'blasphemy' inconceivable. But does this impossibility merely signal a secular reluctance to politicize 'religion', or is it the symptom of an incapacity? (Asad et al. 2009: 56-7)

This is a telling and interesting question, for here Asad comments on how secularism administers and controls discourse through 'the proscription on theological language', while he has noted in previous work (Asad 2003) that Islamic nationalism borrows freely from universalist Islam in its use of theological concepts to describe itself. Is it the case, then, that a West with a limited secular vocabulary cannot comprehend a formation that refuses to have its language proscribed by 'those who use Islamic metaphors to narrate their political projects' (Sayyid 2004: 157)? The Islamists, of which the jihadists represent a militant minority, '[b]y articulating their position by using an ethical vocabulary, empowered by the signifier of Islam, ... have been able to disarm the discourse of their opponents' (Sayyid 2004: 157). This type of disconcertion is noticed by Judith Butler in her response to Asad:

> instead understand how blasphemy and injury function within Muslim religious law and its history, then we are immediately up against a problem of translation: not only the problem of whether the injury of the Danish cartoons is rightly translated by *tajdīf* or *isā'ah* but also of whether the moral framework and discourse within which the outrage took place was not in some key ways at odds with the moral framework and discourse that for the most part controls the semantic operation of 'blasphemy' as a term. The translation has to take place within divergent frames of moral evaluation. (Asad et al. 2009: 103)

Butler acknowledges a critical flaw in the use of one moral framework, as she calls it, or one set of ethical languages, to grasp another ethical tradition. And it is this flaw, this gap in meaning, I will argue, that is accentuated when postsecular criticism reaches outside the framework of secularity to embrace a democratic humanistic engagement with the frameworks of other traditions, most notably Islam. Butler continues: 'what would judgment look like that took place not "within" one framework or another but which emerged at the very site of conflict, clash, divergence, and overlapping?' (Asad et al. 2009: 104). She concludes: 'It would seem that we are being asked to understand this battle as one between, on the one hand, a presumptively secular framework tied to an ontology of the subject as self-owned, and, on the other hand, a nonsecular framework that offers an ontology of the subject as dispossessed in transcendence' (2009: 119). In responding to Butler, Asad explains his reasoning for juxtaposing differing traditions: 'When I look briefly at some conceptions in Islamic thought that overlap liberal ideas, I do so in order to see how the former can shed light on the latter' (2009: 137).

But do such contrapuntal discussions 'shed light' (Asad) or do they continue to 'disarm' (Sayyid)? For example, a similar kind of disjuncture occurs in an equally engaging discussion between Mustapha Chérif, a professor of philosophy and Islamic studies at the University of Algiers, and Jacques Derrida, who initiated a debate on the issue of faith and its role in launching the politics of the future, though it soon becomes obvious that the vocabulary of faith they employ does not intersect at any point. Chérif notes that 'Islam wants engagement with regard to the "Mystery", loyalty to the "revealed Message", and a specific attachment to the religious vision that the last life is the final aim', and asks Derrida 'What can philosophy say today on the subject of the Mystery?' (Chérif 2008: 56). In his reply, Derrida is careful to separate faith and religion, because for him faith is connected to a 'social bond', while religion remains exclusionary. He argues that since the relation to the Other presupposes faith, there is no conflict between the secularization of politics and Chérif's Mystery (2008: 57–8). Derrida displaces the debate about faith, by transporting it from the language of the religious to the language of the social, clearly stating that the language of the religious has no place in the administration of public knowledge:

> I believe that what we must consider as our first task is to *ally* ourselves to that in the Arab and Muslim world which is trying to advance the idea of secularization of the political, the idea of a separation between the theocratic and the political – this both out of respect for the political and for democratization and out of respect for faith and religion. (Chérif 2008: 53–4)

Derrida clearly argues for 'secularization', and in Asad's usage this stands in the way of a dialogue with the universality of Islam.

Vincent Pecora has noted that Said's use of contrapuntal reading is 'not a method particularly well suited to the fruitful synthesis of secular humanist traditions and still-powerful religious ones' (Pecora 2006: 39). However, there are many more examples of attempts to synthesize these traditions in contemporary theory. Here I will limit myself to one further, particularly relevant, example: the discursive usage of 'suicide bombing'. Žižek argues that the postmodern disdain for great ideological causes substitutes the reinventing of ourselves for changing the world, the result being a withdrawal and commodification of the private, the 'radical pursuit of secularization', which turns life, in the absence of any great causes, into an '"abstract" anaemic process' (2002: 88). Referring to Agamben and St Paul, Žižek argues for a messianic dimension to enable eternity to enter the debate; and, drawing upon Alain Baidou's 'ethical act', he longs for 'a gesture of radical and violent simplification' (2002: 101). This ethical and simple act has entered postsecular discourse in the narrative of 'suicide bombing'. Yet the jihadist's own frame of reference in often disregarded when postsecular theory claims his 'suicide' as the ultimate ethical act that holds the promise of a post-human society.

I noted in Chapter 4 that the jihadist humanizes himself for his audience, while committing violence upon himself and his audience. Yet it is not the violence itself, or even the recording of this violence for public consumption, that has placed the jihadist at the centre of theory. The media are replete with far greater examples of mass violence, to which we have become relatively desensitized. It is the willingness of the jihadist to annihilate himself, an act wrongly perceived as suicide, which fascinates the public. The jihadist vehemently rejects the term 'suicide', though analysts, even Muslim ones, favour its use. I want to argue that for the jihadist, his act is one of both secular and sacred intent and can only be fully comprehended within this frame – it is not a 'suicide' but transcendence, a testimony to his faith, his *shahada*.

These considerations are taken up by Talal Asad in *On Suicide Bombing*. Asad traces the genealogy of *jihad* and concludes that modern explanations for suicide bombings focus on the notion of sacrifice, which originates more in Christian tradition than in the Muslim one, where *jihad* is firmly connected to self-defence. He argues that connecting the concept of sacrifice to *jihad* designates it as religious terrorism, which

> defines the bomber as morally underdeveloped – and therefore premodern – when compared with peoples whose civilized status is partly indicated by their secular politics and their private religion, and whose violence is therefore, in principle disciplined, reasonable, and just. (Asad 2007: 45)

To formulate *jihad* as sacrifice, foreign to its Islamic roots, identifies it as a 'perverse form of national politics and permits unhelpful references to a unique "culture of death"' (2007: 50). Instead of tying suicide to a premodern Islamic tradition, Asad argues that suicide bombing is generated by neoliberalism itself. He notes that liberal societies were founded on the Christian notion of sacrifice, with individuals forgoing rights in order to achieve the protection of the state, which is given legitimacy to perpetrate violence on behalf of its citizens:

> I want to suggest that the cult of sacrifice, blood, and death that secular liberals find so repellent in pre-liberal Christianity is a part of the genealogy of modern liberalism itself, in which violence and tenderness go together. This is encountered in many places in our

modern culture, not least in what is generally taken to be 'just' war. (Asad 2007: 88)

He further elaborates that liberalism disapproves of the violent exercise of freedom outside the frame of the law, though it constantly shifts these boundaries, redefining law to address its needs. Suicide bombers, he continues, operate within this ideology of a continually shifting legitimation of violence, of a 'limitless pursuit of freedom' (2007: 91). In this way they confront liberalism with its own internal contradictions. For Asad, not only is 'suicide bombing' a deviation of Islamic theology that cannot be understood by postulating a culture of death and sacrifice inherent to Islam; it is deeply rooted in the metaphysical tradition of liberalism and the socio-political conditions brought about by neoliberal capitalist expansion. Asad accuses Western theorists of reading *jihad* through a neoliberal Christian lens, thereby defining it as a form of sacrifice, implicitly compared to the sacrifice of Jesus.

However, Asad does not elaborate this argument by comparing the Islamic and Christian versions of the death of Jesus, which would, in fact, further support his point and allow him to elaborate on the concept of sacrifice, not just suicide. In Islam, Jesus, Issa, was not actually sacrificed, and instead was made to appear to be sacrificed. He did not die. According to the Quran, the death of Jesus was a collective illusion, instigated by God himself, as he rescued Jesus from death and enthroned him in immortality. Therefore, for Muslims, Jesus was not sacrificed, or even killed, and his death had nothing to do with redeeming the world of its sins. Indeed, he was saved from death and granted immortality, and in this way the transgressions of his opponents remained futile. The Muslim rejection of the notion of sacrifice, as evident in the story of Issa, necessitates, I believe, a more thoroughgoing analysis of this concept, particularly as seen by jihadists themselves.

It is important to note that jihadists consistently refer to their struggle as a *jihad*, and their deaths in its cause as an articulation of their *shahada* or testimony of their belief. Immortality is perceived as a reward for their militant testimony, and those who die as witnesses to this testimony are *shahid*. The problem with Asad's analysis is that he displaces the militancy of the *shahid* from its Islamic tradition and posits it as a secular misreading by the Christian neoliberal tradition in order to highlight how the concept of suicide or sacrifice is not part of the Islamic tradition. However, while 'suicide' is not a concept of the jihadist, militancy is, though this militancy is considered as a testimony, not a sacrifice in the Christian sense. For example, in a September 2009 recording, bin Laden argues,

> Praise be to God, we are carrying our weapons on our shoulders and have been fighting the two poles of evil in the East and the West for 30 years. Throughout this period, we have not seen any cases of suicide among us despite the international pursuit against us. We praise God for this. This proves the soundness of our belief and the justice of our cause. God willing, we will continue our way to liberate our land. (bin Laden 2009b)

Here, bin Laden obstinately rejects the terminology of suicide bombing, instead focusing on the soundness of belief in his struggle for justice, which is protected by the laws and will of the divine. The jihadist dies for a divine cause, and so is not sacrificing himself as an individual for the good of worldly justice alone, but is transforming himself from an individual into immortality. In a 2005 article in the *Guardian*, Terry Eagleton claims that,

> Like hunger strikers, suicide bombers are not necessarily in love with death. They kill themselves because they can see no other way of attaining justice; and the fact that they have to do so is part of the injustice. It is possible to act in a way that makes your death inevitable without actually desiring it. (Eagleton 2005a)

However, jihadists have said time and again 'we love death'. The love of death, as opposed to life, was the key message, for example, in a statement released by al-Qaeda claiming responsibility for the 2004 Madrid bombing,[1] and was expressed by bin Laden himself to describe the *umma* as 'the Nation that desires death more than you desire life' (bin Laden 2005b: 172). This is not to say, of course, that Muslim culture is death-obsessed, as various neoconservatives maintain, but to emphasize that death becomes a form of power for the jihadist, who hopes, by example, to offer it as a testimony to his faith, his *shahada*.

Ali Shariati was seminal in developing a theory of Islamic testimony and sacrifice that is quite different from the Christian notion of martyrdom stemming from the belief that Jesus died to redeem the sins of others. Shariati explains that there is no Islamic notion of martyrdom in the Christian sense, even though, as I have noted, the current debate focuses largely on this concept. Instead, Shariati describes the relationship between the concepts of *shahid* and martyr as that of antonyms. He notes that the root of the word 'martyr' is derived from the Latin root *mort*, and implies death and dying, and so 'martyr refers to 'the one who dies for God and faith':

> Thus a martyr is, in any case, the one who dies. The only difference between his death and that of others is to be seen in the 'cause.' He dies for the cause of God, whereas the cause of the death of another may be cancer. Otherwise, the essence of the phenomenon in both cases, that is to say, death, is one and the same. As far as death is concerned it makes no difference whether the person is killed for God, for passion, or in an accident. In this sense, Christ and those killed for Christianity are 'martyrs.' In other words, they were 'mortals,' because, in Christendom's the term 'martyr' refers to the person who has died [as such].
>
> But a shahid is always alive and present. He is not absent. Thus the two terms, 'shahid 'and 'martyr,' are antonyms of each other. (Shariati n.d. a)

Shariati maintains that the *shahid* is always present, and does not die, unlike a martyr, who actually dies. To support this point, he clarifies that the word *shahid* has a double meaning: one who gives testimony to his faith with his death, and a model or paradigm that is eternal. Therefore a *shahid* dies as a witness to Islam, struggling to institute justice and divine law on earth. If it meant only that, then *shahid* and martyr would be the same. However, the second meaning of a *shahid*'s paradigmatic status indicates that he is immortal. This is demonstrated, for example, in the special Islamic burial procedures for the *shahid*, who because he is rendered free from sin through his act is considered already purified, and therefore is not washed, according to regular Islamic ritual, but is buried in his clothes. He is entitled to immediate immortality, entry into paradise, and enjoys special status. Therefore the notion of the 'present' *shahid* indicates that he is an immortal paradigm and a model, but also that he transcends death and crosses directly over into paradise. Shariati explains:

> A Shahid is the one who negates his whole existence for the sacred
> ideal in which we all believe. It is natural then that all the sacredness
> of that ideal and goal transports itself to his existence. True, that his
> existence has suddenly become non-existent, but he has absorbed
> the whole value of the idea for which he has negated himself. No
> wonder, then, that he, in the mind of the people, becomes sacredness
> itself. In this way, man becomes absolute man, because he is no longer
> a person, an individual. He is 'thought.' (Shariati n.d. a)

Shariati's 'absolute man' refers to the potential of a human being to negate himself for an idea, in this way becoming the thought itself, reproducing the thought. As such, Shariati notes, 'a shahid is always alive and present', and 'a spritual crystallization of that collective spirit which they call "nation"' (Shariati n.d. a). Using the Islamic historical example of Imam Hussein,[2] Shariati further clarifies that, 'When we speak of Hussein, we do not mean Hussein as a person. Hussein was that individual who negated himself with absolute sincerity, with the utmost magnificence within human power, for an absolute and sacred value' (Shariati n.d. a). Therefore it is the act of negating oneself, submission, that is prominent in Shariati's configuration, not sacrifice in a Christian sense, and certainly not suicide.

Shariati is even more concise and categorizes the different types of *shahid* as exemplified by the lives and deaths of Hamzah[3] and

Hussein. He argues that 'Hamzah is a mujahid and a hero who goes (into battle) to achieve victory and defeat the enemy. Instead, he is defeated, is killed, and thus becomes a shahid.' On the other hand, Hussein did not go into battle with the intention of killing the enemy like Hamzah, and neither was he killed accidentally as a victim. Instead he was killed by standing firm in the siege of Kerbala in a power struggle between Muslims themselves. Shariati notes that Hussein 'chooses shahadat as an end or as a means for the affirmation of what is being negated and mutilated by the political apparatus'. While the jihadist, as exemplified in Hamzah, chose to fight as a *mujahidin*, Hussein avoided battle, but yet confronted his enemies willingly to be killed. Both acts are different types of *shahid*: the one who goes to battle, willing to die, but not intending to die; and the one who chooses to make his death a testimony 'even though, between his decision-making and his death, months or even years may pass' (Shariati n.d. a).

Shariati's description of *shahid* is directly relevant to the discourse on 'suicide bombing' and 'sacrifice', since Osama bin Laden, in particular, though Sunni, borrowed quite freely from the Shia doctrine of *jihad* and *shahid*, an argument already explored in depth by Devji in *Landscapes of the Jihad* (2005: 13–32). Therefore bin Laden's references to sacrifice and martyrdom arise from the tradition of the Shi'ism of Shariati and are quite different from the Christian doctrines of sacrificing oneself for the redemption of others. In 'Sacrificial Militancy and the Wars around Terror' Alec Houen, referring directly to Shariati, takes care to avoid the problematic term 'suicide bomber', and examines how 'sacrificial militancy' is both 'substitutive' in nature, substituting the profane for the sacred, and 'constitutive', inasmuch as it is foundational in building community and ideals (Houen 2010: 115–16). In many ways Houen's argument on the 'constitutive' nature of militancy is similar to the one I have presented in Chapter 4, arguing that jihadists' actual articulations of their intentions demonstrate that these intentions are both worldly and other-worldly. However,

Houen makes the mistake, similar to that of Devji, of employing the language of sacrifice, which he claims Islamic tradition holds in common with the other Abrahamic religions, and this leads him to dubious conclusions (2010: 116).

For example, Houen develops Derrida's concept of *qurban* (sacrifice) as a Quranic term to support the idea that the jihadist commits a sacrifice of himself and others (Houen 2010: 115–16). However, the word *qurban* actually refers to an offering to God, in the form of animal sacrifice, not a human one. Indeed, the Quran criticized the pre-Islamic Arabs for thinking that their offerings at the Ka'aba reached God, and in response Islam accepted and encouraged the practice of *qurban*, but made its purpose the feeding of the poor. So, specifically, in Islamic terminology *qurban* refers to the sacrifice of animals on Eid al-Adha, for the worldly purpose of feeding the poor, not human sacrifice.[4] Interestingly, *qurban* is also performed in memory of the bond between Ismael and Ibrahim in submitting to God's will; here the story differs substantially enough from the Judeo-Christian version, in a similar manner as does the narrative of Issa, to render its usage as foundational in a theory of sacrifice nonsensical.

In the Islamic narrative, unlike the Judaeo-Christian one, Ismael (not Ishaq) willingly gave himself up to his father to be killed, for God had ordered it. The story focuses on how both Ibrahim and Ismael discuss the situation and how they both demonstrate total submission to God. Tariq Ramadan, commenting on the common story, notes: 'trials of faith are never tragic in Islamic tradition, and in this sense, the Quran's story of Abraham is basically different from the Bible's when it comes to the experience of sacrifice' (Ramadan 2007: 5). Ramadan argues that the differences in the two narratives have 'essential consequences for the very perception of faith, for the trial of faith, and for human beings' relation to God' (2007: 6). Thus, by accepting Derrida's usage of *qurban*, Houen makes the mistake of assuming the *shahid* views his death as an act of *qurban* or sacrifice, while to the contrary it is an act of submission to God which does not entail a sacrifice of the self but an evolution of the self, as Shariati and bin Laden after him have asserted. These fault lines in Houen's theorization demonstrate the danger of developing theory around Islamic concepts through a faulty synthesis of Judeo-Christian and Muslim histories, without recognizing the difference between them. The stories told differently highlight different metaphysical traditions.

Thus far I have examined some rather problematic attempts to bridge postsecular and Islamic terminologies, particularly regarding discussion of the jihadist. In this regard, Tariq Ramadan's efforts are substantially more encouraging than others, particularly his inventive use of the term 'social *jihad*' and 'abode of testimony', *dar ash-shahadah*. Ramadan has undertaken a complex synthesis of humanist and Muslim traditions and as a result has emerged as a highly contentious figure. He was named by *Time* magazine in 2000 as one of the six religious figures likely to be responsible for Islam's rejuvenation in the new century, and was appointed by former UK prime minister Tony Blair to a government commission on the prevention of extremism. In contrast, the US Department of Homeland Security revoked Ramadan's visa in July 2004, preventing him from taking up a teaching position at Notre Dame University in Indiana, stating as its reason that Ramadan once made a financial contribution to a French charity, Comité de Bienfaisance et de Secours aux Palestiniens (CBSP), which was blacklisted by the US Department of the Treasury in 2003.[5] Ramadan has become a highly controversial figure in Europe and America and is treated with suspicion, particularly on account of his family history – a direct lineage to the Muslim Brotherhood.

Most important for Ramadan is that the Islamic message to which Muslims are expected to bear witness is not primarily the socially conservative code of traditionalist jurists, but a commitment to universalism and the welfare of non-Muslims; it is also an injunction not merely to make demands on un-Islamic societies but to express solidarity with them. In an interview with Peter Connolly of *Salon*, for example, Ramadan describes his own personal positioning as a European Muslim:

> Our values are not based on 'otherness.' Our values are universal. We have to come to the understanding that it's not 'us against them,' it's us on the scale of our own values. This defines the place I live in. That is to say, my role in this world is to understand that I am a witness to the Islamic message before mankind. (Donnelley 2002)

Ramadan's insistence on the universality of Islam's message places him in the humanist tradition, but definitely not in the position of a secularist: 'When I speak about citizenship, I am a Swiss with a Muslim background. But when I speak of philosophy, my perception of life, I am a Muslim with Swiss nationality' (Donnelley 2002).

More than other theorists, Ramadan confronts the role of *jihad* in radical reform. He explicates the now familiar differentiation between the greater inner and spiritual *jihad* and the lesser, outer *jihad* for social justice:

> *Jihad* is the expression of a rejection of all injustice, as also the necessary assertion of balance and harmony in equity. One hopes for a non-violent struggle, far removed from the horrors of armed conflict. ... Resisting the very violent expression of this tendency and trying to implement the necessary balance of forces seem to be the conditions for an order that looks human. The latter being the only situation whereby violence is given legitimacy; situations whereby violence is sustained, repression imposed or rights denied, to the extent, that if one succumbs, one loses one's dignity. (Ramadan 2001: 65)

There is a critical argument here which differentiates Ramadan from other Western Muslim scholars, namely his acceptance of the legitimacy of violence through *jihad* in cases where non-violent means have been exhausted as a means to resist the repression of rights. While Majid focuses on polycentric economic and cultural configurations in a Third World setting and avoids the issue of *jihad*, and Sardar firmly migrates from *jihad* to *ijtihad*, Ramadan asserts the right to violence, under qualification, and uses the explicit and controversial term *jihad* to describe this violence. He argues for an understanding of the reasons behind *jihad*:

> Every day that passes, entire peoples sustain repression, abuse of power, and the most inhumane violations of rights. Until when will these peoples remain silent or see themselves deemed 'dangerous,' by the West, whenever they dare to express their rejection? Here, it is not a question of defending violence but rather of understanding the circumstances wherein it takes shape. North–South imbalances and the exploitation of men and raw materials, combined with the resignation of the peoples of the North, produce a much more devastating violence than that of armed groups, even if the latter are spectacular. As the end of the 20th century draws close, can we call all men to mobilise themselves towards more social, political and economic justice, for it seems to us that this is the only way to give back to men the rights that will silence arms? Such an effort would be the literal translation of the word *jihād*. (Ramadan 2001: 65–6)

While explaining the reasons for *jihad* as residing both in economic imbalance and in the need for a wake-up call of sorts to the cultural and political resignation of the populations of the West, Ramadan calls for a common mobilization of peoples, 'a social *jihad*' (2001: 66). Thus Ramadan asserts the revolutionary terminology of Islam, refashioned to move away from its connotation of violence towards the vocabulary of international social mobilization. Interestingly, the social *jihad* of which Ramadan writes includes *ijtihad* but is not confined to it. For Ramadan, resistance is a dual process: of fighting outward repression of one's rights (social *jihad*) and of internally reforming Muslim societies themselves (*ijtihad*). For Ramadan, *jihad* does not belong to Muslims only; he seeks to internationalize this terminology as a fight against injustice to be held by all people:

> This situation necessitates an urgent response as also a general call for *jihād*. Here, it is about giving from one's own person and property, calling all the forces of all diverse societies and engaging in the work of reform that we have already discussed.
>
> We will not deny that there are struggles wherein circumstances lead us to direct confrontation, in order to oppose a purge here, a

military occupation there, or another type of aggression such as the one we have witnessed in Bosnia and Chechnia. However, it cannot simply be a question of focusing our attention on these events alone and forgetting the broader type of fight which occurs daily and it is, therefore, so much more urgent. Nowadays, our enemies, in the path of God, are hunger, unemployment, exploitation, delinquency and drug addiction. They require intense efforts, a continuous fight and a complete *jihād* which requires each and everyone's participation. (Ramadan 2001: 68)

Ramadan explicitly identifies those whom he hopes will engage in this redefined social *jihad*, which to him, as for Majid and Sardar, is a liberationary movement of the economically dispossessed and those faith-based communities who base their resistance on liberation theology:

the Pope calls for a general mobilisation against poverty and the imbalance of wealth and asserts that it is the duty of Christians to act in this sense. The *jihād* of Muslims is, of course, part of this engagement in the West, but it is equally so in all the countries of the South. It is a wholehearted *jihād* engaged by South American communities who express it in the form of liberation theology, or as it is manifested in the popular and trade unionist forces in the Near East and Asia. (Ramadan 2001: 69)

However, Ramadan's posited universal *social jihad*, which is international, does not mean he does not focus specifically on the responsibilities of Muslims living in the West, 'who must perform the twofold work of deconstruction and reconstruction' (Ramadan 2010: 43). This is the nature of *ijtihad* for Ramadan. This deconstruction is focused on a critique not only of secular liberalism, as is emphasized in the work of Majid and Sardar, but of Islamic sources themselves, which Ramadan is equipped to perform due to his training at Al-Azhar University. Employing Islamic terminology, Ramadan argues that the old binary division of *dar al-islam* (abode of Islam) and *dar al-harb* (abode of war) must be broken down, and suggests the term *dar ash-shahadah* (abode of testimony), which means Muslims and all people of faith should strive to be living witnesses of their beliefs through their presence and behaviour (Ramadan 2010: 51–2). This intriguing appropriation of the term *shahada*, often used by jihadists to describe the militant act of the *shahid*, is described by Ramadan as a space of testimony and responsibility for bearing Islam's universal message:

> the European environment is a *space of responsibility* for Muslims. This is exactly the meaning of the notion of '*space of testimony*' that we propose here, a notion that totally reverses perspectives: whereas Muslims have, for years, been wondering *whether and how they would be accepted*, the in-depth study and evaluation of the Western environment entrusts them, in light of their Islamic frame of reference, with a most important mission. ... Muslims now attain, in the *space of testimony*, the meaning of an essential duty and of an exacting responsibility: to contribute, wherever they are, to promoting good and equity within and through *human brotherhood*. Muslims' outlook must now change from the reality of 'protection' alone to that of an authentic 'contribution.' (Ramadan 1999: 150)

In the abode of testimony, European Muslims must engage in social *jihad* and *ijtihad*. The challenge for Ramadan is to deepen the understanding of Islam among Muslims, in the language of their own terms such as *ijtihad, jihad* and *shariah*, as well as encourage them to query the nature of secularization, citizenship, human rights and democratic models (Ramadan 1999: 56). A clarifying of terminology is critical before a dialogical debate can take place across civilizations. Ramadan argues that he wishes Muslims to belong as citizens who are aware of their own terminology and can negotiate change by engaging with it. To do this, Muslims must be interested in all issues that other citizens are interested in: race, ecology, education, urban violence. In other words, Ramadan argues for a post-integration approach. Likewise, he notes that the West needs to engage in a real dialogue with itself; it cannot go on defining itself by what it is not, with Muslims as its Other.

Ramadan's description of how familiarity with Islamic concepts can transform global society is mapped out in *Radical Reform:*

Islamic Ethics and Liberation, where he draws up an agenda for a radical transformative process, rather than an adaptive one. He insists that his argument is not to modernize Islam or 'Islamize modernity', but to establish that Islamic ethics have universal implications (2009: 145). Ramadan laments the lack of interaction on the part of Islamic scholars with others outside their own field, as well as lack of consultation with actual communities of Muslims, causing them not to understand 'the growing complexity of the Real' (Ramadan 2009: 113). For Ramadan, a dialogue of civilizations is not enough, as one must insist that *a priori* conditions be set in order for the goals of the dialogue to be achieved (2009: 308). These conditions necessarily lead to reflections on the relationship between Islam and capitalism.

Ramadan applies his transformational approach to capitalism on two levels: first, to question the Islamicity of capitalism, and, second, to question the Islamic nature of capitalism itself. Ramadan points to the growing market of Islamic products, and argues that merely putting an Islamic label on products that are produced by an oppressive system, outside of Islamic ethics, cannot make them Islamic. The means of production of commodities through the use of poorly waged workers, unfair trade and the exploitation of the environment are often left unchallenged by contemporary Muslim scholars, who seem content with Islamic labels, such as in Islamic banking, or halal food (2009: 242–7). Indeed, labels of superficial Islamicity have opened up a new market for capitalists in Islamic countries, a case in point being the Islamic banking industry, which operates with a capitalist ethics by merely integrating a few Muslim principles, such as rejecting interest and risk-sharing and providing *zakah* (244–5). In this way, capitalism has been superficially Islamized for the consumption of its commodities. Second, Ramadan argues that Islamic activists have offered no alternatives to capitalism; neither have they been engaged in a sustained critique. He argues that contemporary Muslim societies have not participated, except in cosmetic ways, in the search for better models of overall human development, and instead deal with the issues of global capitalism by integrating into it. Ramadan concedes that at present there is 'no "Islamic" alternative to the dominant neoliberal economic model', but insists there is an ethics upon which a new model can be built (244). Global 'Islamized capitalism' must be resisted because 'the capitalist system has managed to efficiently take over an ideational frame of reference that was supposed to resist it, with the collaboration of its operators and of Muslim consumers themselves' (Ramadan 2009: 250). Ramadan notes that the 'ideational frame' of Islam provides the resistance and Muslims should not allow it to be appropriated. He calls for Muslims to work with non-Muslim critics of capitalism to develop new critiques and new economic forms that engage with other 'universes of resistance to the dominant economic order', even engaging with Marxist and atheist thinkers to work out a critique of a system from within (2009: 248).

It might appear that Slavoj Žižek, as an articulate defender of the importance of atheism, particularly in a strong Europe, would be a potential ally in Ramadan's 'space of testimony'. However, radical reform for Ramadan is quite different from the notion understood by Žižek, whose postsecularism does not actually contain Islam (as discussed in Chapter 4). Appropriating Islamic terminology, Žižek argues that Muslims can be part of radical politics if they can engage in a proper *ijtihad* to reform their societies and a redefined *jihad*. For him, the hope of moving out of a post-political society lies in the excess represented by the jihadist, not in an accommodation to multiculturalism, or a reconfiguration of multiculturalism into a multicivilizational or polycentric model, as propagated by Majid and Sardar. Although Ramadan would claim that multiculturalism is a reality and that a proper framework has not been developed to manage this reality, Žižek posits it as a mere illusion, with identity politics itself a dead end, for it is a diversion from the real class struggle (Žižek 2002:

147–9). Žižek sees multiculturalism as incapable of escaping the model of victimhood, and offers no hope for an inclusive truly multi-civilizational model. Instead, he argues that 'postmodern identity politics of particular (ethnic, sexual, and so forth) lifestyles fits perfectly the depoliticized notion of society', one 'in which every particular group is accounted for and has its specific status (of victimhood) acknowledged through affirmative action or other measures' (Žižek 1998: 1006). Rather than multiculturalism, which contains the Muslim as *Homo sacer*, Žižek argues for a move to the status of 'neighbour'.

In 'Neighbors and Other Monsters: A Plea for Ethical Violence', Žižek argues that if one sticks to 'love thy neighbor', one tries to develop an ethics without violence, instead of recognizing the 'alien traumatic kernel' that forever persists in the neighbour, the 'inert, impenetrable, enigmatic presence that hystericizes me' (Žižek 2005: 140–41), for beneath the neighbour, one's 'mirror image', 'there always lurks the unfathomable abyss of radical Otherness' (2005: 143). Perhaps this is where Žižek's *Homo islamicus* lurks. Žižek's opinions on Eurpean Muslims become more evident in *Violence*, where, in reference to the Paris riots of 2005, the 9/11 bombers and floods of immigrants to Europe, Žižek articulates the difficulty global capitalism and multiculturalism have in dealing with the neighbour, or perhaps what I have argued in this book as the *Homo islamicus*. Muslims in France, for example, protested not because they wanted to be recognized as Muslims, but because they wanted to be French, an argument with which Ramadan would agree (2008: 80). Likewise, Europe's walls against immigration are a sign of the failure of a global capitalism that does not allow people to stay at home (where they belong, perhaps) (2008: 102–4). The bombing of the Twin Towers had no goal other than the performative one of becoming noticed (2008: 92). The same could be said of the Paris riots. Such acts of violence are attempts by the Other, or *Homo islamicus* in this case, to break out of the alienation or the indifference shown to him; to be seen not as a

neighbour but as a citizen. But global capitalism has no citizens,
Žižek would argue; in a sense they are all engaged in a 'zero level
protest' (2008: 81), meaning they want nothing but recognition.
Liberal multiculturalism cannot contain these aimless acts, Žižek
argues, and liberal platitudes will result in 'a society regulated by a
perverse pact between religious fundamentalists and the politically
correct preachers of tolerance and respect for the other's beliefs:
a society immobilised by the concern for not hurting the other'
(2008: 130). The same people who call for the building of mosques
in Europe, for example, also call for the right to print the Danish
cartoons to demonstrate liberalism, thereby creating an irresolvable
knot (2008: 132). Such a paradox, for Žižek, means that Muslims
are showing us the limits of secular 'disenchantment' (2008: 133).
Žižek puzzles as to why Muslims bother with the cartoon issue,
for example, instead of attacking their real enemy, global capitalism, and concludes that those who reprint the cartoons are the
Muslims' only real allies. For Žižek, Muslims are therefore left
with basically only one ethical option:

> This means the choice for Muslims is not only either Islamo-Fascist
> fundamentalism or the painful process of 'Islamic Protestantism'
> which would make Islam compatible with modernization. There is
> a third option, which has already been tried: Islamic socialism. The
> proper politically correct attitude is to emphasize, with symptomatic
> insistence, how the terrorist attacks have nothing to do with the
> real Islam, that great and sublime religion – would it not be more
> appropriate to recognize Islam's resistance to modernization? And,
> rather than bemoaning the fact that Islam, of all the great religions,
> is the most resistant to modernization, we should, rather, conceive of
> this resistance as an open chance, as 'undecidable': this resistance does
> not necessarily lead to Islamo-Fascism, it could also be articulated
> into a Socialist project. Precisely because Islam harbours the 'worst'
> potentials of the Fascist answer to our present predicament, it could
> also turn out to be the site for the 'best.' (Žižek 2002: 133–4)

In the end, Žižek believes that Islam itself may contain the
element of radical energy that is required to lead a socialist
revolution of sorts, but the dangers of a pact with right-wing

fundamentalist cultural values is quite high. Islam, as a pool of mad energy and violence, in the tradition of Nietzsche and Foucault, may be of some service in providing *Homo islamicus* as the sacrifice required for the revolution – the sacrificial violence that atheism cannot offer, since an atheist post-ideological society cannot seem to mobilize its masses for killing and dying. Islam can be employed in a pragmatic manner to spearhead a Euro-centric revolution which is suspiciously empty of real Muslims. In Žižek's view, even this is a harsh compromise, since the atheists have a more highly developed sense of morality than does *Homo islamicus* – the religious, after all, do good deeds to gain God's approval while atheists do them because they believe they are the right thing to do (Žižek 2008: 138). For Žižek, only Europe is capable of using atheism as its moral principle. This is why the only possibility is for the new society to be constructed from a European model, as he posits a unified Europe as the only hope against American-led global capital. In *First as Tragedy, Then as Farce*, Žižek's anxiety with Islam is obvious, as he claims that no matter how anti-imperialist the Islamic movement appears it lacks the dimension of a communal 'utopia' (Žižek 2009: 71). It is only worthy of short-term consideration:

> Although in the long term, the success of the radical emancipatory struggle depends on mobilizing the lower classes who are today often in thrall to fundamentalist populism, one should have no qualms about concluding short-term alliances with egalitarian liberals as part of the anti-sexist and anti-racist struggle. (Žižek 2009: 73)

Therefore, for Žižek, if Ramadan, Rauf, Sardar, Majid and others can prove themselves as 'egalitarian liberals', who are not sexist racists, then his partnership with them will be for the convenience of mobilizing *Homo islamicus*, who can be of use as sacrifices in the communist struggle. Žižek's theological turn is not quite sustained, but is diverted back to European atheism and com-munism when he argues that, instead of renouncing violence and saying religion is good, we ought to renounce religion and continue with violence (2008: 134). Thus, is Ramadan's hope for a cooperative 'universe of resistance' on the left justified? Not if the atheist left is represented by Žižek. This becomes even more evident in Žižek's writings on the Arab revolutions.

To be sure, the left, including Žižek, started out with a particularly euphoric response to the youthful secular messaging of the Arab revolutions, hopeful that they could be appropriated to invigorate leftist politics. For example, Hardt and Negri, in an article in the *Guardian* in February 2011, place hope that the Arab revolutions will be this generation's Latin American struggle, as 'a laboratory of political experimentation', a kind of 'ideological house-cleaning, sweeping away the racist conceptions of a clash of civilisations that consign Arab politics to the past'. They argue:

> This is a threshold through which neoliberalism cannot pass and capitalism is put to question. And Islamic rule is completely inadequate to meet these needs. Here insurrection touches on not only the equilibriums of North Africa and the Middle East but also the global system of economic governance. (Hardt and Negri 2011)

Hardt and Negri are right to note that the revolutions rejuvenate some basic principles of the left that had been discarded as outdated, such as justice, universalism and popular power, but they ignore the fact that the principles they praise are the very basis of Islam itself, the cultural foundation from which these revolutions are being generated. In their haste to condemn 'Islamic rule', without ever defining what that might mean, and in their nostalgia to migrate the revolutions into a communist agenda, they betray the need to leave Islam out of any serious analysis of the reasons behind the revolutions and their likely future achievement. A similar plea for a type of Islamic socialism, which basically leaves out Islam, was made by Žižek in a February 2011 Opinion piece in the *Guardian* titled 'Why Fear the Arab Revolutionary Spirit'.

Indeed, an earlier discussion that took place on *Riz Khan*, where both Tariq Ramadan and Slavoj Žižek offered their insights, is representative of the lenses being used to interpret the events of the revolutions. Ramadan carefully argued that the revolutions are not ideologically inspired and that we must be cognizant of the reality that Western power wants changes in the region which at the same time enable the global situation to remain the same. He confronted head-on concerns about the involvement of Islamist politics, now that Arab dictators are disappearing, and argued that the fear of a monolithic, radical Islam is merely a device whereby the West and Israel maintain hegemony over Muslim populations. Using the example of the Muslim Brotherhood in Egypt, which he argued is ideologically diverse, he looked longingly to the example of Turkey, not Iran, where Islamism and political life have been successfully integrated, albeit under the eye of a watchful military. Žižek used the occasion to comment on universalism, and expressed his admiration for the Arabs, who, he argued, truly understand democracy, more so than the West. Rehearsing his arguments from *Welcome to the Desert of the Real*, and not responding to Ramadan's contention of the diversity contained under the umbrella of Islamist politics, he claimed that the choices open to the revolution are not just 'Muslim fundamentalist Islam' or liberal democracy, but must include a synthesis of Islamic and leftist ideologies. However, Žižek's well-intentioned conclusions betray the same bias as Hardt and Negri – that is, that the Arab revolutions must speak the language of the left.

By August 2011, in an essay largely addressing the London riots, Žižek is already grieving the death of the Egyptian Revolution, stating that 'Its gravediggers are the army and the Islamists'.

> The losers will be the pro-Western liberals, too weak – in spite of the CIA funding they are getting – to 'promote democracy', as well as the true agents of the spring events, the emerging secular left that has been trying to set up a network of civil society organisations, from trade unions to feminists. (Žižek 2011a)

And, in contrast to the hoped-for fusion of Islamism and leftism in *Welcome to the Desert of the Real*, Žižek now wonders 'who will succeed in directing the rage of the poor? Who will translate it into a political programme: the new secular left or the Islamists?' (2011a). Thus there is a choice between 'the new secular left' and the Islamists, though Žižek does not identify the composition of either group. For example, the Islamists comprise socialists, Salafists and capitalists, and cannot be positioned as an ideologically homogeneous group. And what exactly comprises the 'new secular left'? Could it be the Egyptian Bloc? Thus it seems that an alliance between Žižek and Ramadan to promote 'radical reform' with a universal message of 'social *jihad*' will be seriously constrained from the onset.

Perhaps Terry Eagleton, another grandee of postsecular theory, might be a more appropriate accomplice? To his credit, Eagleton confesses in *Reason, Faith and Revolution* that he knows little about theology, and the little he knows is about Christian theology, and so he will confine his work to that for 'it is better to be provincial than presumptuous' (Eagleton 2009: 3). While acknowledging that he may be accused of universalizing Islamic principles about which he knows little, he continues to make various assertions about the role of *jihad* in the contemporary debate and the attack on multiculturalist capitalism. Playing the middle ground, Eagleton surprisingly places himself in a position as interlocutor: 'I also seek to strike a minor blow on behalf of those many millions of Muslims whose creed of peace, justice, and compassion has been rubbished and traduced by cultural supremacists in the West' (2009: 34). He directly aligns himself with Muslims: 'good' moderates whose religion has been hijacked by the Western right and a 'bigoted and benighted Islamism' (2009: 35).

Eagleton's attack on Islamic fundamentalism, while aligning itself with Muslim moderates, is similar to those positions taken by Rauf and Sardar, but, in *Reason, Faith and Revolution*, it is to fellow Marxist Aijaz Ahmad that Eagleton refers to develop his explanation of Islamic radicalism. Eagleton's recourse to Ahmad allows him to place his own discourse within a leftist and secular, but also Muslim, critique.[6] He accepts Ahmad's argument that, being betrayed by their rulers who are seduced by capitalism, with no army to join in to protest, and seeing countless civilians killed by Americans and Israelis, the jihadists do not deem their own killing of civilians to be terrorism, or even comparable to what their own people have suffered. If anything, they would consider themselves counter-terrorists. Eagleton elaborates on Ahmad's point that a combination of domestic, anti-left and mostly autocratic right-wing (Muslim) regimes, on the one hand, and, on the other, determined imperialist Zionist policies (by the West) have created the conditions for extremism (Eagleton 2009: 101–6). Such engagement allows Eagleton to conclude that 'It is rather that, without the vast concentration camp known as the Gaza Strip, it is not at all out of the question that the Twin Towers would still be standing' (2009: 107). Eagleton, however, does not claim that without Western imperialism there would be no Islamic fanaticism, leaving the door open for further reflection on the radical nature of Islamic theology itself. For sure, he argues, the global significance of Islam has brought the West's own internal questions to the forefront, as witnessed in the aggressive new atheism of Christopher Hitchens and Richard Dawkins. Further, Eagleton argues that while the West is in the throes of late capitalism and postmodernity, undermining its own meta-physical foundations, building itself on practical materialism, it is now confronted with another vision which believes in universals and truths (2009: 141–2). Therefore the West is now confronted with its metaphysical foe – Islam. But Eagleton goes no further. He does not theorize exactly how Islam is the metaphysical foe of the West, but merely asserts it as the West's Other, which can facilitate self-reflection and thus progress for the West:

> If the British or American way of life really were to take on board the critique of materialism, hedonism, and individualism of many devout Muslims, rather than Muslims simply to sign on for a ready-made British or American culture, Western civilization would most

certainly be altered for the good. This is a rather different vision from the kind of multiculturalism which leaves Muslims and others well alone to do their own charmingly esoteric stuff, commending them from a safe distance. (Eagleton 2009: 154)

But what should the West do when faced with, in Eagleton's view, the universals of Islam for which Ramadan advocates in his *Radical Reform*? Eagleton answers:

> Either it trusts in the virtues of its native pragmatism in the face of its enemy's absolutism, a risky enough enterprise; or it falls back on metaphysical values of its own, as Western fundamentalists would insist. Yet these values are looking increasingly tarnished and implausible.... Does the West need to go full-bloodedly metaphysical to save itself? And if it does, can it do so without inflicting too much damage on its liberal, secular values, thus ensuring there is still something worth protecting from its illiberal opponents? (Eagleton 2009: 165–6)

Eagleton is, of course, aware of the risk of facing the dilemma from a purely theological view, which is why he depends on a materialist like Ahmad to prove the point. He notes that while theology is part of the problem, it also fosters a kind of critical reflection that might offer some answers. However, the core of Eagleton's dialogue is not with Muslims themselves but with theologians and leftists in the West. If Žižek's objective is to save the world with communism, Eagleton's is to save the West by propagating a form of tragic humanism: 'Tragic humanism, whether in its socialist, Christian, or psychoanalytical varieties, holds that only by a process of self-dispossession and radical remaking can humanity come into its own' (Eagleton 2009: 169). This is surely a rather obscure agenda, and so difficult to assess as an appropriate companion to Ramadan's admittedly rather scattered radical reform. However, it is in his denser earlier work, *Unholy Terror* (2005b), that Eagleton clarifies his notion of 'tragic humanism'.

In *Unholy Terror*, Eagleton posits the figure of the modern tragic protagonist, not unlike *Homo sacer*, caught between desire and consumption, struggling as a Christ-like scapegoat, suffering the sins of global capitalism. Our contemporary tragedy, according to Eagleton, is that we have lost one of the two main components of tragedy, fear and pity: we feel fear but not pity (2005b: 133). When we see the face of terror only in the Other we are unable to see it in ourselves, and so we must dehumanize and exoticize the Other in order to fear him. Because we cannot see ourselves as complicit in terror, we further terrorize the Other, even at the cost of limiting and terrorizing ourselves, in order to try to prevent the terrorist from terrorizing us. Like Butler, Eagleton concludes that unless we can feel pity for the Other, those oppressed for whom the jihadists are supposedly speaking, we are doomed to repeat tragic actions. Eagleton explains terrorism not in a socio-political context, as he opts for in *Reason, Faith and Revolution*, but within a metaphysical framework. *Unholy Terror* does not deal with the reasons for terrorism or *jihad*, per se, but merely seeks to extend the language of the left into metaphysics with concepts such as sacrifice and evil (2005b: v). Interestingly, Eagleton notes, as I have argued above in reference to bin Laden and Shariati, the jihadist is capable of submission as a way of articulating his allegiance to the divine, not as a sacrifice to redeem a community (2009: 39). Eagleton goes on to assert that terror and the sacred have always been connected; and just as creation and destruction are linked in theology, so are the sacred and terror.

The word 'evil', which is often used to describe terror, is not metaphysical for Eagleton, but grounded in the material (Eagleton 2005b: 117), and as such can be transformed by changing material conditions. These changes require sacrifice which is usually made by Eagleton's 'scapegoat', another central figure of the present, and prevalent in tradition since Ancient Greece. The fact that global capitalism requires a 'scapegoat' (2005b: 128) in order to maintain power is evidence for Eagleton that it has indeed failed, and this scapegoat becomes Eagleton's 'tragic protagonist' (2005b: 90) looking for an ethical future, not unlike the ethical strivings of Devji's 'terrorist" in *The Terrorist in Search of Humanity* (2008). For both Devji and Eagleton, the tragic figure sacrifices himself in order to represent all of humanity, in order to remake a humanity that is not tied to a love of life only. Eagleton asserts that the tragic protagonist 'in accepting his death, testifies in his courage to a spirit which cannot be broken by it' (Eagleton 2005b: 27) and Devji asserts that it is 'by stepping out of their bodies in these sovereign acts of sacrifice, violent as well as non-violent, that human beings might represent humanity' (Devji 2008: 219–20). It is this 'tragic protagonist' that reappears as the 'tragic humanist' in *Reason, Faith and Revolution* (2009), where Eagleton argues that the complete transfiguration of the world can be attained only through a 'turbulent passage through death, nothingness, madness, loss, and futility" (Eagleton 2009:24) since 'the traumatic truth of human history is a mutilated body' (2009:27).

The question remains, how can this complete transfiguration occur in the abode of testimony that in Ramadan's formulation is universal? Ramadan argues for Muslims in Europe to take ethical stances in the 'social *jihad*' in their abode of testimony; and while he accentuates the need for radical reform inside Muslim lands, and a connection with radical movements, his hope focuses on a solution spearheaded by European Muslims. Asad perhaps remains more sceptical of the possibility of Muslim participation in an aggressively secularized Europe, noting: 'Muslims, as members of the abstract category "humans," can be assimilated or (as some recent theorists have put it) "translated" into a global ("European") civilization once they have divested themselves of what many of them regard (mistakenly) as essential to themselves' (Asad 2003: 169). To the contrary, Sardar and Majid, as discussed in Chapter 5, place this hope in a conglomeration of anti-imperialist movements that can contain non-violent Islamic dissent. Eagleton's succinct analysis of Europe's problems with Muslims in 'The Scandal of Faith' interestingly questions the 'tediously familiar answers' which are usually given to Europe's Islamophobia – 'they are all potential terrorists, because they are a drain on the social services, because their culture threatens to swamp British civilisation and so on' (Eagleton 2011). Instead Eagleton argues that Muslims represent a challenge to the anaemic faithlessness of capitalism, where faith is privatized rather than integrated into political and social life. He argues:

> Antonio Gramsci maintained that all ordinary people were at a certain level philosophers, but this is a lot more obvious in the Islamic world than it is elsewhere. Islamists are also natural-born internationalists.
> The faith they share is not one confined to national cultures. It links them to a global community of believers and overrides all narrowly parochial concerns. (Eagleton 2011)

He compares this internationalist approach, where all Muslims are expected to have in-depth knowledge of their faith, as a challenge to Western societies, which 'deal with belief primarily by reducing it to a private affair', while 'Islam, by contrast, makes no such absolute distinctions between the personal, the moral, the political and the religious' (2011). Eagleton observes that capitalism is challenged by comprehensive Muslim perspectives, since capitalism is an essentially faithless system, where

> As long as you roll into work, pay your taxes and refrain from beating up police officers, you can believe more or less what you like. Too much conviction smacks of fanaticism, and is bad for business. It is best to get by on as little of the stuff as you can, like a recovering alcoholic. (Eagleton 2011)

The very existence of large Muslim populations in Europe, who live out their faith in an abode of testimony, in all aspects of their individual and socio-political lives, 'reminds the West as a whole of the contradiction between its own need to believe and its inability to do so' (Eagleton 2011). At the end of the article Eagleton has some advice for socialists, which is refreshing considering the anti-Islamism that has permeated the left's responses to the Arab revolutions, as noted above:

Socialists may not agree with the content of Islamic faith, but they are well acquainted by their own history with the idea of millions of ordinary men and women living lives of conviction rather than of pragmatic self-interest. In this, at least, we share a precious tradition with those hounded by the Islamophobes. (Eagleton 2011)

It appears that Eagleton's postsecular turn is profoundly more sustained than Žižek's, and as such he is representative of a new possibility of alliances between Ramadan's 'universes of resistance' for a social *jihad*.

To conclude, the type of humanism propagated by Edward Said in *Humanism and Democratic Criticism* remained secular and incapable of accepting other universals such as Islam into the core of its formation. Similarly, the abstraction and universalization of suicide and Christian notions of sacrifice, which I have argued are alien to Islamic discourse, make Muslims vanish into humanity at the very point of intersection, much in the way Žižek makes them vanish into the impending socialist revolution. Eagleton and Ramadan, on the other hand, offer hope, notwithstanding Eagleton's recourse to the language of sacrifice, that a universal humanist space can contain both Muslim and socialist visions of an imagined future, be it a socialist utopia or an imagined *umma*. So, perhaps Pecora is only partly right: contrapuntality may not be suited for a conversation between secular humanism and religious traditions; nevertheless it is pessimistic to assume that contrapuntality is not suited for a conversation between humanists of diverse traditions, Muslims and socialists, who de-hyphenate the secular from its humanist root. It may be true that postsecularism has not led the way to such an engagement but largely remains trapped in a belief that secularization merely needs to become more transparent to become engaged with diverse traditions, and secularism, as an administrative tool, more pluralistic. However, there is hope that the universalism at the root of humanism will be enriched by the universalism of Islam, which will lead the way in humanism's much needed de-secularization.

CONCLUSION

Universalization of
universes of resistance

The possibility of understanding is dramatized brilliantly by
Mohsin Hamid in *The Reluctant Fundamentalist*, shortlisted for the
2007 Booker Prize. The novel recounts the dramatic monologue
between Changez, a young Pakistani man who studies at Princeton and works for Underwood Samson, but breaks with the
anaemic capitalist world that both Eagleton and Žižek describe.
Throughout the novel only Changez speaks, as he tells to a silent
American listener his story of transformation from Wall Street
executive to a 'reluctant fundamentalist'.[1]

The relationship with Erica, which Changez spends considerable
time describing, demonstrates the violence of the Muslim encounter with the West. Erica is neurotic and hysterical, emotionally
unbalanced and scarred because of the death of her fiancée, Chris.
It is significant that Changez, who feels protective of her, can only
have sexual relations with her by taking on Chris's identity during
their sexual acts, for without this performance Erica is frigid: 'it
reminded me – unwillingly – of a wound, giving our sex a violent
undertone', and after, he says, 'I felt at once both *satiated* and
ashamed' (Hamid 2007: 106). Thus, only by the act of taking on

the identity of a dead lover can the physical relationship between Changez, the Muslim, and Erica, the West, actually occur. At the same time, this relationship facilitates Erica's self-destruction: she apparently starves herself to death (or at least disappears, since her death is not conclusive in the novel). Changez, then, brings on the suicide or disappearance of the West itself.[2]

Yet there is another relationship in this simply written but complex narrative: that between Changez and the nameless American, whom the reader knows only as Changez's silent audience. The conversation between the two men, often described through Changez's perceptions of his silent listener's body language, is based on a shared paranoia and suspicion, yet bound by a certain intimacy and even moments of trust, perhaps also representative of the relationship between Islam and the West. The choice of the dramatic monologue allegorizes the plight of the bad Muslim, who tells his story to an unresponsive and silent audience. Strangely, at the end of the novel, the American and Changez find themselves in an alley being approached by two menacing-looking men. The reader does not know if either of the characters will be a victim or not, and if so which one. Has the American brought Changez to his capture or has Changez brought the American to his demise? Has a conversation occurred and the men reached some type of mutual understanding and compromise? Or has Changez's monologue left the American unmoved? Is the possibility of resolution present in the act of narration itself?

In this book I have suggested that the narration of the figure of the jihadist, particularly over the past decade, offers a fertile area from which to launch an engagement between the supposed universals of Islam and the West. By highlighting the limits of current theory – particularly Orientalism, anti-Orientalism, cultural studies, postcolonialism and postsecularism – in theorizing the rupture presented by the jihadists' universalist discourse from simultaneously particular Islamic identities, I hope to encourage others to chart a way forward from here, where the disjunctures of theory are lessened by genuine contrapuntality that enables understanding. My approach has been to introduce texts that are diverse in genre and theoretical viewpoint and to demonstrate the persistent attempts made to insert the jihadist, as simultaneously an exotic and a familiar figure, into the discourse on the future of democracy, humanism, capitalism and multiculturalism. It is evident that *jihad* has 'travelled' a great deal over the past decade, through a variety of cultural configurations; but it is also evident that the conditions for comprehending it are just beginning to be born.

One of the central queries raised in this study is whether *jihad* is a commodity that is being circulated in a fully charged semiotic circuit, digested through First World interpretation and moderate Muslim interlocutors and regurgitated in a new, digestible form, or whether *jihad* is seriously remedying the political paralysis of radical critique. Two critical conclusions can be drawn. First, we have seen how the binary of secular and religious, prevalent in Said's own work, attaches itself to the newly established binary of 'good' and 'bad' Muslim, raising questions regarding the nature of representation, particularly when the 'bad' Muslims are clearly speaking for themselves. I have argued that it is evident that the global irruption of *jihad* has disrupted the postcolonial privileging of the seminal role of Third World interlocutors in the metropolitan centres, as theory has begun to shift to understanding the internal differences within the field of Islam, rather than merely the relationship of Islam to the metropolitan West. As such, the dethroning of the authority of Western First World intellectuals is a possible site for change. Second, *jihad*, with its insistence on the right and need to use violence to effect change, has raised critical questions about how radical critique has migrated from its radical roots in anti-imperialist movements to its home in secular, First World institutions. This allows a further investigation of how the institutional containment of critique might be usurped through trans-institutional and diverse networks of resistance.

It is important to note that the focus of this book has not been 'postcolonial terror', but *jihad*, a specifically self-defined form of religious violence that has been part of the very formation of postcolonial theory, and has also been largely responsible for the recent postsecular turn in theory towards the theological and the ethical. I argue that *jihad* presents a challenge to the secular bias of contemporary criticism, and subverts the underlying assumptions regarding the necessary representation and mediation of the 'subaltern' by Third World intellectuals located in the metropolitan centres of power. In the rhetoric of resistance on *jihad*, Muslims are assigned value by their position on the continuum of radicality – in other words, whether they are to trying to erase *jihad* as an embarrassing and misguided interpretation of their creed, or asserting the right to practise violent *jihad* to resist oppression. There have been active attempts by both Muslims and non-Muslims to assign the value of good to *al-jihad al-akbar* (the greater *jihad*) and align it with the need for *ijtihad*, or perhaps the secularization and modernization of Muslim societies, and the value of bad to *al-jihad al-asghar* (the lesser *jihad*) on account of its violent and spectacular attacks, misnamed 'suicide' bombings. Just as Said's secular and religious criticism is a displacement of East and West, the binary between 'good' and 'bad' Muslim is a reflection of the persistence of the perceived tension between the secular and the religious. The conditions for the deconstruction of this binary are only now being conceived, as the secular assumptions behind theory come under serious scrutiny and various Muslim theorists become more articulate in clarifying their indigenous theoretical vocabulary.

Giroux, perhaps more than any of the other theorists discussed in this book, notes that the spectacle of terrorism illustrates the degree to which the state and corporate power can be challenged,

while suggesting the importance of what it means to address
audiences through a political discourse:

> The spectacle of terrorism, if examined closely, provides some
> resources for rethinking how the political is connected to particular
> understandings of the social; how distinctive modes of address are
> used to marshal specific identities, memories and histories; and how
> certain pedagogical practices are employed to mobilize a range of
> affective investments around images of trauma and suffering. All
> of these issues raise important questions about how new circuits of
> power, technology, and visual production rearticulate the relationships
> between meaning and action, modes of information and agency, affect
> and collectivity, and the public and the private. (Giroux 2006: 72)

He is quick to point out, however, that this social form must be
reclaimed from the 'necropolitics' of the stateless terrorists (2006:
71). While Giroux applaudes democratic usage of technologies and
visual culture, it is only the *form* of this message that interests him,
not the *content* if it comes from jihadists, since then it 'has no vision
of the future outside of the culture of fear and the discourse of
risk' (2006: 77). While he argues there is need of a sober assessment
of democratic tendencies in Latin America, particularly Argentina,
Brazil and Venezuela, he makes no reference to any movements
across diverse Muslim countries, even those which do not include
the stateless jihadists. His failure to recognize the potential of
Muslim societies to spearhead exactly the types of revolution
that are currently sweeping the Arab world displays a deadening
deafness to the multiplicity of messages that have been contained
in the radical stance of the jihadists over the past decade.

Tariq Ramadan has played a critical role in synthesizing traditions of Islamism and humanism and positing a space, an abode
of testimony, where various universes of resistance can ally to
challenge power. But what are the catalysts for Giroux's and
Ramadan's anticipated solidarities? Are they to be formed through
Baudrillard's 'ruptural events', where the Real irrupts into the
virtual as 'the internal convulsion of history', events which 'appear
no longer the bearers of constructive disorder, but of an absolute

disorder'? (Baudrillard 2007: 126). Was 9/11 such a 'ruptural event' that in a series of sometimes loosely related effects has facilitated both the rupture of the 2010–11 Arab revolutions and the massive Occupy demonstrations across Europe and America?

In *The Terrorist in Search of Humanity* Devji takes a substantial risk in placing faith in radical militants to instigate a series of effects that could propel change. He argues that the real hope to carry change forward lies with the radicals who are capable of revolutionizing Islam more than their liberal counterparts, because their critique represents a kind of democratization, an acting without authority. He claims 'militants are much more creative in their religious thinking and much more imaginative in their means of propagating it' than Western Muslim interlocutors (Devji 2008: 200). Indeed, the 2010–11 militancy across the Arab world required no mediation from Muslim interlocutors living in the West; it has proved that Muslims living in predominantly Muslim countries are capable not only of representing themselves, but of leading global revolutionary – and sometimes violent – change.

At the time of writing, the Occupy movement is growing, and directly referencing the Arab revolutions as inspiration for its civil engagement; the movement remains as ideologically diverse as the struggling Arab revolutions. An often unrecognized fact is that while the Arab revolutions are not particularly Islamist in orientation, they did arise from societies where the Muslim social structure is intricately related to the possibility of revolution against the alienating spiritual and psychological effects of consumer-dominated individualistic capitalism. The struggle against injustice is the root of Muslim civil life, and the young revolutionaries who spearheaded the revolutions and the masses who are carrying them forward have been raised in this tradition. My point is that the revolutions do not need to turn to the principles of secular liberalism or the left to express their vision. The roots of the revolution are in Muslim societies, and therefore in the values of Islam, which are now being articulated to Western audiences through action, in a manner that has been impossible for the past decade under the oppression of the 'war on terror'.

If traditional Islamist political ideology belongs to the last generation, then the living Islam belongs to the present. The achievements of the revolutions thus far have been their re- markable capacity to package this living tradition in a universal language while querying the nature of the societies they envision. In Egypt, Libya and Tunisia, for example, discussions are taking place on the formation of 'civil' societies that are able to contain the diverse ethnic and religious communities of the region, but that are not secular in nature. In all the countries involved, Islam is informing the construction of new governments. This will not necessarily result in the formation of Islamic states, but will allow the necessary space for the people of the region to build governments which incorporate Islamic values into both internal governance and foreign policy. No doubt there is evidence that the ongoing uprisings are challenging the monopolies that both secular tyrants and conservative Islamists have long held on expressions of dissent. And theses fresh articulations are arising from within living Muslim traditions.

Notes

INTRODUCTION

1. The terms 'Islam' and 'the West' have become hopelessly inflammatory. In this study they are used not to agree with the geographical references to which they usually refer, but as imaginary ideological constructs. Much of the study will emphasize the instability of the sign of *jihad*.

2. The war of ideas has become a commonplace to describe the propaganda war between the United States government and Islamic radicals, and frequently appears in policy studies such as various RAND imprints and works by the Washington-based Strategic Studies Institute. Examples of how this terminology is used to describe the binary of *jihad* and democracy can be found in Kamien 2006 and Phares 2008.

3. An excellent overview of the various interpretations of the concept of *jihad* is offered in Esposito and Glenn 2007. Another useful overview source is Peters 1979. Esposito 1999a also provides excellent, in-depth analysis of the various interpretations of *jihad*.

4. Numerous sources attempt either to construct or deconstruct the connection between Wahhabism and al-Qaeda, as well as American involvement in the founding of al-Qaeda. For example, consider Wright 2006; Atwan 2006; Bergen 2001, 2006; Esposito 2002; Sageman 2004.

5. See, for example, Qutb 1964.

6. For example, see a variety of works by these two authors: Esposito 1999b, 2002; Esposito and Voll 2001; Roy 2004, 2008.

7. The term 'native informant' has been popularized in postcolonial studies by Spivak 1998. Spivak claims her purpose in that book is to problematize the figure of the native informant in contemporary theory. Although the aim

here is much less ambitious, the role of the native informant in representing revolutionary politics, as embodied in *jihad*, is a major subject of this study.
8. For Foucault, genealogy refers to how human practices and interpretations change. See particularly Foucault 1977. The contemporary emphasis on both the genealogy of terror and the intentionality of *jihad* counteracts the purely culturalist arguments of Huntington and Lewis, who consider that there is something inherently violent and irreducible in Islam that perpetrates terror.

CHAPTER I

1. Reference here is to Luyendijk's *People Like Us: Misrepresenting the Middle East*, which is a refreshingly personal account of the role of media in misrepresenting the Middle East (Luyendijk 2006).
2. Reports of marijuana being found near bin Laden's compound and the discovery of a vast collection of pornography, as well as a personal diary, have been released in various media sources. See, for example, *Huffington Post* 2011.
3. Various reports suggest that President Obama responded to the killing of bin Laden with the phrase 'We got him'. See, for example, www.cbsnews.com/8301-503544_162-20059009-503544.html.
4. Euben and Zaman provide an excellent discussion of bin Laden's formulation of the 'near' and 'far' enemy in their 'Usama bin Laden' (Euben and Zaman 2009b).
5. Various critics have described how bin Laden's messages have been considered heterodox by 'orthodox' scholars. See Devji 2005, 2008 for a full discussion.
6. See www.huffingtonpost.com/2011/09/12/mustafa-abdul-jalil-libya_n_959202. html.
7. In 'Moment of Opportunity', Obama refers to Ghonim directly: 'It's no coincidence that one of the leaders of Tahrir Square was an executive for Google' (Obama 2011a).

CHAPTER 2

1. For a thoroughgoing and thoughtful overview of globalization theory, see Kellner n.d. a, b, c; Robertson 1992; Turner 1994.
2. Perhaps the best example of this is Said's response to Huntington's 'Clash of Definitions' in *Reflections on Exile* (Said 2001: 569–90).
3. See particularly Majid 2004.
4. See www.irshadmanji.com.
5. Various websites have been set up by Muslims to refute Manji's claims. One of the most interesting and humorous is www.examinethetruth.com/manjism/ Irshad_Manji_propaganda.htm.
6. Gregory documents, for example, that Cubic Applications Inc., a contractor for support services for rehearsal exercises, had a contract valued at $375 million, which expired in 2007 and was renewed for the next ten years for $468 million. Similarly, the ICT was awarded a $45 million US Army contract in 1999, which was renewed in 2004 for another five years for $100 million, to produce videogames for training.

7. For complete coverage of the WikiLeaks story, see the *Secret Iraq Files* on http://english.aljazeera.net.
8. She argues that Western audiences have not heard of people like Vida Hajebi Tabrizi, Fariba Marzban, Nasrin Parvaz or Ashraf Dehghan – all political activists who struggled against and resisted both the Pahlavi tyranny and the Islamic Republic that succeeded it.
9. See the series of interviews at www.farnooshmoshiri.net.
10. For sample reviews, see www.reviewsofbooks.com/kite_runner.
11. See www.khaledhosseini.com/hosseini-bio.html.

CHAPTER 3

1. See http://explore.georgetown.edu/people/jle2.
2. See www.eui.eu/DepartmentsAndCentres/PoliticalAndSocialSciences/People/Professors/Roy.aspx.
3. Campus Watch is an organization led by Daniel Pipes which encourages students to report professors who demonstrate questionable views. It monitors and reports supposed radical discourse on the Middle East on American campuses. See www.campus-watch.org.
4. The Kharijites seceded from the 4th Caliph Ali, believing he was too weak, and developed a new theory of the Caliphate. Patton, at the end of the Second World War, wanted America to confront Germany and the Soviet Union.
5. While Andersen (1983) describes the imaginary homeland as a nationalist construction, Roy and others note the applicability of the term 'imaginary homeland' to internationalist yearning for an imagined better world, including that of Islamic militants.
6. See http://encyclopedia.jrank.org/articles/pages/5594/Bena-ssa-Slimane-1943.html.
7. Public opinion in EU countries generally opposes Turkish membership, though with varying degrees of intensity. The Eurobarometer September–October 2006 survey shows that 59 per cent of EU27 citizens are against Turkey joining the EU, while only some 28 per cent are in favour. European Commission, Eurobarometer 66 – Public Opinion in the European Union, September–October 2006. http://ec.europa.eu/public_opinion/archives/eb/eb66/eb66_en.pdf. Accessed 25 October 2010.

CHAPTER 4

1. Kahan and Kellner (2005) have documented how the 'Total Information Awareness Project' of the Bush administration, a government database, traced the web activities of individuals with a Big Brother surveillance enthusiasm.
2. For example, Žižek makes the absurd argument that Muslims do not use toilet paper because of the 'sacred status of writing' (Žižek 2008: 106).
3. See for example his 3 June 2011 address 'Do Not Rely on Others, Take [the Task] upon Yourself', available from MEMRI.
4. 'Required almsgiving that is one of the five pillars of Islam. Muslims with financial means are required to give 2.5% of their net worth annually as zahat' (Esposito 2003: 345).

CHAPTER 5

1. Anouar Majid replies to Spivak in the essay 'Can the Postcolonial Critic Speak?' (Majid 2000: 22–49).

2. Examples include Breckenbridge and van der Veer 1993, which applies Said's theory to South Asian societies; Kabbani 1988; Lewis 1996; Yegenoglu 1998. Kabbani, Lewis and Yegenoglu all offer feminist contributions to the debate.

3. As W.T.J. Mitchell notes, Said was 'endlessly chastising his would-be followers and younger colleagues for being slaves of fashion and for writing barbarous, jargon-ridden prose (2005: 5). As Spivak succinctly puts it, 'I think he often thought I was a fool, to be so persuaded by theory' (2005: 161).

4. For fuller discussion on Said's lack of engagement with Marxism, see Harootunian 2005; Brennan 2005.

5. Various excellent discussions of the Rushdie affair and the assertion of the secularist master narrative can be found in Majid 2000; Huggan 2001; Brennan 1989; Malak 2005.

6. Recent examples include the Danish cartoon crisis in 2005 and the Sudanese teddy bear incident in 2007, decontextualized to position the freedom-of-expression debate as the antithesis to Islamic totalitarianism.

7. Sardar and Davies (2002) take up this question articulated often by President George W. Bush, various politicians and commentators.

8. The government of Malaysia has organized two conferences on the subject 'Who Speaks for Islam, Who Speaks for the West' since 2002; the United Nations organized a High Level Group with the support of the governments of Spain and Turkey, produced reports and established a special secretariat in the Secretary General's office to explore the issue, offered programming and hosted dialogues; the governments of Canada and Britain have working groups to advise on Muslim relations; and numerous Middle Eastern states have hosted conferences and inter-faith dialogues which address these very issues.

9. Two very useful essays outline some of the arguments of a number of theorists referred to here: Robbins 1997; Viswanathan 1997.

10. This dichotomy is what Viswanathan has identified, I believe correctly, as Said's reinvention of secularism by including heterodoxy in his secular criticism as opposed to dogma. The difficulty, however, lies in the fact that heterodoxy and orthodoxy are deeply unstable categories, changing positions fluidly according to the rhetoric of the war on terror. The orthodox today can be the heterodox of tomorrow, or, perhaps even better put, what is considered as an Islamic orthodoxy in the West can be considered as heterodoxy in Muslim countries, and vice versa.

11. One of Sardar's earlier works was an Icon Books series serving as an introduction to cultural studies, in which he covered the major trends, suitable for an introductory course for undergraduate students: Sardar and Van Loon 1997.

12. The greater *jihad* or *al-jihad al-akbar* focuses on the inner struggle against the ego. The lesser *jihad* or *al-jihal al-asghar* is directed towards freedom from external oppression

13. Campus Watch launched a website to monitor US college campuses for academic pro-Palestinian bias and events. It publishes dossiers on professors, as well as examples of their writings, that it considers anti-American. Campus Watch also encourages students to report on professors and assist in publically highlighting anti-American biases. Horowitz 2006 is representative of this type of political harassment. See www.campus-watch.org.

CHAPTER 6

1. See, for example, BBC News 2004.
2. Hussein ibn ʿAī ibn Abī Ṭālib was the son of ʿAlī ibn Abī Ṭālib and Fātimah Zahrā (daughter of Prophet Muhammad). Hussein is an important figure in Islam, particularly for the Shia, since a seminal event in Shia history is his death in 680 CE at the Battle of Karbala.
3. Hamza ibn ʿAbdul-Muttalib was the paternal uncle of Prophet Muhammad. He died in the Battle of Uhud.
4. One third of the *qurban* of Eid is allocated to the poor, another third to friends and neighbours and the remaining to oneself.
5. In a lengthy article in the *New Republic*, liberal professor Paul Berman details the criticism of Ramadan's views and the criticism they foster. See Berman 2007.
6. Eagleton's references are to Ahmad 2008.

CONCLUSION

1. The narrative of disenchantment with the West is reminiscent of the classics of the growing canon of Muslim literature, such as Tayeb Salih's *Season of Migration to the North* (1969) and Taher ben Jelloun's *Solitaire* (1988). Ben Jelloun's Paris and Salih's London are reflected in Hamid's New York, particularly as women and cities become metaphors for the violence of colonization and postcolonial responses to it.
2. Read allegorically, the novel presents a familiar narrative in postcolonial Muslim fiction. The metaphorical relationship between white women and black men, representative of a larger relationship between the colonizer and the colonized, is theorized by Frantz Fanon in *Black Skin, White Masks*: 'When my restless hands caress these white breasts, they grasp white civilization and dignity and make them mine' (Fanon 1967: 63). Likewise, in *The Season of Migration to the North*, Mustafa Saeed, a Sudanese economist at the London School of Economics, also known as the Black Englishman, is put on trial for murdering a woman, his wife Jean Morris, and for contributing to the suicides of three other women. In his trial, Saeed articulates: 'I came as an intruder into your very homes: a drop of the poison that you have injected into the veins of history. I am no Othello. Othello was a lie' (Salih 1969: 95). In *Solitaire*, ben Jelloun's North African immigrant murders or imagines the murder of (the reader cannot be certain) an imaginary white woman whom he has constructed from images in magazines. In fact, murder, real or imaginary,

becomes a scene for the reconstruction of the self and nation in ben Jelloun and Salih. Hamid's book can be placed in this postcolonial Muslim literary tradition as it reflects on the difficulties of a conversation between Muslims and the West and on the role of violence in such mediation in a post-9/11 world.

References

3arabawy (2011). 'The Myth of Non-Violence'. *Arabawy.org*. 25 January. www. arabawy.org/2011/04/2011/suez-revolution. Accessed 16 May 2011.

Abdel-Malek, Anouar (2000). 'Orientalism in Crisis' (1963). In *Orientalism: A Reader*, ed A.L. MacFie, 47–53. Edinburgh: Edinburgh University Press.

Adams, Tim (2006). 'Portrait of the Terrorist as a Young Aesthete'. Review of John Updike's *Terrorist*. *Observer*, 23 July. www.guardian.co.uk/books/2006/jul/23/fiction.johnupdike. Accessed 6 January 2012.

Afsaruddin, Asma (2007). 'Jihad and its Multiple Meanings in the Early Period'. In *Understanding Jihad: Deconstructing Jihadism*, ed. John L. Esposito and Brian P. Glenn. Georgetown: Georgetown University Press.

Agamben, Giorgio (1998). *Homo Sacer: Sovereign Power and Bare Life*. Trans. Daniel Heller-Roazen. Stanford CA: Stanford University Press.

Ahiska, Meltem (2008). 'Orientalism/Occidentalism: The Impasse of Modernity'. In *Waiting for the Barbarians: A Tribute to Edward Said*, ed. Müge Gürsoy Sökmen and Başak Ertür, 137–54. London: Verso.

Ahmad, Aijaz (1994). *In Theory: Classes, Nations, and Literature*. London: Verso.

——— (2008). 'Islam, Islamism and the West'. *Socialist Register* 44: 1–37.

Ahmed, Akbar (1992). *Postmodernism and Islam: Predicament and Promise*. London: Routledge.

Al Jazeera (2010). 'Interview: Anwar al-Awlaki'. Al Jazeera. 11 February. http://english.aljazeera.net/focus/2010/02/2010271074776870.html. Accessed 10 October 2011.

al-Awlaki, Anwar (2009). '44 Ways to Support Jihad'. 5 February. www.nefafoundation.org/miscellaneous/FeaturedDocs/nefaawlaki44wayssupportjihad.pdf. Accessed 1 October 2011.

———— (2010a). 'A Call to Jihad'. *World Analysis.net*, 20 February. http://world-analysis.net/modules/news/article.php?storyid=1311. Accessed 15 October 2010.

———— (2010b). 'Interview: Anwar al-Awlaki'. Al Jazeera. 7 February. www.aljazeera.com/focus/2010/02/2010271074776870.html/t_blank.

al-Qaeda (2011). 'Al Qaeda Statement on Osama bin Laden's Death'. 6 May. www.reuters.com/article/2011/05/06/us-binladen-qaeda-confirmation-text. Accessed 10 July 2011.

Alatas, Syed Hussein. (1977). *The Myth of the Lazy Native*. London: Frank Cass.

Ali, Tariq (2002). *The Clash of Fundamentalisms: Crusades, Jihads and Modernity*. London: Verso.

———— (2006). *Conversations with Edward Said*. London: Seagull Books.

Almond, Ian (2007). *The New Orientalists: Postmodern Representations of Islam from Foucault to Baudrillard*. London: I.B. Tauris.

Anderson, Benedict (1983). *Imagined Communities: Reflections on the Origin and Spread of Nationalism*. London: Verso.

Andrejevic, Mark (2004). *Reality TV: The Work of Being Watched*. New York: Rowman & Littlefield.

Antonius, George (1938). *The Arab Awakening: The Story of the Arab National Movement*. London: Hamish Hamilton.

Appadurai, Arjun, ed. (1986). *The Social Life of Things: Commodities in Cultural Perspective*. Cambridge: Cambridge University Press.

Appiah, Kwame A. (1996). 'Is the Post- in Postmodernism the Post- in Postcolonial?' In *Contemporary Postcolonial Theory: A Reader*, ed. Padmini Mongia, 55–71. London: Arnold.

Asad, Talal (2003). *Formations of the Secular: Christianity, Islam, Modernity*. Stanford CA: Stanford University Press.

———— (2007). *On Suicide Bombing*. New York: Columbia University Press.

————, Wendy Brown, Judith Butler and Mahmood, Sabah (2009). *Is Critique Secular? Blasphemy, Injury, and Free Speech*. Berkeley: University of California Press.

Atassi, Mohammed Ali (2011). 'What the People Want.' *Perspectives* 2, 'People's Power: The Arab World in Revolt', May: 28–34. http://lb.boell.org/web/52-579.html.

Atwan, Abdel Bari (2006). *The Secret History of al Qaeda*. Berkeley CA: University of California Press.

Atwood, Margaret (2004). 'Headscarves to Die For'. *New York Times*, 15 August. www.nytimes.com/2004/08/15/books/headscarves-to-die-for.html?pagewanted=all&src=pm. Accessed 26 July 2008.

Baudrillard Jean (1994). *Simulacra and Simulation*. Trans. Sheila Faria Glaser. Ann Arbor: University of Michigan Press.

———— (2002). *The Spirit of Terrorism*. Trans. Chris Turner. London: Verso.

———— (2003). 'The Violence of the Global'. Trans. François Debrix. *C-Theory. net*. 20 April. www.ctheory.net/text_file.asp?pick=385. Accessed 21 October 2010.

———— (2004). 'This is the Fourth World War: The *Der Spiegel* Interview with Jean Baudrillard'. *International Journal of Baudrillard Studies* 1 (1) (January). www.ubishops.ca/baudrillardstudies/vol1_1.htm. Accessed 3 September 2010.

————(2005a). *The Gulf War Did Not Take Place*. Trans. Paul Patton. Bloomington IN: University of Indiana Press, 2005.

———— (2005b). *The Intelligence of Evil or the Lucidity Pact*. Trans. Chris Turner. New York: Berg.

Bayat, Asef (2011). 'A New Arab Street in Post-Islamist Times'. *Perspectives 2*, 'People's Power: The Arab World in Revolt', May: 50–53. http://lb.boell. org/web/52-579.html.

BBC News (2004). 'Full text: "Al-Qaeda" Madrid claim'. BBC News online, 14 March. http://news.bbc.co.uk/2/hi/europe/3509556.stm. Accessed 21 April 2007.

ben Jelloun, Tahar (1988). *Solitaire*. Trans. Dareth Stanton and Nick Hindley. London: Quartet.

Benaïssa, Slimane (2004). *The Last Night of a Damned Soul*. Trans. Janice and Daniel Gross. New York: Grove Press.

Bergen, Peter (2001). *Holy War, Inc.: Inside the Secret World of Osama bin Laden*. New York: Free Press.

———— (2006). *The Osama bin Laden I Know: An Oral History of al Qaeda's Leader*. New York: Free Press.

Berman, Paul (2007). 'Who's Afraid of Tariq Ramadan'. *New Republic*, 4 June. www.tnr.com/article/who%E2%80%99s-afraid-tariq-ramadan. Accessed 28 October 2010.

Bhabha, Homi (2005). 'Adagio'. *Edward Said: Continuing the Conversation*, ed. Homi Bhabha and W.J.T. Mitchell, 7–16. Chicago: University of Chicago Press.

Bigrami, Akeel (1992). 'What is a Muslim? Fundamental Commitment and Cultural Identity'. *Critical Inquiry* 18 (Summer): 821–42.

bin Laden, Osama (2005a). 'Nineteen Students'. In *Messages to the World: Statements of Osama bin Laden*, ed. Bruce Lawrence, 145–57. London: Verso.

———— (2005b). 'To the Americans'. In *Messages to the World: Statements of Osama Bin Laden*, ed. Bruce Lawrence, 160–72. London: Verso.

———— (2005c). 'The Towers of Lebanon'. In *Messages to the World: Statements of Osama Bin Laden*, ed. Bruce Lawrence, 237–44. London: Verso.

———— (2007). '"The Solution" – A Video Speech from Usama bin Laden Addressing the American People on the Occasion of the Sixth Anniversary of 9/11 – 9/2007'.SITE Intelligence Group. 7 September. http://counterterrorism-blog.org/site-resources/images/SITE-OBL-transcript.pdf. Accessed November 2010.

———— (2008). 'Bin Laden's Interviews'. In *Al Qaeda in Its Own Words*, ed. Gilles Kepel and Jean-Pierre Milelli. Trans. Pascale Ghazaleh. Cambridge MA: Belknap, Harvard University Press.

———— (2009a). 'Declaration of War against the Americans Occupying The Land of the Two Holy Places'. In *Princeton Readings in Islamist Thought*, ed. Roxanne L. Euben and Muhammad Qasim Zaman, 436–59. Princeton NJ: Princeton University Press.

———— (2009b). 'Transcript: The Latest Bin Laden Statement (September 2009)'. EA Worldview Archives, 15 September. www.enduringamerica.com/september-2009/2009/9/15/transcript-the-latest-bin-laden-statement-september-2009.html. Accessed 22 October 2010.

———— (2011). 'Osama bin Laden's Last Statement'. *New York Times* online, 18 May. www.nytimes.com/2011/05/19/world/middleeast/19binladen.html?_r=1. Accessed 6 June 2011.

Boehmer, Elleke, and Stephen Morton, eds (2010). *Terror and the Postcolonial*. Chichester: Wiley–Blackwell.

Bourdieu, Pierre (1993). *The Field of Cultural Production*. New York: Columbia University Press, 1993.

Bradshaw, Peter (2006). 'Review of *Paradise Now.*' *Guardian*, 14 April. www.guardian.co.uk/culture/2006/apr/14/4. Accessed 10 May 2006.

Brauchli, Christopher (2010). 'The Arms Sale Economy'. *Counterpunch*, 22–24 October. www.counterpunch.org/brauchli10222010.html. Accessed 25 October.

Breckenridge, Carol and Peter van der Veer, eds (1993). *Orientalism and the Postcolonial Predicament: Perspectives on South Asia*. Philadelphia PA: University of Philadelphia Press.

Brennan, Timothy (1989). *Salman Rushdie and the Third World: Myths of the Nation*. New York: St Martin's Press.

———— (2005). 'Resolution'. In *Edward Said: Continuing the Conversation*, ed. Homi Bhabha and W.J.T. Mitchell, 43–55. Chicago: University of Chicago Press.

———— (2008). 'The Making of a Counter-Tradition'. *Waiting for the Barbarians: A Tribute to Edward Said*, ed. Müge Gürsoy Sökmen and Basak Ertür, 3–14. London: Verso.

Butler, Judith (2004). *Precarious Lives: The Power of Mourning and Violence*. London: Verso.

CBS (2001). 'Prominent American Muslims Denounce Terror Committed in the Name of Islam'. Interview with Ed Bradley. *60 Minutes*, 30 September. www.islamfortoday.com/60minutes.htm. Accessed 22 October 2009.

Chérif, Mustapha (2008). *Islam and the West: A Conversation with Jacques Derrida*. Trans. Teresa Lavender Fagan. Chicago: University of Chicago Press.

Chomsky, Noam (2001). *9-11*. New York: Seven Stories Press.

———— (2011a). 'My Reaction to bin Laden's Death'. *Guernica*, 6 May. www.guernicamag.com/blog/2652/noam_chomsky_my_reaction_to_os. Accessed 12 May 2011.

———— (2011b). 'There Is Much More to Say.' *Znet*, 20 May. Accessed 20 May 2011.

Clarke, J.J. (1997). *Oriental Enlightenment: The Encounter between Asian and Western Thought*. London: Routledge.

Clifford, J. (1988). *The Predicament of Culture*. Cambridge MA: Harvard University Press.

CNN (2008). 'Azzam the American Releases Video Focusing on Pakistan'. CNN.com. 4 October. http://edition.cnn.com/2008/WORLD/asiapcf/10/04/gadahn.video/index.html. Accessed 12 October 2009.

Commins, David (2006). *The Wahhabi Mission and Saudi Arabia*. London: I.B. Tauris.

Cole, August (2009). 'Afghan Contractors Outnumber Troops'. *Wall Street Journal*, 22 August. http://online.wsj.com/article/SB125089638739950599.html. Accessed 20 October 2010.

Crooke, Alastair (2009). *Resistance: The Essence of the Islamist Revolution*. London: Pluto Press.

Dabashi, Hamid (2006). 'Native Informers and the Making of the New American Empire'. *Al-Ahram Weekly*, No. 797, 1–7 June. http://weekly.ahram.org. eg/2006/797/special.htm. Accessed 15 July 2009.

——— (2011). 'Delayed Defiance'. Al Jazeera, 26 February. http://english.aljazeera. net/indepth/opinion/2011/02/2011224123527547203.html. Accessed 1 March 2011.

DeLillo, Don (1992). *Mao II*. New York: Penguin.

——— (2007). *Falling Man*. New York: Scribner.

Derrida, Jacques (1994). *Specters of Marx: The State of the Debt, the Work of Mourning, and the New International*. Trans. Peggy Kamuf. New York: Routledge.

Devji, Faisal (2005). *Landscapes of the Jihad: Militancy, Morality, Modernity*. London: Hurst.

——— (2008). *The Terrorist in Search of Humanity: Militant Islam and Global Politics*. New York: Columbia University Press.

——— (2011). 'Politics after Al Qaeda'. Policy paper. Conflicts Forum. July 2011. http://conflictsforum.org/briefings/DrFaisalDevji-PolicyPaper-July2011.pdf. Accessed 1 October 2011.

Dirlik, Arif (1994). 'The Postcolonial Aura: Third World Criticism in the Age of Global Capitalism.' *Critical Inquiry* 20 (2): 328–56.

Donnelley, Paul (2002). 'Tariq Ramadan: The Muslim Martin Luther?' *Salon*, 15 February. www.salon.com/2002/02/15/ramadan_2/. Accessed 17 May 2005.

Drabble, Margaret (2001). 'Why Authors Need a Refuge'. *Guardian*, 8 December. www.guardian.co.uk/books/2001/dec/08/politics. Accessed 10 June 2009.

Eagleton, Terry (2003). *After Theory*. New York: Basic Books.

——— (2005a). 'A Different Way of Death'. *Guardian*, 26 January. www.guardian. co.uk/comment/story/0,3604,1398445,00.html. Accessed 19 June 2008.

——— (2005b). *Unholy Terror*. Oxford: Oxford University Press.

——— (2009). *Reason, Faith and Revolution: Reflections on the God Debate*. New Haven CT and London: Yale University Press.

——— (2011). 'The Scandal of Faith'. *Socialist Review*, September. www.socialist review.org.uk/article.php?articlenumber=11771. Accessed 5 October 2011.

Edemariam, Aida (2006). '"I Want to Continue the Life I Had Before": Interview with Orhan Pamuk'. *Guardian*, 3 April. www.guardian.co.uk/books/2006/ apr/03/fiction.turkey. Accessed 25 October 2010.

El-Ariss, Tarek (2007). 'The Making of an Expert: The Case of Irshad Manji'. *Muslim World* 97 (1) (January): 83–110.

Eley, Tom (2009). 'U.N. Record Number of Afghan Civilian Deaths in 2009'. *World Socialist Website*, 28 September. www.wsws.org/articles/2009/sep2009/afgh-s28. shtml. Accessed 30 October 2009.

Engelhardt, Tom (2011). 'Osama Bin Laden's American Legacy.' 5 May. www. tomdispatch.com/archive/175388. Accessed 20 May 2011.

Esposito, John L., ed. (1999a). *The Oxford History of Islam*. Oxford: Oxford University Press.

——— (1999b). *Islamic Threat: Myth or Reality?* Oxford: Oxford University Press.

———— (2002). *Unholy War: Terror in the Name of Islam*. Oxford: Oxford University Press.

———— (2003). *The Oxford Dictionary of Islam*. Oxford: Oxford University Press.

———— (2007). 'Jihad: Holy or Unholy War?' In *Understanding Jihad: Deconstructing Jihadism*, ed. John Esposito and Brian P. Glenn. Georgetown: Georgetown University Press.

Esposito, John L., and Brian P. Glenn, eds (2007). *Understanding Jihad: Deconstructing Jihadism*. Georgetown: Georgetown University Press.

Esposito, John L., and Dalia Mogahed (2007). *Who Speaks for Islam? What a Billion Muslims Really Think*. New York: Gallup Press.

Esposito, John L., and John O. Voll (1996). *Islam and Democracy*. Oxford: Oxford University Press.

———— (2001). *Makers of Contemporary Islam*. Oxford: Oxford University Press.

Euben, Roxanne L., and Muhammad Qasim Zaman (2009a). 'Introduction'. In *Princeton Readings in Islamist Thought*, ed. Roxanne L. Euben and Muhammad Qasim Zaman, 1–46. Princeton NJ: Princeton University Press.

———— (2009b). 'Usama bin Laden'. In *Princeton Readings in Islamist Thought*, ed. ed. Roxanne L. Euben and Muhammad Qasim Zaman, 425–35. Princeton NJ: Princeton University Press.

European Commission (2007). 'Eurobarometer 66 – Public Opinion in the European Union Sept–Oct 2006', September. http://ec.europa.eu/public_opinion/archives/eb/eb66/eb66_en.pdf. Accessed 25 October 2010.

Fadel, Mohammed (2007). 'Jihad in the Modern World: A Look at Twentieth Century Egyptian Views on Jihad'. In *Understanding Jihad: Deconstructing Jihadism*, ed. John L. Esposito and Brian P. Glenn. Georgetown: Georgetown University Press.

Faith without Fear (2007). America at a Crossroads (PBS series). Narrated by Irshad Manji. WETA, Washington DC. Film.

Fanon, Frantz (1963). *The Wretched of the Earth*. Trans. Constance Farrington. New York: Grove Press.

———— (1965). *A Dying Colonialism*. Trans. H. Chevalier. New York: Grove Press.

———— (1967). *Black Skin, White Masks*. Trans. Charles Lam Markman. New York: Grove Press.

Foucault, Michel (1972). *The Archeology of Knowledge*. Trans. A.M. Sheridan Smith, New York: Pantheon.

———— (1977). *Language, Counter-Memory, Practice: Selected Essays and Interviews*, ed. Donald F. Bouchard. Ithaca NY: Cornell University Press.

———— (1984). *The Foucault Reader*, ed. Paul Rabinow. New York: Pantheon.

Four Lions (2010). Film. Dir. Chris Morris. Warp Films.

Friedman, Thomas (2003). *Longitudes and Attitudes: The World in the Age of Terrorism*. New York: Anchor Books.

———— (2011a). 'This is Just the Start'. *New York Times*, 1 March: A5.

———— (2011b). 'I am a Man'. *New York Times*, 1 May: WK10.

———— (2011c). 'Bibi and Barak'. *New York Times*, 18 May: A19.

———— (2011d). 'Pay Attention'. *New York Times*, 29 May: WK8.

———— (2011e). 'All Together Now'. *New York Times*, 28 August: SR11.

Fukuyama, Francis (1992). *The End of History and the Last Man*. New York: Avon Books.

Gadahn, Adam (2006). 'Invitation to Islam'. Special Dispatch No. 1281, Middle East Media Research Institute, 6 September. www.memri.org/report/en/o/o/o/o/o/o/1867.htm. Accessed 12 October 2008.

Giroux, Henry A. (2004). *The Terror of Neo-liberalism: Authoritarianism and the Eclipse of Democracy*. Boulder CO: Paradigm.

———(2006). *Beyond the Spectacle of Terrorism: Global Uncertainty and the Challenge of the New Media*. Boulder CO: Paradigm.

Goldman, David P. (2011). 'Osama: A Casualty of the Arab Revolt'. *Asia Times online*, 3 May. www.atimes.com/atimes/South_Asia/ME03Df02.html. Accessed 6 September 2011

Gould, Eric D., and Esteban F. Klor, (2010). 'Does Terrorism Work?' *Social Science Research Network*, 11 January. http://economics.huji.ac.il/facultye/klor/DTW. pdf. Accessed 10 October 2010.

Gregory, Derek (2008). 'The Rush to the Intimate: Counterinsurgency and the Cultural Turn'. *Radical Philosophy* 150 (July/August), pp. 8–23.

Gurría-Quintana, Ángel (2005). 'Orhan Pamuk, The Art of Fiction No. 187'. *Paris Review* 175 (Fall/Winter). www.theparisreview.org/interviews/5587/the-art-of-fiction-no-187-orhan-pamuk. Accessed 1 November 2010.

Hardt, Michael, and Antonio Negri (2011). 'Arabs Are Democracy's New Pioneers'. *Guardian*, 24 February. www.guardian.co.uk/commentisfree/2011/feb/24/arabs-democracy-latin-america. Accessed 26 February 2011.

Harootunian, Harry (2005). 'Conjectural Traces: Said's "Inventory'. In *Edward Said: Continuing the Conversation*, ed. Homi Bhabha and W.J.T. Mitchell, 68–79. Chicago: University of Chicago Press.

———(2008). 'Said's Antinomies'. In *Waiting for the Barbarians: A Tribute to Edward Said*, ed Müge Gürsoy Sökmen and Basak Ertür, 155–63. London: Verso.

Hart, William D. (2000). *Edward Said and the Religious Effects of Culture*. Cambridge: Cambridge University Press.

Hashmi, Sohail H. (2007). 'Classical Conceptions of Jihad'. In *Understanding Jihad: Deconstructing Jihadism*, ed. John L. Esposito and Brian P. Glenn. Georgetown: Georgetown University Press.

Herman, Edward S., and Noam Chomsky (1988). *Manufacturing Consent: The Political Economy of the Mass Media*. New York: Pantheon.

Hoffman, Bruce (1998). *Inside Terrorism*. New York: Columbia University Press.

Horowitz, David (2006). *The Professors: The 101 Most Dangerous Academics in America*. Washington DC: Regnery Publishing.

Hosseini, Khalid (2003). *The Kite Runner*. New York: Riverhead Books.

———(2007). *A Thousand Splendid Suns*. Toronto: Penguin.

Houen, Alex (2002). *Terrorism and Modern Literature*. Oxford: Oxford University Press.

——— (2010). 'Sacrificial Militancy and the Wars around Terror'. In Elleke Boehmer and Stephen Morton, eds, *Terror and the Postcolonial*. Chichester: Wiley–Blackwell: 113–40.

Huffington Post (2011). 'Osama Bin Laden's Pakistani Compound's Most Shocking Revelations'. *Huffington Post*, 14 May. www.huffingtonpost.com/2011/05/14/

osama-bin-laden-pakistan-compound-shocking-discoveries_n_861752.html#
undefined.
Huggan, Graham (2001). *The Postcolonial Exotic: Marketing the Margins*. New York:
Routledge.
Huntington, Samuel P. (2003). *The Clash of Civilizations and the Remaking of World
Order*. New York: Simon & Schuster.
Ibn Warraq (1995). *Why I am Not a Muslim*. New York: Prometheus Books.
———— (2007). *Defending the West: A Critique of Edward Said's Orientalism*. New
York: Prometheus.
———— (2010). 'One Imam, Multiple Messages'. *National Review*, 13 September.
Jeffries, Stuart (2005). 'Reader, I'm a He'. *Guardian*, 22 June. www.guardian.
co.uk/books/2005/jun/22/france.world. Accessed 25 July 2009.
Jenkins, Brian Michael (2004). 'Does Terrorism Work?' *Mercury News*, 21 March.
www.rand.org/commentary/2004/03/21/SJMN.html. Accessed 1 October
2009.
Jurgensmeyer, Mark (2000). 'Understanding the New Terrorism'. *Current History:
A Journal of Contemporary World Affairs* 99 (April): 158–63.
Kabbani, Rana (1988). *Imperial Fictions: Europe's Myths of Orient*. London:
Pandora.
Kahan, Richard, and Kellner, Douglas (2005). 'Internet Sub Cultures and Opposi-
tional Politics'. *Cultural Politics* 1 (1). http://gseis.ucla.edu/faculty/kellner/essays/
internetsubculturesoppositionalpolitics.pdf. Accessed 13 September 2006.
Kamien, David (2006). *The McGraw–Hill Homeland Security Handbook*. New York:
McGraw–Hill.
Kaplan, Amy (2002). *The Anarchy of Empire in the Making of U.S. Culture*. Cambridge
MA: Harvard University Press.
Karol, David, and Edward Miguel (2007). 'The Electoral Cost of War: Iraq Casual-
ties and the 2004 American Election'. *Journal of Politics* 69 (3) (August): 633–48.
http://onlinelibrary.wiley.com/doi/10.1111/j.1468–2508.2007.00564.x/abstract.
Accessed 1 November 2010.
Kawash, Samira (1999). 'Terrorists and Vampires: Fanon's Spectral Violence of
Decolonization.' In *Frantz Fanon: Critical Perspectives*, ed. Anthony C. Ales-
sandrini, 235–57. London: Routledge.
Kellner, Douglas (2002a). 'Theorizing Globalization'. http://pages.gseis.ucla.edu/
faculty/kellner/papers/theoryglob.htm. Accessed 20 October 2010.
———— (2002b). 'Theorizing September 11: Social Theory, History, and Globalization'. http://pages.gseis.ucla.edu/faculty/kellner/essays/theorizingsept11essay.
pdf. Accessed 12 October 2010.
———— (2003). 'Globalization, Terrorism, and Democracy: 9/11 and its Aftermath'.
Accessed 12 September 2010. www.gseis.ucla.edu/faculty/kellner/papers/GLO-
BOTY2003.htm#_edn1.
———— (2004). 'Baudrillard, Globalization and Terrorism: Some Comments on
Recent Adventures of the Image and Spectacle on the Occasion of Baudrillard's
75th Birthday'. http://pages.gseis.ucla.edu/faculty/kellner/essays/baudrillard-
globalizationterror.pdf.
———— (2005). *Media Spectacle and the Crisis of Democracy*. Boulder CO: Paradigm
Publishers.

————— (2007). 'Dialectics of Globalization: From Theory to Practice'. http:// gseis.ucla.edu/faculty/kellner/essays/2007_Kellner_DialecticsGlobaltoPrac07. Accessed 19 October 2010.

Kepel, Gilles (2011). 'Bin Laden Was Dead Already'. *New York Times*, 7 May: WK10.

Keshavarz, Fatemeh (2007). *Jasmine and Stars: Reading More than Lolita in Tehran*. Columbia SC: University of North Carolina Press.

Khadra, Yasmina (2003). *Wolf Dreams*. Trans. Linda Black. London: Toby Press.

————— (2004). *The Swallows of Kabul*. Trans. John Kullen. New York: Doubleday.

————— (2006). *The Attack*. Trans. John Cullen. New York: Doubleday.

————— (2007). *The Sirens of Baghdad*. Trans. John Cullen. New York: Doubleday.

Khan, Mohammed Siddique (2005). 'London Bomber: Text in Full'. BBC News online, 1 September. http://news.bbc.co.uk/2/hi/uk_news/4206800.stm. Accessed 23 November 2007.

————— (2008). 'New7/7 Bomber Video'. MSN News, 24 April. http://video. msn.com/video.aspx?mkt=en-gb&vid=10c08352-347c-4cb1-ad9e-5d50d45483ed. Accessed 15 November 2009.

Khoury, Doreen (2011). 'Social Media and the Revolutions'. *Perspectives* 2, 'People's Power: The Arab World in Revolt', May: 80–85. www.lb.boell.org/downloads/ Perspectives_02-12_Doreen_Khoury.pdf.

Laqueur, Walter (2003). *No End to War: Terrorism in the Twenty-First Century*. New York: Continuum.

Laroui, Abdallah (1976). *The Crisis of the Arab Intellectual: Traditionalism or Historicism*. Berkeley: University of California Press.

Leonard, John (2006). 'Rabbit is Radical'. *New York Magazine*, 5 June. http://nymag. com/arts/books/reviews/17120/. Accessed 7 August 2007.

Lewis, Bernard (1990). 'Roots of Muslim Rage'. *The Atlantic* 266 (September). www. theatlantic.com/magazine/archive/1990/09/the-roots-of-muslim-rage/4643. Accessed 12 March 2005.

————— (2002). *What Went Wrong? The Clash between Modernity and Islam in the Middle East*. New York: HarperCollins.

————— (2004). *The Crisis of Islam: Holy War and Unholy Terror*. New York: Random House.

Lewis, Reina (1996). *Gendering Orientalism: Race, Femininity and Representation*. London: Routledge.

Litt, Toby (2007). 'The Trembling Air'. Review of De Lillo's *Falling Man*. *Guardian*, 26 May. www.guardian.co.uk/books/2007/may/26/fiction.dondelillo. Accessed 9 August 2008.

Little, Donald (2000). 'Three Arab Critiques of Orientalism' (1979). In *Orientalism: A Reader*, ed. A.L. MacFie. Edinburgh: Edinburgh University Press: 123–41.

Lockman, Zachary (2005). *Contending Visions of the Middle East: The History and Politics of Orientalism*. London: Hurst.

Lumbard, Joseph, ed. (2004). *Islam, Fundamentalism and the Betrayal of Tradition: Essays by Western Scholars*. Bloomington IN: World Wisdom.

Lütticken, Sven (2009). 'Monotheism and the New Image Wars'. In *The Aesthetics of Terror*, ed. Manon Slome, Joshua Simon, and Eric Stryker. Milan: Edizioni Charta: 48–53.

Luyendijk, Joris (2006). *People Like Us: Misrepresenting the Middle East*. Trans. Michele Hutchinson. New York: Soft Skull Press.

MacFie, A.L. (2002). *Orientalism*. London: Longman.

———, ed. (2000). *Orientalism: A Reader*. Edinburgh: Edinburgh University Press.

MacKenzie, John M. (1995). *Orientalism: History, Theory and the Arts*. Manchester: Manchester University Press.

Majid, Anouar (2000). *Unveiling Traditions: Postcolonial Islam in a Polycentric World*. Durham NC: Duke University Press, 2000.

——— (2004). *Freedom and Orthodoxy: Islam and Difference in the Post-Andalusian Age*. Stanford CA: Stanford University Press.

——— (2007). *A Call for Heresy*. Minneapolis: University of Minnesota Press.

Makdisi, Saree (2008). 'Edward Said and the Style of the Public Intellectual'. In *Waiting for the Barbarians: A Tribute to Edward Said*, ed. Müge Gürsoy Sökmen and Basak Ertür, 53–65. London: Verso.

Malak, Amin (2005). *Muslim Narratives and the Discourse of English*. New York: State University of New York Press.

Mamdani, Mahmood (1995). *Good Muslim, Bad Muslim: America, the Cold War and the Roots*. Manchester: Manchester University Press.

——— (2008). 'On Blasphemy, Bigotry, and the Politics of Culture Talk'. In *Waiting for the Barbarians: A Tribute to Edward Said*, ed. Müge Gürsoy Sökmen and Basak Ertür, 176–83. London: Verso.

Manji, Irshad (2003). *The Trouble with Islam Today*. Toronto: Vintage.

McGrath, Charles (2006). 'In "Terrorist," a Cautious Novelist Takes on a New Fear'. *New York Times*, 31 May. www.nytimes.com/2006/05/31/books/31updi. html?_r=3&oref=slogin&oref=slogin. Accessed 9 October 2008.

Milvy, Erika (2007). 'The "Kite Runner" Controversy'. *Salon*, 9 December. www. salon.com/2007/12/09/hosseini. Accessed 3 June 2009.

Mitchell, W.T.J. (2005). 'Secular Divination: Edward Said's Humanism'. In *Edward Said: Continuing the Conversation*, ed. Homi Bhabha and W.J.T. Mitchell, 99–108. Chicago: University of Chicago Press.

Moshiri, Farnoosh (2001). *The Bath House*. Boston MA: Beacon Press.

Mufti, Aamir R. (2005). 'Global Comparativism'. In *Edward Said: Continuing the Conversation*, ed. Homi Bhabha and W.J.T. Mitchell, 109–26. Chicago: University of Chicago Press.

Nafisi, Azar (2004). *Reading Lolita in Tehran: A Memoir in Books*. London: Harper Collins.

Newsmax.com (2008). 'French Prisons: Up to 70% of Inmates Are Muslims'. *Newsmax.com*, 28 April. http://newsmax.com/InsideCover/French-Prisons-muslims/2008/04/29/id/323551. Accessed 10 November 2009.

Obama, Barack (2011a). 'Moment of Opportunity'. 19 May. www.whitehouse. gov/the-press-office/2011/05/19/remarks-president-barack-obama-prepared-deli very-moment-opportunity. Accessed 9 September 2011.

——— (2011b). 'Remarks by the President at the AIPAC Policy Conference 2011'. 22 May. www.whitehouse.gov/the-press-office/2011/05/22/remarks-president-aipac-policy-conference-2011. Accessed 22 May 2011.

O'Rourke, Meghan (2005). '*The Kite Runner*: Do I Really Have to Read It?' *Slate*,

25 July. www.slate.com/articles/news_and_politics/the_highbrow/2005/07/
the_kite_runner.html. Accessed 12 September 2007.

Pamuk, Orhan (2004). *Snow*. Trans. Maureen Freely. New York: Alfred A.
Knopf.

Pape, Robert A. (2005). *Dying to Win: The Strategic Logic of Suicide Terrorism*. New
York: Random House.

Pappé, Ilan (2008). 'The Saidian Fusion of Horizons'. *Waiting for the Barbarians:
A Tribute to Edward Said*, ed. Müge Gürsoy Sökmen and Basak Ertür, 83–92.
London: Verso.

Paradise Now (2005). Film. Dir. Hany abu Asad. Warner Independent Pictures.

Pearson, Keith Ansell, Benita Parry and Judith Squires (1997). *Cultural Readings
of Imperialism: Edward Said and the Gravity of History*. London: Lawrence &
Wishart.

Pecora, Vincent P. (2006). *Secularization and Cultural Criticism: Religion, Nation and
Modernity*. Chicago: University of Chicago Press.

Peters, Rudolph (1979). *Islam and Colonialism: The Doctrine of Jihad in Modern History*.
Mouton: The Hague.

Phares, Walid (2008). *The War of Ideas: Jihadism against Democracy*. New York:
Palgrave Macmillan.

Piore, Adam (2004). 'The Death of Humanity: A Bleak Portrait of Life under the
Murderous Taliban: *The Swallows of Kabul*'. *Newsweek International*, 28 March.
www.newsweek.com/2004/03/28/the-death-of-humanity.html. Accessed 25
July 2009.

Qureshi, Emran, and Michael A. Sells (2003). *The New Crusades: Constructing the
Muslim Enemy*. New York: Columbia University Press.

Qutb, Sayed (1964). *Ma'alim fi al-Tariq* [*Milestones*]. Cairo: Kazi Publications. Available in English at http://majalla.org/books/2005/qutb-nilestone.pdf.

Rabbani, Mouin (2011). 'The Arab Revolts: Ten Tentative Observations'. *Perspectives*
2, 'People's Power: The Arab World in Revolt', May: 10–13. www.lb.boell.
org/downloads/Perspectives_02-01_Mouin_Rabbani.pdf.

Ramadan, Tariq (1999). *To Be a European Muslim*. Leicester: Islamic Foundation.

——— (2001). *Islam, the West and the Challenges of Modernity*. Leicester: Islamic
Foundation.

——— (2004). *Western Muslims and the Future of Islam*. Oxford: Oxford University
Press.

——— (2007). *The Messenger: The Meanings of the Life of Muhammad*. London:
Allen Lane.

——— (2009). *Radical Reform: Islamic Ethics and Liberation*. Oxford: Oxford University Press.

——— (2010). *What I Believe*. Oxford: Oxford University Press.

Rauf, Imam Feisal Abdul (2004). *What's Right with Islam is What's Right with America*.
New York: HarperCollins.

Redfield, Marc (2009). *The Rhetoric of Terror: Reflections on 9/11 and the War on Terror*.
New York: Fordham University Press.

Rich, Frank (2007). 'The Clear Blue Sky'. Review of DeLillo's *Falling Man*. *New
York Times*, 27 May. www.nytimes.com/2007/05/27/books/review/Rich-t.
html?pagewanted=1. Accessed 3 August 2008.

Risen, James (2008). 'Use of Iraq Contractors Costs Billions, Report Says'. *New York Times*, 11 August. www.nytimes.com/2008/08/12/washington/12contractors. html?_r=1. Accessed 25 October 2010.

Robbins, Bruce (1997). 'Secularism, Elitism, Progress and Other Transgressions'. In *Cultural Readings of Imperialism: Edward Said and the Gravity of History*, ed. Keith Ansell Pearson, Benita Parry and Judith Squires, 67–87. London: Lawrence & Wishart.

Robertson, Roland (1992). *Globalization: Social Theory and Global Culture*. London: Sage.

Rodinson, Maxime (1987). *Europe and the Mystique of Islam*. Trans. Roger Veinus. Seattle: University of Washington Press.

Roy, Olivier (2004). *Globalised Islam: The Search for a New Ummah*. London: Hearst.

———— (2008). *The Politics of Chaos in the Middle East*. New York: Columbia University Press.

———— (2011a). 'The Tunisian Revolt: Where Have All the Islamists Gone?' 21 January. *Christian Science Monitor*. www.csmonitor.com/Commentary/Global-Viewpoint/2011/0121/The-Tunisian-revolt-Where-have-all-the-Islamists-gone. Accessed 25 May 2011.

———— (2011b). 'The Paradoxes of the Re-Islamization of Muslim Societies'. *The Immanent Frame*, 8 September. http://blogs.ssrc.org/tif/2011/09/08/the-paradoxes-of-the-re-islamization-of-muslim-societies. Accessed 15 October 2011.

Rushdie, Salman (1991). *Imaginary Homelands: Essays on Criticism 1981–1991*. London: Granta.

Sageman, Marc (2004). *Understanding Terror Networks*. Philadelphia: University of Pennsylvania Press.

Said, Edward (1979). *Orientalism*. New York: Vintage.

———— (1983). *The World, the Text, and the Critic*. Cambridge MA: Harvard University Press.

———— (1992). *The Question of Palestine*. New York: Vintage.

———— (1994a). *Culture and Imperialism*. New York: Vintage.

———— (1994b). *The Politics of Dispossession: The Struggle for Palestinian Self-Determination 1969–1994*. New York: Pantheon.

———— (1995a) *Orientalism*. 25th anniversary edition. New York: Vintage.

———— (1995b). *Peace and Its Discontents: Essays on Palestine in the Middle East Peace Process*. New York: Vintage.

———— (1996). *Representations of the Intellectual: The 1993 Reith Lectures*. New York: Vintage.

———— (1997). *Covering Islam: How the Media and the Experts Determine How We See the Rest of the World*. Rev. edn. New York: Vintage.

———— (2000). *Reflections on Exile and Other Literary and Cultural Essays*. London: Granta.

———— (2001). 'Islam and the West are Inadequate Banners'. *Observer*, 16 September: 27.

———— (2002a). *Power, Politics and Culture: Interviews with Edward Said*, ed. Gauri Viswanathan. New York: Vintage.

———— (2002b). 'Thoughts About America'. *Al-Ahram Weekly* online 575, 28

February–6 March. http://weekly.ahram.org.eg/2002/575/op2.htm. Accessed 10 August 2005.

———— (2003a). 'Give Us Back our Democracy. *Counterpunch*, 18–20 April. www.counterpunch.org/said04212003.html. Accessed 22 October 2006.

———— (2003b). 'The Appalling Consequences of the Iraq War Are Now Clear'. *Counterpunch*, 22 April. www.counterpunch.org/said04222003.html. Accessed 29 September 2006.

———— (2003c). 'Dreams and Delusions.' *Al-Ahram Weekly* No. 652, 21–27 August. http://weekly.ahram.org.eg/2003/652/op1.htm. Accessed 10 August 2005.

———— (2004a). *Humanism and Democratic Criticism*. New York: Columbia University Press.

———— (2004b). *From Oslo to Iraq and the Road Map*. New York: Pantheon.

Salih, Tayyeb (1969). *Season of Migration to the North*. Trans. Denys Johnson-Davis. London: Quartet.

Sardar, Ziauddin (1999). *Orientalism*. Buckingham: Open University Press.

———— (2002). *The A–Z of Postmodern Life: Essays on Global Culture in the Noughties*. London: Vision.

———— (2003). *Islam, Postmodernism and Other Futures: A Ziauddin Sardar Reader*. Ed Sohail Inayatullah Sohail and Gail Boxwell. London: Pluto Press.

———— (2006). *How Do You Know?* London: Pluto Press.

———— (2008). 'On Franz Fanon: Forward to Black Skin, White Masks'. www.nakedpunch.com/articles/47. Accessed 12 December 2010.

———— (2010). 'Islam, Colonialism and Resistance'. Interview by Bux Qalandar Memon. *Naked Punch* 14 (Summer). www.nakedpunch.com/articles/61. Accessed 17 December 2010.

Sardar, Ziauddin, and Borin Van Loon (1997). *Introducing Cultural Studies*. Cambridge: Icon Books.

Sardar, Ziauddin, and Merryl Wyn Davies (2002). *Why Do People Hate America?* Cambridge: Icon.

Sayyid, Bobby (2004). *A Fundamental Fear: Eurocentrism and the Emergence of Islamism*. London: Zed Books.

Scanlon, Margaret (2001). *Novelists and Terrorists in Contemporary Fiction*. Charlottesville VA: University Press of Virginia.

Scheinin, Martin (2010). 'Report of the Special Rapporteur on the Promotion and Protection of Human Rights and Fundamental Freedoms while Countering Terrorism'. United Nations Human Rights Council. Sixteenth session. A/HRC/16/51/Add.2. 28 December. http://daccess-dds-ny.un.org/doc/UNDOC/GEN/G10/179/33/PDF/G1017933.pdf?OpenElement. Accessed 12 March 2011.

Schwartz, Moshe and Joyprada Swain (2011). 'Department of Defense Contractors in Afghanistan and Iraq: Background and Anaysis'. Congressional Research Service. 13 May. www.fas.org/sgp/crs/natsec/R40764.pdf. Accessed 19 December 2011.

Shariati, Ali (n.d. a). 'Jihad and Shahadat'. In *The Works of Dr Ali Shariati*. Iran Chamber Society. www.iranchamber.com/personalities/ashariati/works/jihad_shahadat.php. Accessed 13 November 2010.

———— (n.d. b). 'The Free Man and Freedom of Man'. In *The Works of Dr Ali*

Shariati. Iran Chamber Society www.iranchamber.com/personalities/ashari-ati/works/free_man_freedom_man.php . Accessed 10 October 2011.
——— (n.d. c). 'Maryrdom: Arise and Bear Witness'. Trans Ali Asghar Ghaseemy. *Ahlul Bayt and Digital Islamic Library Project* www.al-islam.org/arisewitness/. Accessed 10 October 2011.
——— (n.d. d). 'Where Shall we Begin". In *The Works of Dr Ali Shariati.* Iran Chamber Society. www.iranchamber.com/personalities/ashariati/works/where_shall_we_begin.php. Accessed 10 October 2011.
Shatz, Adam (2008). Adonis Interview. *New York Times.* 2 November. Accessed 4 December 2009.
Simon, Steven, and Daniel Benjamin (2000). 'America and the New Terrorism'. *Survival* 42 (1) (Spring): 59–75. www.eusec.org/su0001te.pdf. Accessed 10 November 2010.
Singh, Amardeep (2007). 'Republics of the Imagination'. *Minnesota Review* 68 (Spring). http://theminnesotareview.org/journal/ns68/singh.shtml. Accessed 23 October 2010.
Slisli, Fouzi (2008). 'Islam: The Elephant in Fanon's *The Wretched of the Earth'. Critical Middle Eastern Studies* 17 (1) (March). http://ouraim.blogspot.com/2008/03/absence-of-islamism-in-fanons-work.html. Accessed 10 July 2009.
Smith, Adam (2006). 'Interview with Orhan Pamuk'. www.nobelprize.org.
Der Spiegel (2005). 'Orhan Pamuk and the Turkish Paradox'. 21 October. www.spiegel.de/international/spiegel/0,1518,380858-2,00.html. Accessed 3 November 2010.
Spivak, Gayatri (1988). 'Can the Subaltern Speak?' In *Marxism and Interpretation,* ed. Cary Nelson and Lawrence Grossberg, 271–308. Urbana: University of Illinois Press.
——— (1998). *In Other Worlds: Essays in Cultural Politics.* New York: Routledge.
——— (2005). 'Thinking About Edward Said: Pages from a Memoir'. In *Edward Said: Continuing the Conversation,* ed. Homi Bhabha and W.J.T Mitchell, 156–62. Chicago: University of Chicago Press.
Stoda, Kevin (2001). 'Review of *Snow'. The Teacher,* 25 February. http://the-teacher.blogspot.com/2007/02/part-1book-review-snow-faber-faber.html. Accessed 12 August 2007.
Stone, Robert (2006). 'Updike's Other America'. Review of *Terrorist. New York Times,* 18 June. www.nytimes.com/2006/06/18/books/review/18stone.html. Accessed 25 October 2007.
Tamdgidi, Mohammad (2007). 'Intersecting Autobiography, History, and Theory: The Subtler Global Violence of Colonialism and Racism in Fanon, Said, and Anzaldúa'. *Human Architecture: Journal of the Sociology of Self-Knowledge* 5 (Summer): 113–36. www.okcir.com/Articles%20V%20Special/Mohammad TamdgidiEdNote.pdf. Accessed 16 June 2009.
Tanweer, Shehzad (2006). 'Video of 7 July Bomber'. BBC News online, 6 July. http://news.bbc.co.uk/2/hi/uk_news/5154714.stm. Accessed 13 October 2007.
Tibawi, A.L. (1964). 'English Speaking Orientalists'. In *Orientalism: A Reader* (2000), ed A.L. MacFie. Edinburgh: Edinburgh University Press: 57–76.
——— (1979). 'Second Critique of the English Speaking Orientalists'. *Islamic Quarterly* 23: 2–54.

—— (1980). 'On the Orientalists Again'. *Muslim World* 70 (1): 56–61.

Traboulsi, Fawwaz (2008). 'Orientalizing the Orientals: The Other Message of Edward Said'. In *Waiting for the Barbarians: A Tribute to Edward Said*, ed. Müge Gürsoy Sökmen and Basak Ertür, 33–43. London: Verso.

—— (2011). 'Revolutions Bring Down Ideas as Well'. *Perspectives* 2, 'People's Power: The Arab World in Revolt', 20 May: 14–21. www.lb.boell.org/downloads/Perspectives_02-02_Fawaz_Traboulsi.pdf.

Tremlett, Giles (2002). 'I Thought Only Soldiers Liked Fighting. But Intellectuals Hit Harder and Hurt More'. *Guardian*, 3 January. www.guardian.co.uk/culture/2002/jan/03/artsfeatures.fiction. Accessed 22 August 2009.

Turner, Brian (1978). *Marx and the End of Orientalism*. London: George Allen & Unwin.

—— (1994). *Orientalism, Postmodernism and Globalism*. London: Routledge.

Updike, John (2006). *Terrorist*. New York: Knopf.

Van Auken, Bill (2007). 'The US War and Occupation in Iraq – the Murder of a Society'. *World Socialist Web Site*. 19 May. www.wsws.org/articles/2007/may2007/iraq-m19.shtml. Accessed 12 October 2008.

Viswanathan, Gauri (1997). 'Secular Criticism and the Politics of Religious Dissent'. In *Cultural Readings of Imperialism: Edward Said and the Gravity of History*, ed. Keith Ansell Pearson, Benita Parry and Judith Squires, 151–72. London: Lawrence & Wishart.

—— (2008). 'Said, Religion, and Secular Criticism'. In *Waiting for the Barbarians: A Tribute to Edward Said*, ed. Müge Gürsoy Sökmen and Basak Ertür, 164–75. London: Verso.

Wolfe, Michael. ed. (2002). *Taking Back Islam: American Muslims Reclaim Their Faith*. New York: Rodale.

Wright, Lawrence (2006). *The Looming Tower: Al-Qaeda and the Road to 9/11*. New York: Knopf.

Wright, Robin (2008). 'Since 2001, A Dramatic Increase in Suicide Bombing'. *Washington Post*, 18 April. www.washingtonpost.com/wp-dyn/content/article/2008/04/17/AR2008041703595.html. Accessed 15 October 2009.

Yale Office of Public Affairs and Communications (2008). 'Award-winning Iranian Author Azar Nafisi To Lecture at Yale'. Press release, 28 January. http://opa.yale.edu/news/article.aspx?id=2309. Accessed 9 September 2009.

Yegenoglu Meyda (1998). *Colonial Fantasies: Towards a Feminist Reading of Orientalism*. Cambridge: Cambridge University Press.

Žižek, Slavoj (1992). 'In His Bold Gaze My Ruin Is Writ Large'. In *Everything You Always Wanted to Know about Lacan but Were Afraid to Ask Hitchcock*, ed. Slavoj Žižek, 211–72. London: Verso.

—— (1998). 'A Leftist Plea for Eurocentrism'. *Critical Inquiry* 24 (4) (Summer): 988–1009.

—— (1999). *The Ticklish Subject*. London: Verso.

—— (2000). *The Fragile Absolute, or Why is the Christian Legacy Worth Fighting For?* London: Verso.

—— (2002). *Welcome to the Desert of the Real: Five Essays on September 11 and Related Dates*. New York: Verso.

—— (2004). *Iraq: The Borrowed Kettle*. London: Verso.

——— (2005). 'Neighbors and Other Monsters: A Plea for Ethical Violence'. In *The Neighbor: Three Inquiries in Political Theology*, ed. Slavoj Žižek, Eric L. Santer and Kenneth Rinehard. Chicago: University of Chicago Press.

——— (2008). *Violence*. New York: Picador.

——— (2009). *First as Tragedy, Then as Farce*. London: Verso.

——— (2010a). *Living in the End Times*. London: Verso.

——— (2010b). 'Are We Living in the End Times?' *Riz Khan Show*. Al Jazeera International, 12 November 2010. http://videowap.org/video/YIpiXJW3dYE/Riz-Khan-Are-we-living-in-the-end-times.html. Accessed 23 December 2010.

——— (2011a). 'Shoplifters of the World Unite'. *London Review of Books*, 19 August. www.lrb.co.uk/2011/08/19/slavoj-zizek/shoplifters-of-the-world-unite. Accessed 1 October 2011.

——— (2011b). 'Why Fear the Arab Revolutionary Spirit?' *Guardian*, 1 February. www.guardian.co.uk/commentisfree/2011/feb/01/egypt-tunisia-revolt. Accessed 10 February 2011.

Žižek, Slavoj, and Tariq Ramadan (2011). 'Egypt'. *Riz Khan Show*. Al Jazeera. 1 February. www.youtube.com/watch?v=29NffzEh2bo&feature=relmfu. Accessed 15 February 2011.

Zurayk, Rami (2011). 'Feeding the Arab Uprisings.' *Perspectives* 2, 'People's Power: The Arab World in Revolt', 20 May: 119–25. www.lb.boell.org/downloads/Perspectives_02-18_Rami_Zurayk.pdf.

Index

Abdel-Malek, Anouar, 146–7, 150, 167
Abu Ghraib prison, 2; torture images circulation, 114–15, 121, 124
academics, post 9/11, 168
Aden bombing, 132
Adonis, Syrian poet, 152–3
Afghanistan, 1, 8, 30, 49, 62–3, 68, 71, 77, 81, 124, 134, 136; demonized Islamists, 67
Afsaruddin, Asma, 4
Agamben, Giorgio, 7–8, 189
Ahmad, Aijaz, 209–11
AIPAC, 38
Ajami, Fouad, 50
Al Jazeera, TV station, 62, 110, 130; beheading videos broadcast, 115; US threat to bomb, 114
al-Awlaki, Anwar, 21, 25, 35–6, 46, 129, 136; Internet use, 34; video messages of, 139; Yemen assassination of, 138
al-Azhar Mosque, 5
al-Azhar University, 200
al-Bahr, Nasser Ahmad, 57
al-Gaddafi, Muammar, 28, 31
al-Qaeda, 12, 28, 39–41, 47, 62, 80–81, 173, 192; composition of, 86; recruitment strategy, 113
al-Rawandi, Ibn, 165

al-Sadr, Mohammed Baqer, 43
al-Sadr, Musa, 43
al-Sheikh, Sheikh, 5
al-Turabi, Hassan, 172
al-Wahhab, Muhammad Ibn Abd, 4
al-Warraq, Muhammad, 165
al-Zawahiri, Ayman, 5, 81, 110
Alatas, S.H., 146
Algeria, 41, 173–4; civil war, 70, 90, 91; FLN, 177–8, 180; indigenous culture, 176; national liberation struggle, 175; political Islam, 172
Almond, Ian, 119–23; *The New Orientalists*, 18
'altruistic suicide', 84
American Immigration Law Foundation, 64
Amnesty International, 28
Amr, Mohamed Kamel, 39
Andrejevic, Mark, 108
anti-globalization movement, 94
anti-Orientalists, 131
Antonius, George, 36
Aoun, Michel, 42
Appadurai, Arjun, 11
Appiah, Kwame Anthony, 63
Arab 'Awakening'/Spring/revolutions, 2, 18, 21, 23, 36, 47, 221; non-violence

packaging, 29
Arab world, American imperialism, 32; Ottoman colonization of, 4
Arab–Israeli Six Day War 1967, 81
Arafat, Yasser, 171
Argentina, 220
Armenians, massacre of, 98
Asad, Hany Abu, 88
Asad, Talal, 7, 19, 185–92, 213
Association Beaumarchais, 90
Association of Muslim Scholars, 177
Atassi, Mohammad Ali, 26
atheism, new, 210
Atta, Mohammed, 60, 73, 93–4; psychologizing of, 57
Attwood, Margaret, 64, 99
Abu Ghraib, torture pictures circulation, 115
Auerbach, Erich, 153
Austen, Jane, 64
'authenticity', 70
Azzam, Abdulla, 81

Baghdad, 72, 74–5
Bahrain, 39
Badiou, Alain, 189
Baudrillard, Jean, 111–12, 117, 127, 139, 220; jihad configuration, 118; Saddam Hussein admiration, 119; *The Intelligence of Evil* 121; *The Spirit of Terrorism*, 120
Bayat, Asef, 34
Bedouin code of ethics, 73
beheading videos, 112; censored, 114–15
Beirut, 72, 75
Belhaj, Abd al-Hakim, 28
Ben Ali, Zine El Abidine, 31
Benaïssa, Slimane, 18, *The Last Night of a Damned Soul*, 90–97
Benda, Julien, 151–2
Benjamin, Daniel, 117
Berg, Nick, beheading of, 115
Berlin Film Festival, 88
Bhabha, Homi, 144, 163, 176
bin Laden, Osama, 3, 5, 8, 17, 18, 23–4, 26–7, 33, 34, 37–8, 57, 75, 80, 86, 101, 120, 125, 128, 180, 192, 195, 197, 212; address to American mothers, 129; American mental lethargy accusation, 132–3, 135; assassination, 21, 25, 39; call for critical thinking, 136; CIA

support, 83; contextualized, 81; death of responses, 22–3; exoticized, 28; historical context, 82; multiple audiences awareness, 130; 'The Solution' address, 36; 'Towers of Lebanon' address, 131; *ulama* opposing, 46; Western populations positioning, 134
biopolitics, humanitarian, 9
Blair, Tony, 36, 197
Bouazizi, Mohamed, 26–8, 32, 45
Bourdieu, Pierre, 11
Bradley, Ed, 82
Brazil, 220; Workers' Party, 43
Brown, Gordon, 36
Brown, Wendy, 186
Bush, George W., 36, 66, 116, 133, 137
Butler, Judith, 8, 186–8, 212

Cairo, Israeli embassy attack, 39
Campus Watch, 79, 142, 169
Camus, Albert, 71
capitalism, 202, 214; global 205; 'Islamized', 203
Caspian Sea region, oil, 62
Catholic Church, 43
Centre National de la Récherche Scientifique, 147
Chérif, Mustapha, 188
Chechenya, 86
Chirac, Jacques, 90
Chomsky, Noam, 23, 37, 65, 136, 139
CIA (US Central Intelligence Agency), 22, 65; bin Laden support, 83; 'extraordinary rendition' programme, 30; hit list of, 138
Clarke, J.J., *Oriental Enlightenment*, 118
Clifford, J., 161
Clinton, Bill, 129–30
Clinton, Hillary, 39
CNRS, Paris, 79
codes: of honour, 77; of practice, 87
Coetzee, J.M., 70
colonialism, 1, 4, 178; Islamic resistance to, 177
Comité de Bienfaisance et de Secours aux Palestine, 197
Commission Internationale des Francophonies, 90
'comprador intellectual', 63–4
Conflicts Forum, 23

Connolly, Peter, 198
contrapuntality, 15–16, 164, 215, 218
cosmopolitanism, utopian, 163
Crooke, Alastair, 43
cultural capital, concept of, 11
cultural imperialism, 49
cultural industries, 11
culturalism, 124; culturalization, 42
culture of fear, 169

Dabashi, Hamid, 40–41, 64
Danish cartoon crisis, 124, 186, 205
Dar es Salam, 125
Dawkins, Richard, 210; 'selfish gene'
    theory, 84
death, form of power, 193
decolonization, 175; violence of, 179
deculturation, 42, 95
dehumanization, 8
DeLillo, Don, 58–9, 61, 94; Falling Man,
    60
democracy, 169; 'democratic' criticism,
    162
Derrida, Jacques, 118, 188–9, 196
Devji, Faisal, 18, 22–4, 117, 125–8, 132,
    136, 139, 195–6, 213, 221
Dirlik, Arif, 63
discursivity, founders of, 145
Dostoevsky, Fyodor, 71
Durkheim, Émile, 84

Eagleton, Terry, 19, 192, 209–10, 212–16;
    Unholy Terror, 211
École des Hautes Études en Sciences
    Sociales, 79
Egypt, 32–4, 43, 222; Internet use, 35;
    Israel August 2011 incident, 39;
    Muslim Brotherhood, 44; nationalist
    intellectuals, 42; postcolonial, 5;
    revolution, 30
El-Ariss, Tarek, 55–6
elites, secular indigenous, 157
Emerson, Steven, 137
Englehardt, Tom, 23
Enlightenment, the, 156
Esposito, John, 5–6, 18, 22, 79–83, 85, 88,
    91, 98, 131
Euben, Roxanne L., 6, 33
Europe: Eurocentrism, 122; European
    Union, 22; Muslimness of, 51, 55, 99
exile, 95–6

Fadallah, Sayyed Mohammad Hussein,
    43
Fadel, Mohammed, 5
faith, vocabulary of, 188
'false consciousness', 36–7, 134
family honour, Bedouin codes, 17
Fanon, Frantz, 41, 170, 174–80, 182–4;
    theory of violence, 143
'fascism', 169
Fatah, 42
fiction, Muslim, 20
'field', concept of, 12, 15
filiation/affiliation, 155
Fils de l'amertume, Les, 90
Fiske, Robert, 137
Fitzgerald, F. Scott, 64
Fort Hood shooter, 137
Foucault, Michel, 118–19, 145, 206;
    'enunciative modality', 144
Freedom House, 65
Friedman, Thomas, 44–5, 50–51, 53, 56,
    71–2, 119, 124
Fukuyama, Francis, 48, 50
'fundamentalists', Islamic, 86

Gadahn, Adam (al-Amriki), 18, 110, 129;
    American economic crisis focus, 137;
    videotaped messages, 136
Gaddafi, see al-Gaddafi
Galloway, George, 137
game theory, 84
Gandhi, Mohandas, 174
Gaza: Islamic militants, 173; siege of, 2,
    124
Georgetown University, 79
Ghanooshi, Rashid, 44
Gharbeia, Ahmed, 35
Ghonim, Wael, 32
Giroux, Henry, 7–8, 18, 112–14, 120, 136,
    139, 219–20; The Terror of Neo-
    liberalism, 169
Goldman, David P., 39–40
'good'/'bad' Muslims, 3, 10–13, 18, 21–2,
    30, 39, 47, 54, 62–3, 67, 142, 145, 170,
    209, 218–19
Gould, Eric D., 115
Gramsci, Antonio, 151–2
Grand Prix Francophone de la SACD, 90
Guantánamo Bay prison, 2, 124
Guevara, Ernesto 'Che', 177
Gulf War, 157

Hamas, 5, 38, 42, 171–2
Hamid, Moshin, 217; *The Reluctant Fundamentalist*, 216
Hamzah, 194
Hardt, Michael, 207–8
Hart, William D., 155–7
Hashmi, Sohail, 4
Haut Conseil de la Francophonie, 90
Havel, Vaclav, 70
Hazara, ethnic group, 66
heresy, 11
Herman, Edward, 65
Hezbollah, 38, 42
Hitchens, Christopher, 210
Hobsbawm, Eric, 172
Hoffman, Bruce, 117
Homo islamicus, 9–10, 58, 63, 67–8, 125, 180, 204, 206; code of honour, 73; denigration of, 115
Homo sacer, 7–10, 204, 211
Hosseini, Khalid, 18; *The Kite Runner*, 63, 66–8, 75, 77
Houen, Alec, 127, 143, 195–7
Huggan, Graham, 11
Hugo, Victor, 91–2
human rights, Islamic discourse, 163
humanism, 184; humanitarian aid, 8, 68; 'tragic', 211
Huntington, Samuel, 3, 18, 51–2, 57, 65, 119, 124; militarism, 53
Hussein, Saddam, 52, 62, 72, 75, 119

Ibn Hazm, 160, 184
Ibn Khaldun, 158–9
Ibn Warraq, 83
identity: crisis of, 87; politics, 204
ijtihad, 125, 152, 166, 168–70, 198, 200–201, 203
imaginary community, 86
Imam Hussein, 194–5
IMF (International Monetary Fund), 22, 31
imperialism, 1
intellectuals: cosmopolitan, 145; credibility, 142–3; religious, 173; Third World, 144; 'utopian border', 149; Western speaking for 'subaltern', 141
intentionality, issue of, 146–7
interlocutors, Muslim, 116
International Parliament of Writers, 70

Iran, 32, 38, 65, 68, 118, 208; Iranian Revolution, 119, 177
Iraq, 30, 49, 124, 134, 136, 180; American failure, 133; jihadists, 76; oil reserves, 62; socio-political reality marginalized, 122; threat to Filipino contractors, 112; US invasion of, 65; war, 1, 50, 58, 77, 116, 119, 121
Iron Dome anti-rocket system, 38
Islam, 182; anti-capitalist ethics, 165; anti-essentialist understanding, 106; anticolonial tradition, 177; 'authoritarian' nature, 56; banking industry, 202; burial procedures, 194; cultures, 164; 'dehumanized functionality', 122; foundational texts interpretation, 14; global spectacle, 127; globalization discourse, 48; heterodox elements, 157; higher rates of Western conversion, 113; metaphorical use, 120; Orientalist narratives, 75; property and marriage laws, 55; revolutionary terminology of, 199; scholarship, 160, 162; secularism relationship, 100, 154; unitary assumption, 3; universality, 181, 185, 198
Islamaphobia, 22, 45, 213
Islamic Jihad, 172
Islamism/Islamists, 43, 174, 209; governments failure causation, 80; political, 41, 208; 'post', 46; significance denial, 46
Israel, 22, 32–3, 38, 44–5, 55; attacks on, 115; US support for, 131; Wall building, 122

Jalil, Mustapha Abdul, 28
Jamaat Islamiya, 172
James, Henry, 64
Jefferson, Thomas, 165
Jerusalem, Mufti of, 5
Jesus (Issa), 196; death of, 191
jihad, 120, 168–70, 173, 198–9, 212; ambiguous meanings, 5; American voyeurism, 24; challenge of, 154; code of, 61; cultural configuration, 14; dehistoricized, 56; discourse interpretations, 34, 117; Edward Said disdain for, 145; effects on West, 113;

essentializing of, 106; exile connections, 97; for peace, 84–5; globalized concept, 33; interpretation role, 126; philosophy, 81; psychologizing of, 57; public discourse, 4; role of, 209; serious analysis of, 80; social, 197, 200–201, 213, 215; social justice struggle, 6; socio-political contextualized, 82, 88, 137; testimony to faith, 131; theorizations, 2–3, 19, 179; videos, US government fear, 114; Žižek romanticizing, 124

jihadist(s), 180, 190, 210; as universal mediator, 127; dishonour motive, 74; ethical performances, 108, 128; intentionality, 79, 88, 90; Islamic terminologies, 142; media representation awareness, 109–10; mediations of, 140; performers, 111, 116; psychologizing, 17; romanticized, 123; shahada, 191–2; shahid, 193–4; spectacle, repoliticizing theory, 114; universalist discourse, 217; Western, 95

journalism, 104; violence mediating, 102

Kaplan, Amy, 61
Karol, David, 116
Kawash, Samira, 179
Kellner, Douglas, 3, 8, 28, 48, 114, 121
Kepel, Gilles, 23
Kerbala, siege of, 195
Keshavarz, Fatemeh, 64
Khadra, Yasmina, 18, 69–70, 72, 75–6, 97; The Attack, 63
Khan, Mohammed Siddique, video statement by, 18, 108–11
Kharijites, 83
Khomeini, Ruhollah, 43
Khoury, Doreen, 35
Klor, Esteban F., 115
knowledge, indigenous revival, 42
Kristeva, Julia, 118
Kurds, massacre of, 98

Lacquer, Walter, 117
Laroui, Abdallah, 146
Latifeh Yarsheter Book Award, 64
Latin America, democratic tendencies, 220

Lebanon, Israeli attack on, 124, 132
'left', the, anti-Islamism, 214
Lewis, Bernard, 18, 51–4, 58, 64, 71, 82, 119, 124
liberation theology, South American Catholic, 43
Libya, 44, 222; Libyan Islamic Fighting Group, 28
Little, Donald, 149–50
Lockman, Zachary, 52, 144
London 7/7 bombings, 2, 17
Lukács, Georg, 174–5

Maarri, Abu al-Ala, 165
Macfie, A.L., 149–50
Madrid, train bombing 2004, 2, 17, 116, 192
Mahmood, Sabah, 186
Majid, Anouar, 19, 163–6, 168, 170, 173, 181, 198, 200, 203, 206, 213
Makdisi, Saree, 151
Malak, Amin, 20
Mamdani, Mahmood, 5, 12
Manji, Irshad, 18, 51, 53, 56–8, 62, 65, 71–2, 74, 77, 82–4; self-heroizing, 54
martyrdom, Christian notion of, 193
Marx, Karl, 181; Marxism, 52, 94, 143, 146, 203, 209; Third World Marxism, 85
Masion du Théâtre, 90
Masjid al-Farah mosque, New York City, 82
Mearsheimer, John, 37
media: and 'martyrdom' relationship, 127; mass violence desensitizing, 190
memoirs, market for, 66
Mesha'al, Khaled, 43
Middle East, militarization of, 49, 65
Miguel, Edward, 116
military targets, legitimacy differences, 5
Mitchell, W.J.T., 157
modernity, 52, 62; critiques of, 118; Islam's supposed challenge, 2; jihad as antithesis, 62; Kemalist, 6
Mohammed, Khaleel, 55
Le Monde, 70
Moral Courage project, 53
Morris, Chris, Four Lions, 89
Moshiri, Fanoosh, 66
Moulessehoul, Mohammed, 69–71

Mu'tzalites, 165
Mubarak, Hosni, 31
Mufti, Aamir, 15–16
mujahidin, 134; American desertion of, 68
multiculturalism, 124, 203–5
Muslim Brotherhood, 41, 45, 197; Egypt, 172, 208; Palestine, 81
Muslims; authoritarian regimes, 82; autobiographical fiction, 61, 69; European, 55; intellectual positioning, 154; interlocutors, 16, 41, 53–4
Muslim Spain, collapse of, 165
Muslimness, concept of, 12

Nabokov, Vladimir, 64
Nafisi, Azar, 18, 64–6, 68–9, 71, 77; *Reading Lolita in Tehran*, 63
Naipaul, V.S., 153
Nairobi bombing, 132
Nakba, 63rd anniversary killings, 37
Nasrallah, Sayyed Hassan, 43
Nasser, Gamal Abdel, 5
nationalism, 157–9, 161, 175; Islamic, 187
'native informants', 10, 63, 65, 68, 83
NATO (North Atlantic Treaty Organization), 67, 98
Negri, Antonio, 207–8
neoconservatives, 48, 50, 64, 82, 85
neo-fundamentalism, 87
neo-Orientalism, 85
New York University, Robert F. Wagner Graduate School, 53
Nietzsche, F.W., 71, 118–19, 206
9/11, attacks, 1, 82, 221; attackers, 17, 84, 130, 204; victims, 59
Nobel Prize for Literature, 98
non-violence, narrative of, 28
Notre Dame University, Indiana, 197

Obama, Barack, 24–6, 29, 31–2, 35, 37, 39, 44–5, 47; bin Laden exoticizing, 28; Bouazizi appropriation, 27; Palestine state blocking, 38
Occupy Wall Street, 221
oil embargo, 1973, 81
Olmert, Ehud, 44
'Operation Ijtihad', 85
Operation Iraqi Freedom, 56
Orientalism(s), 1, 10, 44, 49, 51, 72, 76, 78, 118, 161; 'postmodernist', 119;

dehistoricized, 148; displaced version of, 156; intention of, 147; re-emergence, 18; Western, 157
Orientalists, 20
Orientalization, USA, 50
orthodoxy, 11
Other, the, 12, 123, 188, 212; Islamic/ Arab, 118
Otherness, 150; exotic manufactures of, 11
Ottoman Empire, 4

Paine, Tom, 165
Pakistan, 40, 137; nationalist intellectuals, 42
Palestine, 41, 77, 86, 176; female jihadists, 76; intifada, 171; issue of, 170, 174; Muslim Brotherhood, 81; occupied territories, 75, 89; state blocking, 38
Pamuk, Orhan, 18; *Snow*, 90, 98–104, 107, 110
Pape, Robert, 116
Pappé, Ilan, 170
Paradise Now, 88–90, 107
Paris, 2005 riots, 204
Park 51, 83
Pashtuns, ethnic group, 66–7
Patton, General, 83
Pecora, Vincent, 189, 215
philology, Islamic tradition of, 162
Pipes, Daniel, 137
PLO (Palestine Liberation Organization), 38
Poland, Solidarity movement, 43
'polycentricity', 164, 166
post-secular theory, jihad repoliticized, 114
postcolonial theory, 11, 219; intellectuals, 61; jihad repoliticized, 114, 164; Muslim critics, 163
Prophet Muhammad, 181; authenticity questioned, 148

Qaradawi, Shiekh Yusuf, 5
Quran, 56–8, 84, 93, 148, 191, 196; reinterpreted, 95
qurban, Islamic terminology, 19
Qutb, Mohammad, 81
Qutb, Sayyid, 4–5, 43, 81, 143

Rabbani, Mouin, 31

Ramadan, Tariq, 19, 196–204, 206–9, 211, 213, 215, 220; US visa refusal, 13
Rauf, Imam Feisal Abdul, 18, 82–4, 88, 206, 209
'real', 220; thrill of the, 112
reality TV, 110–11, 113; jihadist subverted, 128
recruitment, 128
reification, 174
representation, 144; issue of, 141
Rich, Frank, 59
Robbins, Bruce, 157
Rodinson, Maxime, 9
Roy, Olivier, 6, 18, 22, 41–2, 45–6, 79, 86–8, 91, 94, 97, 125
Rushdie, Salman, 70, 153–4

Sabri, Akram, 5
sacrifice, 191, 212–13; Christian notions, 215
Said, Edward, 1, 3, 16, 20, 41, 49–51, 63–4, 96, 106, 127, 147–50, 161–2, 164, 170–71, 173–4, 176, 178, 181, 184, 189, 218–19; Arab rejection of *Orientalism*, 151; critiques of, 167; elitist dichotomy, 163; Enlightenment terminology accusation, 158; humanism, 168; humanism critique, 146; intellectual role definition, 152–5; Islamism critique, 172; Islam relationship, 19; legacy of, 144; nationalism critique, 157; post-9/11, 159; religious criticism opposition, 156; Rushdie allegiance, 154; secular humanism, 145; 'worldliness' of texts, 15
Saint Paul, 189
SAIS Dialogue Project, Johns Hopkins University, 63
Salafism, 6
Salon, 198
Sardar, Ziauddin, 166–8, 170, 173–4, 181, 198, 200, 203, 206, 209, 213
Sarkozy, Nicolas, 36
Sartre, Jean-Paul, 181
Saudi, Arabia, 39, 180; bin Laden view of, 33–4; Grand Mufti, 5; US arms purchases, 62; Wahhabi, 81; Yemeni policy, 40
Sayyid, Bobby, 6, 14, 19, 105, 106

Scanlon, Margaret, 18
'scapegoat', 212
Scheinin, Martin, 30
Scheuer, Michael, 37, 137
secularism, 161, 185, 187; secular criticism, 144, 156; secular–jihadist binary, 104
shahid, 26, 193–4; types of, 195
sharia, 86
Shariati, Ali, 43, 143, 177, 180–2, 193–5, 197, 212
Simon, Steven, 117
Slisli, Fouzi, 176–7
social media, 35
Solzhenitsyn, Aleksandr, 91
Sorbonne, Paris, 147
Soyinka, Wole, 70
Spain, Muslim history of, 55
Spencer, Robert, 137
Spivak, Gayatri Chakravorty, 141–2, 144, 163
Sudan, 81, 172
Sufism, 6
'suicide bombing', 2, 5, 76, 84, 88, 189–92, 195
suicide, widow, 141, 142

Tahrir Square, Cairo, 25
Taliban regime, 12, 66–7
Tamdgidi, Mohammed, 175
Tantawi, Sheikh Muhammad Sayad, 5
Tanweer, Shehzad, 18; video of/by, 110–11
terrorism: genealogy construction, 18; 'spectacle' of, 113, 139, 219–20; studies, 16; Western science 'appropriation', 51
terrorist(s): government negotiations with, 115; policy change achievements, 116; religious–secular division, 117; 'the terrorist', 7
theatre, 103, 104, 110; violence mediating, 102
Théâtre International de Langue Français, 91
Third World, 123; challenge to global capital, 166, development approach, 168, resistance literature, 147, unification, 177; women, 142
Tibawi, A.L., 146–51, 167

Traboulsi, Fawaz, 33
tragedy, 212
Tunisia, 32–4, 43, 118, 222; Al-Nadha
    Party, 44; Internet use, 35;
    revolution, 30
Turkey, 208; EU entry debates, 98–9,
    104

UAR (United Arab Republics), 67
umma, 185; as global community, 159;
    conceptual, 186
UN (United Nations), 38; Office of the
    Coordinator for Afghanistan, 79
UNHCR, 68
University of Algiers, 188
University of Houston, 66
Updike, John, 58–9, 61, 92, 94, 97
USA (United States of America), 22, 65;
    arms sales to Saudi Arabia, 33;
    congressional elections 2006, 133;
    Department of Homeland Security,
    197; military contractors, 63;
    presidential election 2004, 131; Saudi
    arms deals, 62; University of Notre
    Dame, 13

van der Veer, Peter, 156
Venezuela, 220
Vico, Giambattista, 153, 157–8
victimology, Western culture of, 24
violence, 172, 174–5, 177–80, 218;
    legitimacy of, 198; political, 176
Viswanathan, G., 157
Voll, John, 80

Wahhabism, 6
Walesa, Lech, 43
Walsh School of Foreign Service, 79
Walt, Stephen, 37
'war on terror', 1, 14–15, 21, 24, 42, 49, 58,
    62, 69, 114; Orientalism
    underwritten, 63; theorization of, 2
Washington DC, 165
Western technology, Muslim
    'appropriation', 51
Western Third World interlocutors,
    privileged, 218, 219
Whitman, Walt, 165
WikiLeaks, 62
Wolfowitz, Paul, 64–5
Woolsey, James, 65
World Bank, 22, 31
worldliness, 155; Said use of, 160
WTO (World Trade Organization), 22

Yasin, Sheikh Ahmad, 5
Yemen, 39, 138; destabilization, 40

Zahirites, Andalusian linguists, 160, 162,
    184
Zaman, Muhammad Qasim, 6, 33
Znet, 23
Zionism, politics of, 210
Žižek, Slavoj, 3, 8–9, 19, 25, 68, 108, 117,
    119, 125, 127, 139, 189, 203–4, 206–9,
    211, 215–16; jihad appropriation, 118,
    123, 125; post-9/11 work, 122;
    Welcome to the Desert of the Real, 107
Zurayk, Ramy, 31